SPORTS
STYLE GUIDE
& REFERENCE
MANUAL

The Complete Reference for Sports Editors, Writers, and Broadcasters

Jennifer Swan, Editor

TRIUMPH
BOOKS

CHICAGO

To Mom, Dad, Kris, and my friends
for their never-ending support and encouragement.
—J. S.

© 1996 Triumph Books

All rights reserved.

ISBN: 1-57243-101-6

Cover design: Sam Concialdi
Typesetting: Sans Serif, Inc.
Book design: Vivian Bradbury
Copy editors: Anne Roby and Sarah Burgundy

All inquiries and comments on style guidelines should be addressed to:

Triumph Books
Editorial Office
644 South Clark Street
Chicago, Illinois 60605

Due to volume of mail, all inquiries may not be answered individually.

CONTENTS

PREFACE

While attending graduate school at the University of Kansas, I worked part-time as a sports copyeditor at the *Kansas City Star*. With a solid background in sports broadcasting and writing, I thought editing sports copy would be easy.

I soon found that having a knowledge of sports did not mean knowing the first thing about editing. When I asked where I could find a book to answer my questions about spelling and usage of sports terms, I was told that one did not exist. Instead, I was directed to a room full of books and press information about every team, league, and sport. Searching through this room for the correct way to use punctuation in a given situation or to check the spelling of a stadium name was time-consuming. Soon this practice gave way to asking others in the sports department for answers.

It has been a tradition in sports departments to pass along style rules by word of mouth, using the "best guess" approach when no rule exists for a particular situation. Evidence of this is plentiful when examining the use of the same term in different publications. Take RBI for example. This often is found three different ways:

He has 35 RBIs.
He has 35 RBI's.
He has 35 RBI.

This type of inconsistency isn't only found when comparing two different publications. A study of several newspapers showed that quite often a word is spelled or used differently on the same day in a single publication.

A survey of 52 newspaper sports editors across the country

showed 73 percent did not have a written set of sports style rules. Many editors stated that their only reference source was the *Associated Press Stylebook*, which contains only a small section devoted to sports.

The *Sports Style Guide and Reference Manual* is designed to help bring clarity and continuity to the sports page. I've asked several sports editors for their suggestions, many of which are included in this book.

More than just providing style rules, this book supplies writers and editors with spellings, definitions of unfamiliar terms, team and association names and the leagues in which they play, lists, and other information to make sports publications more consistent, accurate, and free of errors.

My goal is to answer as many style, usage, spelling, and punctuation questions as possible. Although I am certain more questions remain, it is my hope that this guide will serve as the first step toward the universal use of many words and terms and will promote consistency in sports publications.

There is more to be discussed and included in the second edition of the *Sports Style Guide and Reference Manual*. Your suggestions and comments are welcome.

Jennifer Swan
Editor

ACKNOWLEDGMENTS

The following people and organizations contributed to the *Sports Style Guide and Reference Manual.*

American Professional Soccer League
Associated Orthopedics, Overland Park, Kan.
Association of Professional Sports Editors
John Bisognano, *Times Advocate*, Escondido, Calif.
Steve Blust, *Sacramento Bee*, Sacramento, Calif.
Rich Bolas, *Daily New-Sun*, Sun City, Ariz.
Harry Bryan, *Courier-Journal*, Louisville, Ky.
Richard Bush, *Charlotte Observer*, Charlotte, N.C.
Bill Coats, *St. Louis Post-Dispatch*, St. Louis, Mo.
Continental Indoor Soccer League
Stuart Courtney, *Chicago Sun-Times*, Chicago, Ill.
Dan Cunningham, *Houston Chronical*, Houston, Texas
Owen Davis, *Detroit Free Press*, Detroit, Mich.
Steve Doyle, *Orlando Sentinel*, Orlando, Fla.
Sean Duff, *Fort Collins Coloradoan*, Fort Collins, Colo.
Mike Fitzgerald, *Honolulu Star-Bulletin*, Honolulu, Hawaii
Barry Forbis, *Rocky Mountain News*, Denver, Colo.
John Garrett, *The Press-Enterprise*, Riverside, Calif.
Brad Hall, *Appeal-Democrat*, Marysville, Calif.
Bruce Hammel, *San Jose Mercury News*, San Jose, Calif.
Bill Huffman, *Arizona Republic*, Phoenix, Ariz.
International Boxing Federation
Kansas City Star Sports Department
Andy Knobel, *Baltimore Sun*, Baltimore, Md.
Kathy Kudraui, *Plain Dealer*, Cleveland, Ohio
David Little, *Record Searchlight*, Redding, Calif.

Dave Lyghtle, *Modesto Bee*, Modesto, Calif.
Patrick McKee, *Indianapolis Star*, Indianapolis, Ind.
Major League Baseball
Bob Morrissette, *Meriden Record-Journal*, Meriden, Conn.
Tim Mowry, *Daily News-Miner*, Fairbanks, Alaska
National Basketball Association
National Collegiate Athletic Association
National Football League
National Hockey League
Jim O'Connell, *Greeley Daily Tribune*, Greeley, Colo.
Howard Owen, *Richmond Times-Dispatch*, Richmond, Va.
Doug Pittman, University of Iowa, Iowa City, Iowa
Pro Bowlers Association
Professional Golfers Association
Leah Reiter, *San Bernardino County Sun*, San Bernardino, Calif.
Jim Rice, *Times-Picayune*, New Orleans, La.
Roller Hockey International
Rugby Press
Mark Scarp, *Progress Tribune*, Scottsdale, Ariz.
Don Shelton, *Seattle Times*, Seattle, Wash.
Brad Steinhope, *Daily Republic*, Fairfield, Calif.
Kevin Turbeville, *Jonesboro Sun*, Jonesboro, Ark.
United States Polo Association
University of Kansas School of Journalism
USA Boxing
Joan Weiner, *Herald*, Monterey, Calif.
Vern Williams, *Merced Sun-Star*, Merced, Calif.
David Wilson, *Miami Herald*, Miami, Fla.
World TeamTennis
Kerry Young, *California Delta Newspaper*, Antioch, Calif.
John Zant, *Santa Barbara News-Press*, Santa Barbara, Calif.
Mark Zeligman, *Kansas City Star*, Kansas City, Mo.

PART I

INTRODUCTION

Part I consists of an alphabetical list of words used commonly in sports stories. This list is designed mainly as a usage guide. Most entries include correct spelling, part of speech, usage and spelling rules, and, if necessary, a definition or a sample sentence.

This section is not intended to be a sports dictionary. Only obscure words or words with definitions that affect their usage are defined.

Part I also contains information on several sports, such as field dimensions, events, major tournaments, corporate sponsors, team nicknames, awards, and slang terms.

At the end of Part I, you will find a punctuation guide specific to sports terms.

Terms and Their Usage

A

AAU Spell out Amateur Athletic Union on first reference.

abbreviations

cities/states
Do not abbreviate the name of a city as a modifier on first reference.

> WRONG: Johnson plays for L.A. Dodgers.
> RIGHT: Johnson signed with Los Angeles. He plays for the
> L.A. Dodgers.

When used alone, don't abbreviate the name of a city or state. *See* cities, states.

> WRONG: Evelyn is from Ill.
> WRONG: Clark lives in N.Y. City.
> RIGHT: Clark lives in New York City.

junior/senior
Abbreviate junior and senior when they appear at the end of a person's name. Do not use a comma to separate the word from the name.

> The record was broken by Ken Griffey Jr.

Do not abbreviate junior if it is a person's first name.

> Junior Seau was voted the team's captain.

a.m./p.m.
Abbreviate a.m. and p.m. when used with figures. Do not use alone.

> WRONG: The doubleheader will be played in the p.m.
> RIGHT: The doubleheader will be played in the evening.

Do not use the redundant a.m. in the morning or p.m. in the evening.

street/avenue/boulevard
Abbreviate and capitalize St., Ave., and Blvd. as part of a complete address.

> Market Square Arena is located at 300 E. Market St.
> America West Arena is on Jefferson Street.

No.
Use the abbreviation No. in reference to a rank or position.

> Stevens was the No. 1 qualifier.
> The Bulldogs are No. 2 in the poll.
> There were a number of former athletes present.

ABC Spell out American Bowling Congress on first reference.

ABC Masters Tournament ABC Masters is acceptable in headlines when space is limited, but spell out ABC Masters Tournament on first reference. The tournament is sponsored by the American Bowling Congress.

ability Do not assume that an athlete has relied solely upon natural talent to reach his or her position. This suggests that he or she has attained success through a stroke of luck, rather than hard work.

absolute necessity This phrase is redundant. Use necessity.

Academic All-America Award given to college athletes who excel athletically and academically. *See* All-America.

Armstrong was an Academic All-America selection.
He is an Academic all-American.

ACC Spell out Atlantic Coast Conference on first reference, then ACC. *See* college, Part II.

ace (n., v.) Lowercase ace when referring to a perfect serve in tennis or a hole in one in golf.

Wong had 11 aces during the match.
Sanchez aced her opponent seven times.

Ace Capitalize the trademark name of elastic bandage.

Crane is wearing an Ace bandage.

Achilles' heel An Achilles' heel refers to a vulnerable spot. It is not part of the body.

Thomas can hit a fastball, but the curve is his Achilles' heel.

Achilles' tendon The large tendon that joins muscles in the calf of the leg to the bone of the heel.

Banks was unable to play after injuring his Achilles' tendon.

acronyms Spell out words that an acronym represents on first reference with the following exceptions. These abbreviations do not need to be spelled out because they are widely recognized. Note that all are capitalized without periods.

ABC (American Broadcasting System)
AFC (American Football Conference)
CBS (former Columbia Broadcasting System)
FIFA (Fédération Internationalé de Football Association)
LPGA (Ladies Professional Golf Association)
NASCAR (National Association for Stock Car Auto Racing)
NBA (National Basketball Association)
NBC (National Broadcasting Company)
NCAA (National Collegiate Athletic Association)
NFC (National Football Conference)

NFL (National Football League)
NHL (National Hockey League)
PGA (Professional Golfers' Association)
UCLA (University of California-Los Angeles)

When an acronym is used as a possessive, use a lowercase *s* with an apostrophe.

The NFL's best player is injured.

active consideration This phrase is redundant. Use consideration.

acute Acute means short and relatively severe. For example, a sprained ankle may be considered an acute injury. One cannot have an acute back problem for 20 years. *See* chronic injury.

Adams Award Award given to the NHL Coach of the Year. *See* hockey, Part II.

adapt To change.

Antonic quickly adapted to the new rules.

See adopt.

ad-in Always hyphenate this tennis term, which indicates that the player who is serving holds advantage.

adopt Adopt means to take possession of something.

Coach Lungren adopted a new set of principles.

See adapt.

ad-out Always hyphenate this tennis term, which indicates that the player receiving the serve holds advantage.

adrenaline Do not capitalize the name of the secretion produced by the adrenal glands. Capitalize Adrenalin in reference to the trademark name for the adrenaline preparation.

advantage rule Rule allows a soccer referee to continue play after a foul when stopping the play would take away an advantage held by the non-offending team.

adverse Adverse means unpleasant or hostile.

> Bankston played well despite adverse weather.

See averse.

aerial (n., adj.) Movement in which a gymnast turns over while in the air without touching the floor with his or her hands.

aerobic exercise Exercise with oxygen. The word *aerobic* is associated with sustained periods of exercise. In contrast, anaerobic exercise is exercise without oxygen and is associated with short duration, high intensity exercise.

AFC Use AFC on first reference for American Football Conference. *See* football, Part II.

affect To influence. *See* effect.

> This shot will affect the game's outcome.

AFL Spell out Arena Football League on first reference. *See* football, Part II.

African American Most publications have their own rules about the use of African American vs. black. Neither is incorrect when using the adjective form to refer to a person; avoid using black as a noun.

> WRONG: Dennis is a black.
> RIGHT: Dennis is black.
>   He is an African American.

Hyphenate African-American as a modifier.

> Paul is a member of an African-American organization.

aft Toward the stern of a boat.

afterward Not afterwards.

ages Always use figures.

> The stadium is 21 years old.
> The players are all in their 20s.
> Kelly, 26, is hoping his team will improve.

When using an age as a modifier or in place of a noun, use a hyphen between the number and year.

> The Lakers traded the 34-year-old center.
> Older players complained after being beaten by a 16-year-old.

agent Do not capitalize agent as a title when referring to an athlete's agent.

> WRONG: Is Agent Lekan Dawson's representative?
> RIGHT: Lekan is Dawson's agent.
>   Gunnar asked player agent Tom Kaegel about the trade.

Capitalize Agent when referring to an FBI agent.

> The FBI sent Special Agent Brundy to investigate the rumors.

aggravate Do not use as a synonym for annoy. Only existing conditions can be aggravated.

> WRONG: Long aggravated his teammates.
> RIGHT: Long aggravated his knee injury.
> RIGHT: Janson annoyed the other players with his whining.

ahold This is not a word.

> WRONG: The tackle grabbed ahold of the running back's jersey.
> RIGHT: He grabbed the running back's jersey.

AIDS Capitalize. Acceptable in all references for Acquired Immune Deficiency Syndrome. People infected with the virus that causes AIDS do not have AIDS until they develop particular symptoms. In this case, a person is HIV-positive.

aikido Note spelling of this Japanese art of self-defense. *See* martial arts, Part II.

air ball (n.) A shot in basketball that doesn't hit any part of the basket or backboard before falling to the floor.

Air-Dyne Note spelling of this trademark Schwinn stationary exercise bicycle.

airtight (adj.) One word, no hyphen.

AL Spell out American League on first reference. Do not use AL as a noun. *See* baseball, Part II.

ALCS Spell out American League Championship Series on first reference, then AL Championship Series or ALCS. *See* baseball, Part II.

All- Capitalize All when it is part of a proper name.

> Keating was named an All-American.
> Earls was All-Big Ten last year.
> The National League won the All-Star Game 1-0.

All-America Use All-America in reference to a team or honor.

> He made the All-America team.
> He was an All-America selection.

See Academic All-America.

All-American Use All-American in reference to an individual.

> He is an All-American.

All-American Soap Box Derby Coasting race features small gravity-powered cars built by their drivers and assembled according to specific guidelines. There are three divisions: Stock Cars, Kit Cars, and Masters.

all-around (n., adj.) Gymnastics event is made up of all the apparatuses.

> The women's all-around competition is made up of the balance beam, uneven bars, floor exercise, and vault.
> The men's all-around competition is made up of the pommel horse, parallel bars, floor exercise, rings, high bar, and vault.
> Entsminger won the gymnastics all-around competition.
> She was first in the all-around.

Use all-round, not all-around, to describe a person who is adept at many tasks.

> Lyons is an all-round athlete.

allege Use said. *Allege,* as a word of attribution, implies skepticism. *See* said.

alley-oop (n., adj.) Always hyphenate.

> The crowd cheered when the team scored on the alley-oop.
> Gibbs received an alley-oop pass from Gipson.

All-League Capitalize League and hyphenate this distinction in all references.

> Sarge was voted All-League.
> She was selected for the All-League team.

All-Metro Capitalize Metro and hyphenate this distinction in all references.

> Rosenlof was selected for the All-Metro team.
> She was named All-Metro.

All-Pro Capitalize Pro and hyphenate this distinction earned by an NFL football player who has been chosen for the Pro Bowl.

> Jenkins is an All-Pro lineman.

all-purpose yards Note the hyphen in this term for all yards gained by a player or team.

all right Always two words, never alright.

all-round Use all-round to describe a person who is adept at many tasks. *See* all-around.

> He is an all-round athlete.

All-Star Capitalize as part of a proper name.

> When is the NHL All-Star Game?
> Armstrong was chosen to be an NBA All-Star.

Lowercase all-star in other references.

> The NFL all-star game is the Pro Bowl.
> Several high school all-stars were selected for our team.

All-Star break Lowercase break. *See* All-Star.

all-terrain vehicle Spell out on first reference, then ATV.

all that Use *all* alone in phrases.

> Their quarterback isn't all he's cracked up to be.

all time

> Steele was the best receiver of all time.

all-time Hyphenate all-time as a modifier.

> He is the all-time leader in rebounds.

It is not redundant to refer to a record as an all-time record in an effort to avoid confusion between, for example, a meet record or an American record. *See* record.

allude To refer to something. *See* elude.

> The General Manager alluded to the possibility of a trade.

allusion An allusion is a reference. *See* illusion.

> Schott made an allusion to the strike's potential implications.
> She alluded to the fact that people might lose their jobs.

alma mater Lowercase.

> Princeton is Ryan's alma mater.

Alpine skiing The events that make up Olympic Alpine skiing are downhill, super giant slalom, giant slalom, slalom, and Alpine combined. *See* skiing.

also ran (v.)

> Charlie ran the race. His brother Steve also ran.

also-ran (n.)

> I don't consider Gorden an also-ran.

alumni Use alumni to refer to more than one graduate of a college or university.

> Bradley and Anne are University of Iowa alumni.
> The alumni are sponsoring an event to raise money.
>
> One female graduate is an alumna.
> One male graduate is an alumnus.
> Two female graduates are alumnae.
> Two male graduates are alumni.

To avoid confusion, graduate can be used in all references.

a.m. Lowercase or specify small caps. Do not use the redundant a.m. in the morning.

WRONG: Practice begins at 8 a.m. in the morning.
RIGHT: Practice begins at 8 a.m.

amateur Use amateur to refer to a person who plays a sport for fun or as a hobby rather than as a profession. Amateurs are not paid for their participation in a sport. *See* professional.

> Minor-league baseball and hockey players are not amateurs.

Amateur Athletic Association Spell out on first reference to avoid confusion with the American Automobile Association. Use AAA on second reference.

Amateur Athletic Union Spell out on first reference, then AAU.

amateur draft Lowercase amateur draft in reference to the major-league selection process.

American Automobile Association Spell out on first reference, then AAA.

American Basketball Association Spell out on first reference, then ABA.

American Bowling Congress Spell out on first reference, then ABC.

American Football Conference AFC is acceptable on first reference. *See* acronyms.

American League Spell out on first reference, then AL as a modifier. Avoid using AL as a noun.

> The American League Championship Series begins tonight.
> Who will win the AL Championship?

American Professional Soccer League Spell out on first reference, then APSL.

American Softball Association Spell out on first reference, then ASA.

American West Conference *See* college, Part II, for members.

Americas Cup There is no apostrophe in the name of the golf event.

America's Cup Note the apostrophe in the name of the yachting event.

amid Preferred to amidst.

> Amid the confusion, the players still were able to concentrate.

among, between Use among to mean throughout or within a group of three or more.

> The team members discussed the issue among themselves.

Use between for two people or items.

> The owner said the matter was between him and the manager.

amphetamine A stimulant drug.

anaerobic exercise Exercise without oxygen. This term is associated with short duration, high intensity exercise. In contrast, aerobic exercise is associated with exercise over a sustained period of time.

anaerobic threshold The point at which exercise intensity increases to such a level that the body's energy requirements can no longer be met completely by the aerobic energy pathway. At this point, lactic acid is produced faster than it can be cleared from the body.

anabolic steroid A steroid hormone resembling testosterone that stimulates anabolism in the body.

anchor (n., v.) Anchor is acceptable in reference to a person who serves as the host of a newscast.

> He is the 10 p.m. anchor.
> She anchors the 10 p.m. news.

Anchor also is acceptable when referring to an anchorman or anchorwoman, the last person on a relay team.

> Gerard was the relay's anchor.
> He anchored the relay.

anchor leg (n.) The last position on a relay team.

> Rob will run the anchor leg.

anchorman, anchorwoman A person who serves as the host of a newscast also can be referred to as an anchor.

> Holtzman is the evening anchor.

Anchorman, anchorperson, and anchorwoman also refer to the last person on a five-person bowling team or four-person relay team, but anchor is acceptable as well.

> Thome was the relay team's anchor.

androgenic steroid A substance producing or stimulating male characteristics.

animals Do not use a personal pronoun unless gender has been established or the animal has a name.

> The dog won its race.
> Holy Bull won his third race.

annual Yearly. Do not hyphenate annual as a modifier.

> Tomorrow is the third annual relay meet.

Biannual refers to an event that occurs twice in one year.
Biennial refers to an event that occurs once every two years.
Quadrennial refers to an event that occurs once every four years.

anterior cruciate ligament A stabilizing ligament within the center of the knee joint that prevents hyperextension and exces-

---

sive rotation of the joint. Spell out on first reference, then ACL. *See* posterior cruciate ligament.

anticipate To anticipate is to look forward to and prepare for something. To expect something requires no preparation.

> We expect the game to start on time.
> I anticipate 30 people will come to dinner.

anti-inflammatory (n., adj.) A drug that prevents inflammation, such as ibuprofen.

> Samuels required anti-inflammatory medication for her knee.
> The doctor prescribed an anti-inflammatory.

anxious Worrisome. Do not use anxious as a synonym for eager, which implies positive anticipation.

> George is eager for the game to begin.
> Crews was anxious about giving his speech.

any more Means any additional.

> The Knicks aren't accepting any more applications for the coaching position.

anymore Means any longer.

> Reynolds won't be playing anymore.

anyway Not anyways.

> It rained, but Gapen went to the game anyway.

AP Spell out Associated Press on first reference, then AP.

> Kansas is ranked No. 1 by the Associated Press.
> Massachusetts is No. 2 in the AP Poll.

APBA Spell out American Power Boat Association on first reference.

APSL Spell out American Professional Soccer League on first reference.

AP Poll *See* Associated Press Poll.

apron (n.) The grass fringe that borders the green on a golf course.

arbitrate, mediate Professional athletes often file for arbitration, where one person hears two sides of an argument and hands down a decision. In mediation, one uses reason to persuade two parties to agree.

arc An arch or curve.

archery *See* Part II.

archrival (n., adj.) Use to describe a team's or individual's main competitor.

> The Bears defeated archrival Green Bay 33-0.

ARCO Arena Note capitalization in the name of this arena in Sacramento, Calif.

Arena Football League Spell out on first reference to avoid confusion with the old American Football League. *See* football, Part II.

armchair quarterback Slang term for a football fan who comments on a game while watching it on television.

armlock (n.) One word. In wrestling, use armlock to describe a hold in which a wrestler's arm is held in such a way that it cannot be moved.

armstand Use one word for the type of dive that begins with the diver standing on his or her hands.

around Do not use around as a synonym for about or approximately.

Thurman skated around the rink.
He arrived at the game about 10 minutes late.
The courts are approximately three miles from here.

arrhythmia An irregularity in the rhythm of the heartbeat.

arthroscopy This surgical procedure to examine the internal structures of a joint uses an arthroscope to diagnose, remove, or repair damaged tissue.

Art Ross Trophy *See* hockey, Part II.

ashiwaza Note the spelling of this foot-and-leg throw in judo.

assemble together This phrase is redundant. Use put together or assemble.

assistant coach Do not capitalize even when the title precedes a name. *See* coach.

She got advice from assistant coach Reinhart.

assistant general manager Do not capitalize even when the title precedes a name. *See* general manager.

The decision was made by assistant general manager Jones.

assists per game Spell out in text. Use apg only in agate.

Associated Press Poll Use Associated Press Poll or Associated Press Top 25 on first reference, then the AP poll, AP Top 25, or the poll. Do not refer to the poll simply as the Writers' Poll.

Is the Associated Press Poll out yet?
The Big Ten has six teams in the AP Top 25.

Association Do not abbreviate. Capitalize as part of a proper name.

Association of Intercollegiate Athletics for Women Spell out on first reference, then AIAW.

Association of Tennis Professionals Spell out on first reference, then ATP.

assure Assure means to make sure. *See* ensure.

> Reinsdorf assured us there wouldn't be a strike.

Astroturf Capitalize the trademark name of artificial grass.

at-bat (n.)

> This is Ripken's third at-bat.

athlete's foot Note apostrophe in the name of this condition characterized by itching and cracking skin between the toes.

Athletes in Action Capitalize the name of this Christian organization made up of collegiate athletes.

athletic club Spell out athletic club in all references in a story. Use the abbreviation AC only in headlines when space is limited and in agate. Capitalize as part of a proper name.

athletic conference Spell out conference names on first reference. *See* college, Part II.

> Arizona is a member of the Pacific-10. The team is in the Pac-10.

athletic director Capitalize Athletic Director as a title before a name. A.D. is acceptable in headlines when space is limited.

> Western Athletic Director John Johnson is present.
> Kim Kelly, Central's athletic director, was not there.

athletic team Capitalize team names and associations. *See* team.

> The Chicago Cubs play today at Wrigley Field.
> The Oakland A's are in third place.

Athletics, Oakland Oakland A's or the A's is acceptable on all references.

Atlanta-Fulton County Stadium Note hyphenation.

Atlantic Coast Conference Spell out on first reference, then ACC. *See* college, Part II.

Atlantic Ten Conference Spell out on first reference, then Atlantic 10. *See* college, Part II, for members.

at-large

> The coach is an at-large member of the voting committee.

ATP Spell out Association of Tennis Professionals on first reference.

attack line Two words. In volleyball, an attack line is drawn on each side of the court, 9 feet, 10 inches from the center line.

ATV Spell out all-terrain vehicle on first reference, then ATV.

audible (n.) A play called at the line of scrimmage in order to adjust to the opponent's formation.

> Thinking that the defense might blitz, Rypien called an audible.

Auerbach Trophy Award given to the NBA Coach of the Year is named after Arnold "Red" Auerbach. Auerbach Trophy is acceptable on second reference.

Australian rules football Do not hyphenate. Australian rules football is played on an oval playing field by two teams, each with eighteen players on the field. Players attempt to score goals, worth six points, and behinds, worth one point. Throwing the ball is not allowed.

author (n.) Do not use author as a verb.

> WRONG: McGuire authored the book.
> RIGHT: McGuire is the author.

auto racing Speeds are listed in miles per hour.

> A. J. Foyt set a record going 123.474 mph.

Turns are banked in degrees not percentages. Use figures in the names of specific turns.

> He crashed on Turn 2.
> He took the lead near the third turn.

Use figures in the names of specific row names.

> Mears will start on the inside of Row 3.
> He will start in the fifth row.

See Part II.

avenge (v.) To take revenge.

> The Vikings will try to avenge last season's 21-10 loss to the
> Lions.

average Average is determined by adding all quantities and then dividing the sum by the number of quantities. *See* batting average, ERA, goals against average.

> 2, 5, 8, 9, 12   Average 2 + 5 + 8 + 9 + 12 /5 = 7.2

Mean is the midpoint.

> 2, 5, 8, 9, 12   Mean = 7

The median is the point with an equal number of items above and below.

> 2, 5, 8, 9, 12   Median = 8

averse Opposed to.

> Coach May is averse to using a playbook.

Avia Capitalize the name of this athletic apparel company.

award Capitalize the proper names of awards.

> Kris will be chosen the Player of the Month.
> Joyce was voted Most Valuable Player.
> Al is once again Coach of the Year.
> T. J. was the team's Most Improved Athlete.

ax Note spelling. A tool used to chop is not an axe. The plural spelling of ax is axes.

axel Note the spelling of this figure skating movement in which a skater jumps from the outside edge of one skate, turns in the air and returns to the back edge of the other skate. Use single, double, triple, or quadruple to describe the number of rotations.

> Rosing performed a triple axel.

axle A rod on which a wheel turns.

B

Babe Ruth Baseball Youth summer baseball league.

back and forth

> The argument went back and forth for hours.

back-and-forth Not a synonym for the basketball term, over and back.

> The boat moved in a back-and-forth motion.

back board (n.) Use two words in reference to the board used to stabilize someone with neck or back injuries.

backboard (n.) One word in basketball and hockey references.

back-check (n., v.) Hyphenate this hockey term, which means to skate backward while defending one's own goal.

backcourt In basketball, the two guards make up the backcourt.

> Armstrong and Jordan will start in the Bulls' backcourt.

back dive (n.) Acceptable in all references to backward dive.

backdoor (adj.) Use in basketball references when a player quickly moves away from his or her defender and runs behind the defense to get in position for a quick pass under the basket.

> Manfield was fooled on the backdoor play.
> Crawford came in the back door.

backfield In football references, use one word to refer to players lined up behind the line of scrimmage.

backfire (v.)

> The team captain's plan backfired.

backhand Do not use the slang back-hander in baseball, tennis, or hockey references.

> Vail has a powerful backhand.
> Roberts scored with a backhand shot past the goalie.
> Phillips made a backhand catch in the outfield.
> He backhanded the ball.

back judge In football, the back judge's duties include counting the number of defensive players and watching all the eligible receivers on his or her side of the field.

back line Use two words for the out of bounds line in curling.

backpack (n., v.)

> The hikers took their backpacks.
> Koppel went backpacking in the woods.

backpedal (v.) To move backward while facing the play.

> Allen had to backpedal to catch the ball.

---

back-row players The three players farthest from the net in volleyball.

backspin (n.) Use backspin to describe the backward motion of a ball that causes it to stop quickly or reverse its direction.

> Brown's shot landed beyond the flag, but had so much backspin that it rolled into the hole.

backstop (n.) Do not use this slang term for goalie or catcher.

backstretch (n.) The straight part of a track opposite the homestretch.

backstroke (n.) In a medley relay, backstroke is the first leg of the race. In the individual medley, backstroke is the second leg after butterfly and before breaststroke and freestyle.

backswing (n.) Use one word.

back-to-back Hyphenate in all uses.

> The Bulls won back-to-back titles.
> The Braves won two games back-to-back.

backtrack (v.) Use one word to describe an athlete running backward. Synonym for backpedal.

back up (v.)

> Traffic backed up outside the stadium about noon.

backup (n., adj.)

> Clay was Jones' backup.
> Clay is a backup player.

backward (adj.) Not backwards.

> He bent over backward.
> Powter threw a backward pass.

badminton A match usually is three games. Games are won by the first player to score 15 points. In a one-game match, the game may consist of 21 points.

Events are men's singles, men's doubles, women's singles, and women's doubles. *See* Part II.

bagel job Avoid using this term in reference to a 6-0 score in tennis.

balaclava Note the spelling of this fire-resistant hood or mask worn by some race car drivers.

balance beam Spell out on first reference, then beam. *See* gymnastics.

> Miller placed first in the balance beam.
> Last year she was fifth in the beam.

balk (n., v.)

> Eldred was called for a balk.
> The runners advanced after the pitcher balked.

ball-and-socket joint Note hyphens.

ballast Note the spelling of the load used to stabilize a boat.

ballboy, ballgirl One word in reference to the person responsible for retrieving and storing equipment during a baseball game.

ball carrier (n.) Two words, no hyphen.

ballclub (n.) One word.

ballfield (n.) Synonym for ballpark.

ballgame (n.) One word.

ball-handler

> Armstrong is an excellent ball-handler.

---

ball-handling (adj.)

> He has improved his ball-handling skills.

ballpark (n.) Use one word in this synonym for ball field.

ballplayer (n.) One word.

banana heat Avoid using this slang term in swimming for a consolation final.

banana shot (n.) A soccer shot on goal where the ball spins on an arc in mid-air.

Band-Aid Capitalize this trademark name, but lowercase bandage.

> The trainer put a Band-Aid on the cut.
> I need a bandage for my cut.

bank (v.)

> Stockton banked a shot off the backboard.

bank shot (n.) A shot in basketball that bounces off the backboard.

> Don made a bank shot.

bantamweight Olympic class is 113–119 pounds. IBF/WBA/WBC class is 116–118 pounds. *See* boxing.

Baretta Capitalize this brand name of gun.

Baseball Writers Association of America Spell out in first reference, then BBWAA.

base hit Do not use the redundant base hit single.

base line The line that runs from base to base in baseball. *See* baseline.

baseline In basketball and tennis, the line that marks the end of the court. *See* base line.

base on balls Walk is acceptable in all references.

base runner (n.) Runner is acceptable.

base running (n.)

> Edwards is the best on the team at base running.

base-running (adj.)

> He has committed several base-running errors.

Basic Agreement Capitalize the proper name of the Major League Baseball agreement.

basic summary A system of summarizing games and events with more than two competitors or teams.

BASS Masters Classic Note capitalization of BASS. Spell out on first reference, then the Classic.

> The 36 top-ranked professional fishermen and five amateurs participate in this three-day event.

batboy, batgirl *See* ballboy, ballgirl.

batsman In baseball and cricket, the batter is not the batman.

batter's box The box is 4 feet wide and 6 feet long.

battery In baseball, the battery refers to the pitcher and catcher.

batting average Calculate by dividing the number of at-bats by the number of hits. Walks are not counted as at-bats and are not calculated into a player's batting average.

battle royal (n.) Acceptable in all references to a contest between two strong contenders.

Bay Area Capitalize in reference to the region surrounding and including San Francisco.

beam In sailing the beam refers to the greatest width of a boat.

In gymnastics, spell out balance beam on first reference, then beam.

> Rhonda won the balance beam event with a 9.75.
> Miller was first in the floor exercise and second in beam.

beanball A pitch thrown at a batter's head.

because Use because to indicate a cause-effect relationship. *See* since.

> Clements left because of the controversy.

belay (v.) Climbing term refers to method of protecting a climber by passing a rope around oneself or an object and paying it out as necessary to the climber.

Belmont Stakes Thoroughbred race held at Belmont Park in New York is one of the three races along with the Kentucky Derby and Preakness Stakes that make up the Triple Crown. Three-year-old horses compete in this 1 1/2-mile race. The Belmont Stakes is held three weeks after the Preakness Stakes. *See* Triple Crown.

bench press (v.)

> Shannon is able to bench press 240 pounds.

bench-press (adj.)

> He won the bench-press competition.

benchwarmer (n.) Avoid using in reference to a player who rarely plays in games.

beside Next to.

> The spectator stood beside the gate.

besides In addition to.

> Besides Wilkinson, only Rapp can throw a slider.

best-ball tournament In golf, a best-ball tournament is a team competition using the best individual score of the group on each hole. *See* golf.

best-of Hyphenate when using in phrases such as best-of-five series.

betting odds Use figures and a hyphen.

> The odds are 5-1 King will win.

Use a hyphen when expressing odds with the word *to*.

> The odds are 3-to-1.
> John took the bet despite 5-to-1 odds.

bettor One who bets.

between Use between with two people or items. *See* among.

> The owner said the matter was between Earle and Muller.

biannual Twice a year.

> The biannual picnic takes place in March and September.

A biennial event occurs once every two years.

biathlon Olympic competition combines shooting and skiing. A miss of the target adds two minutes to the total elapsed course time. The winner is decided on the basis of the lowest elapsed corrected time. *See* Part II.

bicycle kick (n.) Soccer kick in which the player does a back somersault and kicks the ball while his or her feet are pointing skyward.

Big East Conference Abbreviate Big East. *See* college, Part II.

Big Eight Conference Not Big 8. *See* college, Part II.

Big Four Capitalize when referring to the following Grand Slam tennis events as a group: Australian Open, French Open, Wimbledon, and U.S. Open.

big-league Hyphenate as a modifier.

> The high school shortstop made a big-league play.

big-leaguer Use major-leaguer or minor-leaguer when referring to a professional baseball player.

Big Sky Conference *See* college, Part II, for members.

Big South Conference *See* college, Part II, for members.

Big Ten Conference Not Big 10, Big Eleven, or Big 11. *See* college, Part II.

Big West Conference Abbreviate Big West. *See* college, Part II.

bike (n., v.) Acceptable for bicycle in all references.

> They will race on mountain bikes.
> The competitors will bike through a wooded area.

billiards The name of the sport is billiards, but the game is played on a billiard table with billiard balls. *See* Part II.

billion Use figures when expressing a specific dollar amount.

> The league made $2.1 billion last year.
> The league made more than a billion dollars last year.
> More than seven billion people saw the game.

bird Acceptable in badminton references to a shuttlecock. Do not use the term *birdie.*

birdie (n., v.) One under par in golf.

> Trevino had a birdie on the second hole.
> He doesn't have a chance to birdie the next one.

Daly birdied No. 6.
He can win by birdieing the last hole.

black (adj.) Black can be used as an adjective when referring to a person's race, but avoid using it as a noun.

> WRONG: Dennis is a black.
> RIGHT: Dennis is black. He is an African American.

See African American.

In bowling, this term refers to a player's ability to keep his or her average above 200. If a player is in the red, his or her average is below that mark.

Black Coaches Association Spell out on first reference, then BCA.

black out (v.) To refrain from televising a sporting event.

> They plan to black out the game in Kansas City.

blackout (n.)

> Will they go through with the blackout of the game?

blind side (n.) The side of person to which his or her attention is not turned.

> Hargrove was hit from the blind side.

blind-side (adj.)

> The blind-side hit forced Osborn into the wall.

blindside (v.)

> Jovic blindsided Zoran.

blitz (n., v.)

> We expect a blitz.
> The Raiders blitzed.

blow out (v.)

> The car's tire blew out on the second turn.

blowout (n.)

> The blowout sent Ware's car into the wall.

Blue Jays Spell out Blue Jays on second reference to the Toronto Blue Jays. Avoid using Jays alone except in headlines when space is limited.

blue line Hockey term is two words.

board In hockey and soccer, boarding means to force an opponent into the boards surrounding the playing area.

> The hockey player was penalized for boarding.
> Walters lost control of the soccer ball after he was boarded.

Do not use board to mean rebound in basketball.

> WRONG: George had 10 boards.
> RIGHT: George had 10 rebounds.

board-checking (n.) In hockey, board-checking is pushing an opponent into the boards.

> Jagr's board-checking has gone out of control.

boatswain (n.) The crew member on a boat assigned to maintain the boat's gear.

bobsled, bobsledding Use one word in reference to this winter sport.

> We watched the bobsledding competition.
> Walker was on the bobsled team.

See Part II.

body building (n.) Use two words in reference to the sport.

---

body check (n.)

> Rohan hit Recheiv with a body check.

body-check (v.)

> He body-checked Rone.

body English Always capitalize English in this phrase.

bogey, bogeys, bogeyed One stroke over par in golf.

> Palmer bogeyed the first hole.
> He had a double bogey on the second, and he triple-bogeyed
> the third.

bomb (n.) In general, do not use war imagery in sports stories. In football, however, the bomb is an exception, but use it sparingly in reference to a long pass.

> Redman threw a bomb to a wide-open receiver.

bootleg (n., adj.) Use one word to describe a football play or an illegal item.

bore Note spelling for the interior diameter of a gun barrel.

BoSox Do not use as a synonym for Boston Red Sox.

bow (n.) The front of a boat. The rear is the stern.

Bowl Alliance Participating teams come from the Atlantic Coast, Big East, Big Eight, Southeastern, and Southwest conferences, plus Notre Dame. The top six college football teams meet in three bowl games at the end of the season. The selection process rotates between the Fiesta, Sugar, and Orange bowls each year.

Sample Selection Order

> Sugar selects first and second
> Fiesta selects third and fifth
> Orange selects fourth and sixth

Bowl Coalition Poll In the past, the final Bowl Coalition Poll was determined by the combined point totals of the Associated Press and USA/CNN polls.

bowl games Note corporate sponsor on first reference. *See* college, Part II, for games and participating teams. Always capitalize the name of a bowl.

> The Jeep Eagle Aloha Bowl is today.

box-and-one Hyphenate this basketball zone defense in all uses.

bowling Highest score is 300, or a perfect game. Avoid the redundant perfect 300 game. *See* Part II.

boxing There are several professional boxing organizations, including the International Boxing Federation, United States Boxing Association, North American Boxing Federation, World Boxing Association, and World Boxing Council.

There are 17 weight divisions recognized by the WBC, WBA, and IBF. Following are these classes and the weight limit of each.

Mini-Flyweight (IBF)	
Minimumweight (WBA)	
Strawweight (WBC)	105 pounds
Junior Flyweight	108
Flyweight	112
Junior Bantamweight	115
Bantamweight	118
Junior Featherweight	122
Featherweight	126
Junior Lightweight	130
Lightweight	135
Junior Welterweight	140
Welterweight	147
Junior Middleweight	154
Middleweight	160
Super Middleweight	168
Light Heavyweight	175
Junior Heavyweight	190
Heavyweight	191 +

The Olympics have 12 weight classes, as follows:

Light flyweight	106 pounds
Flyweight	112
Bantamweight	119
Featherweight	125
Lightweight	132
Light welterweight	139
Welterweight	147
Light middleweight	156
Middleweight	165
Light heavyweight	178
Heavyweight	201
Super heavyweight	202+

box office (n.)

Bull Durham did well at the box office.

box-office (adj.)

Have you seen the box-office receipts?

box score (n.) *See* Part II for examples of different box scores.

boys Boys does not require an apostrophe when used descriptively. *See* men, women, girls.

The boys basketball team won the state championship.

BP Do not use as a synonym for batting practice.

brakeman Note the spelling for the member of the bobsled team who operates the brake.

break away (v.)

Lavris broke away from the field.

breakaway (n.) In sports such as basketball, hockey, and football, a player on a breakaway is in control of the ball with no opposition between the player and the goal.

> Snook scored on a breakaway.

break point (n.) Use two words when describing the point the receiver needs to break the serve in tennis.

breakwater The structure built to keep water out of a boat cockpit or a harbor.

breaststroke Breaststroke is one of the four competitive swimming strokes. In the individual medley event, breaststroke is the third stroke performed. In a medley relay, breaststroke is the second leg of the race. *See* swimming.

Breeders' Cup Note apostrophe. The Breeders' Cup features thoroughbreds competing at seven distances.

Juvenile/Juvenile Fillies	1 $1/16$ miles
Sprint	6 furlongs
Mile	1 mile
Bistaff	1 $1/8$ miles
Turf	1 $1/2$ miles
Classic	1 $1/4$ miles
Steeplechase	2 $5/8$ miles

bring to a head Avoid using this cliche.

British Open PGA event is held at golf courses in England and Scotland. It is one of the four Majors. *See* golf.

broodmare (n.) A female horse used for breeding.

brushback pitch An inside pitch.

bucket Avoid using bucket as a synonym for basket in basketball references.

Bucs Acceptable in headlines when space is limited for a team whose full name is Buccaneers. Do not use as a synonym for Pirates.

bullfight, bullfighter (n.) One word.

bullpen The bullpen is the warm-up area for pitchers in baseball, a staging area for athletes waiting to compete in an event, such as swimming or track, or an area that holds cattle.

bull's eye (n.) Note the apostrophe.

bump-and-run (n.) Note the hyphens.

bungee cord (n.) Note the spelling of this elasticized cord.

bunker (n.) Hazard area on golf course.

buoy (n., v.)

> Connor steered the yacht away from the buoy.
> The cheers buoyed the marathoner's spirits.

bush league Use minor league.

Butkus Award Acceptable in all references to the award established in 1985 and named for Dick Butkus. The honor is given to the top collegiate linebacker by the Downtown Athletic Club of Orlando, Fla. *See* college, Part II.

butt-ending In hockey, butt-ending is using the end of the stick in a jabbing motion.

> Vidal was called for butt-ending.
> He received a butt-ending penalty.

butterfly Spell out on first reference to the swimming event, then fly. Butterfly is the first event performed during the individual medley. It is the third leg of a medley relay. *See* swimming.

bye (n.) A position in a tournament that allows a team to advance through a round without facing an opponent.

Byng Trophy *See* hockey, Part II.

C

Cactus League Use sparingly in reference to the major-league baseball exhibition season in Arizona. The exhibition season in Florida often is referred to as the Grapefruit League.

caddie (n.) Note the *ie* ending

caddie, caddied, caddying (v.) Note the spelling.

Calder Memorial Trophy Award given to NHL Rookie of the Year. *See* hockey, Part II.

caliber, calibre Use a hyphen between a number and caliber.

> Barnes fired a .22-caliber rifle.

calisthenics (n.) Exercises.

called game A baseball game terminated by the umpire-in-chief.

called strike (n.) A strike at which a batter doesn't swing.

call letters Capitalize.

> KRUI-FM will broadcast the game.
> The game will be on KJHK-90.7.

call up (v.)

> The Rangers called up Moore from the minor leagues.

call-up (n., adj.)

> Hansen is the team's fifth call-up from Class A.

Camden Yards The full name of the Orioles ballpark is Oriole Park at Camden Yards. Spell out on first reference.

Camp Award Award is given to NCAA Division I Player of the

Year and Coach of the Year. On first reference, use the Walter Camp Award, then Camp Award. *See* college, Part II.

Canada goose Not Canadian goose when referring to the bird.

Canadian Football League Spell out on first reference, then CFL. *See* football, Part II.

cancel Do not use as a synonym for postpone. A canceled game isn't made up. A postponed game is rescheduled.

canned Do not use as a synonym for hit or made.

> WRONG: Ritter canned a three-point shot.
> RIGHT: Ritter made a three-point shot.

cannon Do not use as a synonym for arm when referring to a person's throwing ability.

> WRONG: The shortstop has a cannon.

canoe, canoed, canoeing *See* Part II.

cap Baseball players wear caps, not hats, as a part of their uniform.

capitalization Capitalize the first word in a sentence.

> Sacramento will have the first pick in the draft.

Capitalize titles of books, newspapers, TV shows.

> The ad will run during "Monday Night Football."

Capitalize proper names.

> Kyle Jackson played his first game at Candlestick Park.

Capitalize a common noun when it is part of a proper name.

> I would like to see a game at Jack Murphy Stadium.

Capitalize trademarks.

> The trainer put a Band-Aid on the quarterback's hand.
> Duke advanced to the NCAA Final Four.

Capitalize titles before a name.

> General Manager Carl Peterson informed us of the trade.
> Information on the trade was provided by Kurt Larsen, general
> manager.
> Club President John Dewy makes the financial decisions.

Capitalize Coach before a name when it appears without a qualifying term.

> Kings coach Rob Paravonian.
> Coach Ara Hagopian called the plays.

captain In reference to a team's leader, do not capitalize captain when it precedes a name.

> Chicago captain Scottie Pippen led the team meeting.

Capitalize Captain as a title when a person is in the military or the captain of a ship or airplane.

> Headquarters informed Captain Thompson of the crisis.
> Robinson was once a captain in the Navy.

carabiner (n.) Metal snaplink device used in mountain climbing is placed in a piton so that a rope may pass through.

carbohydrate loading Technique used by athletes preparing for competition in which foods rich in carbohydrates are eaten to build up fuel in the body. Spell out on first reference, then carbo-loading.

card Do not use as a verb in golf stories.

> WRONG: Simms carded a 4-under-par 71.
> RIGHT: Simms shot a 4-under-par 71.

cardinal points The north, south, east, and west points on a compass.

Cardinals Cards is acceptable in headlines when space is limited, but Cardinals should be spelled out in other references to a team's name.

carry over (v.)

> Do you think the momentum will carry over?

carry-over (n.)

> Watson experienced some carry-over.

casual water On a golf course, casual water is a temporary accumulation of water. It is not considered a water hazard.

casualty Avoid using war imagery to refer to an injured player. *See* war.

> WRONG: He was the third casualty of the game.

catamaran (n.) Note spelling for this boat.

catcher's box (n.) Note the apostrophe.

catch fire Avoid using this phrase to describe a player or team that suddenly begins doing well.

catch up (v.)

> Charlotte was able to catch up in the fourth quarter.

catch-up (n., adj.)

> Hartford had to play catch-up throughout the game.
> They found themselves in a catch-up situation.

cat rig (n.) Note the two-word spelling for a sailboat with one sail.

CAT Scan *See* CT Scan.

Cavaliers Cavaliers is preferred in all references, but Cavs is acceptable in headlines when space is limited.

CBA Spell out Continental Basketball Association on first reference, then CBA. *See* basketball, Part II.

CBS Acceptable in all references to the former Columbia Broadcasting System.

CD-ROM Capitalize and hyphenate.

center back Football term is two words.

center court Two words. Do not spell as "centre."

center field, center fielder Hyphenate as a modifier.

> Josh plays center field.
> Justin is a center fielder.
> He ran into the center-field fence.

center forward Hockey position is two words.

center/forward Use a slash when referring to a basketball player who is known to play both positions.

> Gipson, a center/forward, is being recruited by several schools.

center line In hockey, it is the line that runs the width of the ice.

> In volleyball, the center line runs under the net and divides the court into two halves.

centerline Use one word for the imaginary line that runs along the center of a boat.

center mark The mark on the baseline of a tennis court that defines the limit of the serving area.

champion Capitalize the trademark name of the athletic apparel company.

Lowercase champion as a title before a name.

> The national champion Washington Huskies visited the White House.

change of pace Do not hyphenate.

change over (v.)

> Agassi and Sampras will change over during this set.

changeover (n.)

> Agassi and Sampras spoke during the changeover.

change-up (n., adj.) Use a hyphen when referring to this slow baseball pitch.

> Sheridan throws a change-up.
> His change-up pitch fooled many batters.

channel Capitalize when referring to a specific channel. Use figures.

> The game is on Channel 7.
> Gertrude Ederle was the first person to swim the English Channel.

Lowercase channel when referring to more than one channel or in general uses.

> We watch channels 5 and 9 at night.

charity stripe Avoid using as a synonym for foul line or free-throw line.

charley horse (n.) A pain or stiffness in the leg.

chassis (n.) The chassis is the rectangular steel frame attached to the axles of a vehicle that holds the body and motor.

check (n., v.) Note the usage of this chess term for a king in danger.

> Fischer put the white king in check.
> Marley checked the black king.

check (v.)

> Rogers checked his swing.

checked swing (n.) Note spelling. It is not check swing.

checked-swing (adj.)

> Oscar hit a checked-swing foul.

checkmate (n.) Use one word to refer to the winning check in chess.

chess *See* Part II.

ChiSox Do not use as a synonym for Chicago White Sox.

choke Do not use to describe the inability of a team or athlete to perform because of pressure.

chronic injury A long-term injury often associated with overuse. This is different from an acute injury, which is often sudden and short-term.

chukker In polo, there are six chukkers, or periods, in each match.

CISL Acceptable on second reference to the Continental Indoor Soccer League.

cities Do not abbreviate the names of cities on first reference.

> WRONG: He plays for the L.A. Dodgers.
> RIGHT: He plays for Los Angeles Dodgers.

Use a comma to separate a city from its state. *See* states.

The tournament will be held in Springfield, Mo.

The following cities are large enough and familiar enough to be recognized without their state.

Atlanta	Houston	Philadelphia
Baltimore	Indianapolis	Phoenix
Boston	Las Vegas	Pittsburgh
Chicago	Los Angeles	St. Louis
Cincinnati	Miami	Salt Lake City
Cleveland	Milwaukee	San Antonio
Dallas	Minneapolis	San Diego
Denver	New Orleans	San Francisco
Detroit	New York	Seattle
Honolulu	Oklahoma City	Washington

Include the name of a state with any U.S. city not on the above list.

The team traveled to Anaheim, Calif., for the tournament.

Use parentheses when inserting a state name into an unfamiliar proper name.

The Panora (Iowa) Hawks won the football game.

Do not insert a state name into the proper name of a well-known professional team.

WRONG: The Jacksonville (Fla.) Jaguars play tomorrow.

claim Claim, as a form of attribution, implies skepticism. Do not use as a substitute for said. *See* said.

Class A Use Class A, Class AA, and Class AAA when referring to minor-league baseball classifications. Hyphenate when used as a modifier.

Jackson moved up from Class A to Double A.
Jones plays for a Triple-A team in the International League.

clean-and-jerk (n.) Note the hyphens in this weightlifting event where the lifter pulls the weight to the waist, then lifts it above the head.

clean up (v.)

> Howser will clean up the stadium.

cleanup (n., adj.)

> Ward bats cleanup for the Expos.
> Donahey is the cleanup hitter.

cliche, cliché A cliche is an overused expression that often fails to enhance a sentence, confuses the reader, and creates clutter. Many of the sports editors who contributed to this book suggested the following cliches as ones to be avoided.

between the pipes	launch an attack
bring to a head	one-bagger
circles the bases	reach the century mark
dented the scoring column	ticks on the clock
dodged a bullet	unanswered points
got on the board	

cliffhanger (n.) An exception to *Webster's Tenth Collegiate Dictionary,* spell cliffhanger without a hyphen.

clip (n., v.) In football, a clip occurs when a player throws his or her body across the back of an opponent's legs or falls into the back of an opponent below the waist from behind.

> Xavier was called for a clip.
> He was called for clipping in the first quarter.
> Word clipped the running back.

In baseball references, use clip as a noun.

> Shadel is hitting at a .345 clip.

clubhouse In baseball, the locker room is referred to as the clubhouse. Other sports use locker room.

---

coach Capitalize coach when it is used in place of a first name or without a qualifying term.

> Ask Coach Riggins who is up next.
> Coach Janet Lundeen is a great motivator.
> Mike Hewitt, the team's coach, will present the award.

Do not capitalize coach when it is preceded by a qualifying term.

> Chiefs coach Marty Shottenheimer was here.
> First-base coach Ritter told him to run.

Use head coach only when it is necessary to distinguish between two coaches.

> James is the head coach and Kevin is the assistant coach.

Coach of the Year Capitalize this award and others like it. *See* awards.

> Wallace was voted Coach of the Year.
> Craig was Player of the Month.

coach's box In baseball, the box is 10 feet wide and 20 feet long.

co-captain Hyphenate in all uses. Do not capitalize as a title before a name.

> Stacey Peterson is a co-captain of the team.
> The decision will be made by co-captain Joan Baker.

coed A coed team or organization is made up of male and female participants. Do not refer to a female student as a college coed.

> They play softball in a coed league.

co-leader (n.) Always hyphenated.

> Anderson and Williamson are the co-leaders.

Coliseum, Colosseum Note the difference in spellings.

The Raiders play at the Los Angeles Coliseum.
Have you ever visited the ancient Roman Colosseum?

collected Do not use collected as a synonym for got or had. Athletes do not collect hits, runs, or points.

WRONG: The Expos collected 10 hits.

Collective Bargaining Agreement In the NFL, this agreement outlines the terms under which a player becomes a restricted or unrestricted free agent.

collective nouns Most collective nouns, such as team, organization, class, and group, take a singular verb.

The team is in first place.
The class presented its findings.

college Always capitalize as part of a proper name.

Griffen plays football at Columbia College.

college division There are six major divisions in college athletics: NCAA Division I-A and I-AA, NCAA Division II, NCAA Division III, and NAIA Division I and II. *See* college, Part II.

College World Series Use in reference to the NCAA Men's Baseball or Women's Softball championships. Spell out on first reference, then the series, never CWS. This differs from the World Series, where Series is capitalized on second reference. *See* college, Part II.

collision A collision takes place between two moving objects, not one moving object and one stationary object.

WRONG: The player collided with the fence.
RIGHT: The players collided while running for the ball.

Colonial Athletic Association *See* college, Part II, for members.

colored Do not use colored to describe a person's race.

colorman Refer to a person who works with a play-by-play announcer as the colorman or color commentator.

Colosseum, Coliseum Note the difference in spellings.

> The Raiders play at the Los Angeles Coliseum.
> Have you ever visited the ancient Roman Colosseum?

colt A young male horse.

comebacker A ground ball hit back at the pitcher in baseball.

commissioner Capitalize Commissioner when it is used as a formal title before a name.

> NBA Commissioner David Stern issued a ruling.
> Gary Bettman, NHL commissioner, led the meeting.

Commission on Olympic Sports Spell out on first reference, then COS.

commit, committed, committing (v.)

commodore A yacht club's highest officer. Capitalize as a formal title before a name.

complement A complement makes up part of a complete set. *See* compliment.

> The players' skills complement each other.

complete game A pitcher must start and finish a game to record a complete game.

complete-game shutout (n.) Shutout alone is acceptable. A shutout occurs when a pitcher throws a complete game in which no runs are scored.

compliment A compliment is praise. *See* complement.

> Coach Reinhart complimented us on our game.

compose To compose is to put together. *See* comprise.

> The league is composed of 10 teams.

compound fracture A broken bone that has cut through the soft tissue near it.

comprise To comprise is to be made up of. A whole comprises its parts. *See* compose.

> The league comprises 10 teams.
> The team is made up of nine players.

compulsory routine (n.) A routine, as in figure skating, that is required of all participants.

concussion This injury to the brain can be graded as mild, moderate, or severe depending on loss of consciousness, amnesia, and loss of equilibrium.

conference Capitalize as part of a proper name.

> The Bulls are in the Midwest Division of the Eastern Conference.

Conference USA *See* college, Part II, for members.

Conn Smythe Trophy *See* hockey, Part II.

consecutive games Do not hyphenate as a modifier when used with a number.

> The Jayhawks have won five consecutive games.

contest The word *contest* should be reserved for competitions in which individuals perform separately. Avoid using contest to describe a competition between teams.

> WRONG: The Chicago Cubs won the contest.
> RIGHT: The Cubs won the game.
> RIGHT: Meyer won the diving contest.

Style and Usage

Continental Basketball Association Spell out on first reference, then CBA. *See* basketball, Part II.

Continental Indoor Soccer League Spell out on first reference, then CISL.

continuing action foul Do not hyphenate. In football, a continuing action foul is spiking the ball or a personal foul that occurs immediately after a down ends.

contusion A bruise usually caused by a blow from a blunt object.

cornerback (n.) Use one word in reference to this football defender.

corporate sponsors Include the name of a corporate sponsor when its name is part of the event's official title.

> The Virginia Slims tennis tournament was exciting.
> The Weiser Lock Copper Bowl is this week.

corps The term for a group of people is not corp.

COSD Committee on Sports for the Disabled is a bylaw committee of the United States Olympic Committee. Spell out on first reference, then COSD.

Cotton Bowl Use Mobil Cotton Bowl on first reference. *See* bowl games.

council (n.) An assembly of people.

> Starbird was treasurer for the intramural sports council.

counsel (v.) To give advice.

> She counseled the batter during his hitting slump.

counterattack (n., v.) One word.

counterpunch (n.) One word.

country club Spell out and capitalize as part of a proper name. C.C. is acceptable as part of a name on second reference, but do not use it alone as a noun.

> We played golf at Glen Flora Country Club.

coupé Note the accent in this fencing attack made by passing a blade over the opponent's blade.

courtesy titles Do not use courtesy titles unless it is general practice for a specific publication.

coxswain (n.) Note no hyphen.

cox-swain (v.) Note the hyphen in the verb form.

crackback (adj.)

> Richie was penalized for a crackback block.

Cracker Jack Capitalize the trademark name of caramel popcorn candy.

crackerjack Lowercase when referring to a person who is particularly skilled at his or her sport.

> Howard is a crackerjack shooter.

crevasse (n.) A deep chasm.

crevice (n.) A narrow crack or opening.

cricket This game, which remotely resembles baseball, is played by two teams of 11 players. The field is called a pitch, which features two wickets placed 22 yards apart. Scoring is in runs. *See* Part II.

crippled Do not refer to a team as crippled by injuries.
When referring to a person with a physical impairment, use disabled or handicapped.

crisscross (v.) One word.

crossbar (n.) The crossbar is the horizontal bar on a goal post.

cross-check (n., v.) The act of hitting an opponent with both hands on the stick and no part of the stick on the ice.

> Fite hit Roney with a cross-check.
> He cross-checked the defenseman.

cross-country (adj.) *See* skiing.

> Michelle is a cross-country runner.
> The American team won a medal in cross-country skiing.

cross-court (adj.)

> Skiles threw a cross-court pass.

cross service line There is no hyphen in the tennis term for the line that runs parallel to the baseline at the edge of the service court.

cross-town (adj.)

> The schools are cross-town rivals.

CT scan Preferred to CAT scan. A CT scan is a method of taking multiple X-rays of the body and creating cross-sectional views. It is not the same as Magnetic Resonance Imaging, an imaging process that uses radio waves.

curling *See* Part II.

curveball A right-handed pitcher's curveball breaks to the left.

cut off (v.)

> Brock cut off the throw from left field.

cutoff (n., adj.)

> Dorn was the cutoff man.
> Lang was unable to hit the cutoff.

cut-throat (adj.) The tournament featured cut-throat competition.

CWS Do not use in reference to the College World Series. *See* College World Series.

cycle In baseball, the term used to describe a single, double, triple, and home run hit by the same player during a game.

> McRae hit for the cycle.

cycling Olympic events include:

> individual road race
> sprint
> individual points race
> 4,000 team pursuit
> 4k individual pursuit
> 1k time trial

See Part II.

cyst Medical term for an abnormal sac containing liquid or semi-solid matter.

Cy Young Award Always spell out. Do not refer to the award simply as the Young Award. The Cy Young Award is given to the major-league pitcher of the year. *See* baseball, Part II.

D

D Avoid using D as an abbreviation for defense.

dark horse (n.)

> Cervano is the dark horse in the race.

---

dark-horse (adj.)

> Milwaukee is the dark-horse team in the American League Central.

dates Always use figures.

> The Royals play road games from June 1 to June 9.

Capitalize days of the week and months.
Abbreviate Jan., Feb., Aug., Sept., Oct., Nov., and Dec. when used with a specific date. Spell out other months in all references.

> Practice begins Monday, March 7.
> The stadium will open Aug. 15, 1997.

day's rest (sing.)

> Harris will pitch on one day's rest.

days' rest (pl.)

> Hal pitched on three days' rest.

day-to-day Hyphenate in all uses.

> Pena is listed as day-to-day.

dead end (n.) Two words.

dead-end (adj.) Note hyphen when used as a modifier.

deadlock (n., v.)

> Negotiations are in a deadlock.
> The score was deadlocked at 20-20.

debut (n.) Do not use debut as a verb.

> WRONG: The pitcher debuted yesterday.
> RIGHT: The pitcher made his debut yesterday.

Terms and Their Usage

decades Use figures and an apostrophe when numbers are omitted.

> Ryan was the best pitcher of the '70s.

Use figures without an apostrophe when writing out the entire number.

> Ryan was the best pitcher of the 1970s.

decathlete, decathlon Note there is no *a* between the *b* and *l*.

> Events:
>
> | | |
> |---|---|
> | 100-meter dash | 110-meter hurdles |
> | long jump | discus |
> | shot put | pole vault |
> | high jump | javelin |
> | 400-meter run | 1,500-meter run |

decline to comment Use only if a person has actually declined to comment. Do not use the phrase about a person who is unavailable for comment or could not be reached for comment. Be specific.

defense Do not use defense as a verb.

> WRONG: The Rockets defensed the Suns.
> RIGHT: The Rockets' defense kept the Suns from scoring.

defenseman In hockey and lacrosse, the term is one word.

dehydrate (n., v.) To suffer excessive water loss.

> The triathlete was dehydrated at the end of the race.
> Jacobson could be suffering from dehydration.

deke (v.) Acceptable for a fake in hockey.

> Lemieux was able to deke the first defender.

delay of game (n.) Football penalty is not delay of the game.

Style and Usage

delay-of-game penalty Note the hyphens. The penalty in the NFL is 5 yards.

DeLong Athletic apparel company.

deltoid muscle This muscle is located at the top of the arm, just below the shoulder.

derogatory terms Avoid using derogatory terms. If a word that might be offensive to a segment of the population appears in a quote, determine whether the quote is really necessary to the story. If the quote is relevant, determine whether the word is acceptable for print. If it is not, follow your publication's practice for omitting a word in a quote.

Following is just a small sample of words that may be considered offensive by some readers.

bimbo	fag
chick	hillbilly
colored (or other even	powwow
more offensive words	redneck
aimed at African	savage
Americans)	squaw
cripple	token

Derby Use on second reference to the Kentucky Derby.

designated hitter Avoid using DH in text. Abbreviation is acceptable in agate and in headlines when space is limited.

destroy In general, don't use war imagery in sports stories. An exception to this is bomb. *See* bomb.

If using the word *destroy,* do not use completely destroyed or partially destroyed. Something is either destroyed or isn't.

deuce The score of a tennis match tied at 40 is deuce. Do not use the redundant deuce at 40/40.

Deuce Avoid using the Deuce in reference to ESPN2.

DH Use only in headlines when space is limited and in agate for designated hitter.

diagnose To distinguish or identify an injury or illness. A person cannot be diagnosed. *See* prognosis.

> WRONG: Kimble was diagnosed with a sprained ankle.
> RIGHT: The doctor diagnosed Kimble's injury as a sprain.

dimension *See* numbers.

Dinah Shore LPGA event is played at Mission Hills Country Club in Rancho Mirage, Calif. The event is one of the LPGA Majors. *See* golf.

dinger Do not use as a synonym for home run.

direct-free kick (n.) Note the hyphen when referring to this soccer kick that can score as a goal without touching another player. *See* indirect-free kick.

directions Do not capitalize a direction unless it refers to a specific region or the name of an athletic conference.

> The wind is blowing from the west.
> Park north of the stadium.
> Who is No. 1 in the Midwest regional?
> They live in the Southwest.
> The Southwest Conference is tough this year.

director Capitalize as a formal title before a name.

> Personnel Director Barb Taylor hired two new workers.
> The trade wasn't made, according to director of player personnel Rich Gunnar.

disabled list DL is acceptable in headlines when space is limited and in agate, but spell out in other references. Do not change if in a quote.

> Horn was put on the 15-day disabled list.

disc Note spelling of connective tissue in backbone.

dislocation (n., v.) A complete displacement of the joint surfaces.

> The lineman suffered a dislocation.
> He dislocated his elbow.

dive, diving, dived The past tense is not dove.

> Melissa dived into the pool.

Use figures for the heights of boards used in diving events.

> Wirth won the 1-meter and 3-meter events, and she was second
> in 10-meter platform.

Division I Always use Roman numerals and do not hyphenate as a modifier.

> Are they a Division I or Division II team?

It is not necessary to distinguish between Division I-A and I-AA unless relevant, for example, when teams from different divisions are mentioned in the same story.

> Division I-A Miami defeated Division II Southern. *See* college,
> Part II.

DL DL is acceptable in headlines when space is limited and in agate, but spell out disabled list in other references.

DNF Use only in agate for Did Not Finish.

dogleg A curving fairway.

dog racing Greyhound races are usually 3/8 or 5/16 of a mile.
Use a personal pronoun only when the gender of a dog has been established.

> Kansas Sue won her first race.

---

dollars Always use figures and a dollar sign for specific amounts.

> Pete will make $8 million this year.
> He made $100,000 last year.
> Ticket prices could increase to $15.
> The race car will cost thousands of dollars.

Double A Use instead of Class AA when referring to the minor-league baseball classification. *See* Class A, Triple A.

> Taylor was moved up to Double A.
> Taylor excelled in Double-A baseball.

double bogey (n.)

> Yang had a double bogey on the eighth hole.

double-bogey (v.)

> He double-bogeyed the 10th hole.

double coverage (n.)

> Sanders ran into double coverage throughout the game.

double-cover (v.)

> The Eagles doubled-covered Isaacs.

double eagle (n.)

> Richie had a double eagle on the eighth hole.

double-eagle (v.)

> He double-eagled the 10th hole.

double-elimination

> The team won the double-elimination tournament.

double fault (n.)

The momentum shifted after Becker's double fault.

double-fault (v.)

Veslavic double-faulted twice.

doubleheader A doubleheader is two games played back-to-back on the same day.

double play (n.)

Mueller hit into a double play.

double-play (adj.)

He hit another double-play ball.

double-pump (v.)

Price double-pumped before taking the shot.

double-team (v.)

We double-teamed O'Neil.

dove (v.) A bird. Dived is the past tense of dive. *See* dive.

Tracy dived from the 3-meter board.

down Spell out first, second, third, and fourth down. Use figures when referring to yard lines.

The Bears had a first down at the 4-yard line.

down-and-in Football play is hyphenated in all uses.

He ran a down-and-in.

down-and-out Hyphenate in all uses.

He ran a down-and-out.
Jones feels down-and-out.

downcourt (n., adj.) One word.

downfield (n., adj.) One word.

downhill (n., adj.)

Evans saw her sled downhill.
Marcus enjoys downhill skiing.

downstream (n.) One word.

downwind

It was loud downwind from the Packers' fans.

draft Do not capitalize draft when referring in general to the selection process of various professional leagues.

The NFL draft begins today.
Patrick was chosen in the first round of the draft.
He was a first-round pick.
I expect Harris will be the No. 4 pick.

Draft Day Capitalize Draft Day when referring specifically to the first day of the draft in the NFL, NBA, and NHL.

April 22 is Draft Day.

drafting Technique in which an athlete, such as a runner, biker, swimmer, or the driver of a car, maneuvers behind a competitor to reduce resistance and conserve energy.

Andretti has been drafting off Unser for several laps.

drain Do not use drain as a verb for made.

WRONG: Hagopian drained a three-pointer.
RIGHT: Hagopian made a three-pointer.

Style and Usage

draw In golf, a draw is a shot that curves slightly to the left. A shot that makes a severe curve to the left is a hook. A draw also is a tie score.

> We played to a 12-12 draw.

drop back (v.)

> Barker dropped back to throw.

drop-back (adj.)

> He is a drop-back quarterback.

drop goal In rugby, a drop goal, worth three points, is scored when the ball is drop-kicked over the crossbar and between the posts in open play.

drop kick (n.)

> Crociani decided to try a drop kick.

drop-kick (v.)

> Plantier drop-kicked the ball.

dual (n., adj.) Use dual to refer to something of double character, such as a dual meet.

duel (n., v.) Use duel to refer to a contest.

> The men met in a duel to decide the champion.

dugout The area in which a baseball team resides during a game is one word. *See* bullpen, clubhouse, locker room.

DUI In some states, a person can be charged with Driving Under the Influence. In other states, the offense is an OUI, OWI, or DWI. Be careful when reporting a drunken driving incident to use the correct acronym.

du Maurier Classic This LPGA event is played at Ottawa Hunt Club in Ottawa, Ontario. It is one of the four LPGA Majors. *See* golf.

dumbbell (n.) Note the spelling of this weightlifting implement. Do not use as a derogatory term.

E

each and every Redundant. Each or every can be used alone.

eager Eager denotes enthusiasm. Do not use eager as a synonym for anxious. *See* anxious.

eagle (n., v.) Two under par in golf.

> Swan had an eagle on the third hole.
> He eagled No. 12 as well.

earned-run average (n.) ERA is acceptable in all references. *See* ERA.

Easton Athletic equipment company.

easy Do not assume that winning by a wide margin was easy. For example, in basketball, a game that ends with a 15-point final margin may have been tied only two minutes earlier.

echelon Note the spelling of a staggered line of cyclists in a pace line.

Eclipse Award Award given to the outstanding jockey of the year.

eddy Patch of water less disturbed than surrounding water.

elicit (v.) To elicit is to create action or information. *See* illicit.

> The letter elicited a strong response.

eligible, eligibility Note spelling.

encroachment (n.) Encroachment occurs when any part of a football player's body enters the neutral zone and contact with an opponent occurs before the snap.

end around (n.)

> Smith ran an end around.

end line (n.)

> The ball sailed over the end line.

end zone (n.)

> Stallworth reached the end zone on a 50-yard run.

English Capitalize English in phrases.

> He put English on the ball.

en guard Or on guard. In fencing, the official says en guard as a warning that the match will begin.

ensure (v.) Ensure means to guarantee. *See* insure.

> The free throw ensured the victory.

enveloppement Note the spelling of this fencing movement when an opponent's blade is carried for at least one full circle.

épée Note spelling of the sword used in fencing.

epicondylitis Inflammation in the elbow due to overuse.

equestrian There are three paces: walk, trot, and canter. *See* Part II.

ERA Earned run average. ERA is acceptable in all references. Use a decimal point and figures.

> Appier finished the season with a 2.25 ERA.

Calculate an ERA using the following formula:

> Add the number of runs scored before the third out that are not scored because of an error.
> Divide by the total number of innings pitched.
> Multiply by 9.

Eskimo roll Capitalize the name of this kayaking maneuver.

ESPN Acceptable in all references.

ESPN2 Do not use a space between ESPN and 2. Avoid referring to ESPN2 as the Deuce.

ESPY Awards Spell out on first reference, then ESPYs.

> Berman was awarded an ESPY.

ethyl chloride This chemical coolant is sprayed onto an injury to act as local anesthesia.

explode, erupt Do not use these terms to describe a team's scoring ability.
Avoid using war imagery in sports stories. An exception is the word *bomb,* which has come to mean a long pass in football. *See* war.

extra-base hit (n.) Note the hyphen.

extra-inning game (n.) Note the hyphen in this term for a tied baseball game.

extra point Extra point or points after are preferred to PAT.

even par This is redundant. Use par.

every day (n.)

> Randle practices every day.

everyday (adj.)

> This is not an everyday occurrence.

exhibition game Use exhibition or spring training when referring to the professional baseball spring training season, not preseason.

> The Marlins and Reds will meet in an exhibition game.
> It is their second spring training game.

Preseason is acceptable for basketball, hockey, and football games played prior to the regular season.

F

face mask (n.)

> Marcus broke the face mask on his helmet.

face-mask (adj.)

> Phillips was called for a face-masking penalty.

face off (v.)

> The country's leading players will face off tonight.

face-off (n., adj.)

> Quebec won the face-off.
> Upson skated to the face-off circle.

fade Golf term refers to a ball that curves slightly to the right.

fadeaway (adj., v.)

> Matt fooled the defender with a fadeaway jump shot.
> Animosity toward the striking players began to fade away.

---

fair ball (n.) Two words.

fair catch (n.)

> Lockhardt signaled for a fair catch.

fair-catch (adj.)

> Splitt gave the fair-catch signal.

fairway

> Goodwin's drive landed in the fairway.

fall classic Lowercase, but capitalize World Series. *See* World Series.

false motion Motion at a point in a limb where it normally doesn't occur, indicating a bone fracture.

false start Use false start in swimming and track stories when a competitor starts a race before the starter's signal. In drag racing, refer to an early start as a foul start.

fan (v.) Do not use fan as a synonym for strikeout.

> WRONG: Johnson fanned three batters.

fantasy league baseball *See* Rotisserie League baseball.

farmhand Minor-leaguer is preferred.

farm team A team in the minor-league baseball system. Refer to those who play on these teams as minor-leaguers, not farmhands or bush-leaguers.

farther Farther refers to distance. *See* further.

> DeJarld can throw the ball farther than Cooper can.

Fartlek training Capitalize this Swedish term, which means "speed play." Athletes, often triathletes, who use the Fartlek training technique alternate periods of sprinting with jogging.

far turn Do not capitalize far turn as you would the name of a specific turn.

> The car crashed on the far turn.
> Hansen took the lead in Turn 3.

fastball (n.) Use one word when referring to the baseball pitch.

fast break (n.)

> Lougherty scored on a fast break.

fault (n., v.)

> He had three double faults.
> Gary double-faulted.

faze To embarrass or disconcert. *See* phase.

> Matty was not fazed by the comment.

featherweight Olympic boxing class is 120–125 pounds. IBF/WBA/WBC boxing class is 123–126 pounds. *See* boxing.

Fédération Internationalé de Football Association FIFA is acceptable in all references to world soccer's governing body.

feels Do not use as a substitute for said. We don't know how people feel until they tell us. *See* said.

feetfirst Not footfirst.

> Brady jumped into the pool feetfirst.

feign (v.) To fake.

> Ben feigned an injury.

feint (v.) To fake in fencing.

Fellowship of Christian Athletes Spell out on first reference, then the fellowship.

femur The thigh bone is the longest bone in the body.

fencing Classes are épée, foil, and saber.

fewer Use fewer for countable items. *See* less.

> He was gone fewer than 20 days.

field Capitalize as part of a proper name.

> The game is on Field 4.
> Did you ever play at Wrigley Field?

fielder's choice When a fielder handles a fair ground ball and, instead of throwing to first base to put out the batter, throws to another base in an attempt to put out the runner.

Charge a batter who hits into a fielder's choice with an at-bat, not a base hit.

field goal (n.)

> Pann kicked a field goal.

field-goal (adj.)

> Shane has the highest field-goal percentage.

field hockey *See* Part II.

field house Capitalize if part of a proper name.

> The game is at Allen Field House.
> We held practice in the school's field house.

fielding average Calculate the ratio of putouts and assists to the number of chances.

> 600 putouts and assists / 624 chances = .962 average

fieldsman (n.) In cricket, the players on the field are the fieldsmen, not the fieldmen.

Fiesta Bowl Refer to as the OS/2 Fiesta Bowl on first reference. *See* bowl games.

FIFA Fédération Internationalé de Football Association. The international governing body of soccer. FIFA is acceptable in all references.

fifth-year senior Note the hyphen.

figure eight Skating maneuver in which a performer skates in the pattern resembling an 8.

figure skating Do not hyphenate as a modifier. Competition includes men's, women's, pairs, and ice dancing.

fill in (v.)

> Who will fill in for Ritter?

fill-in (n.)

> We'll need to find a fill-in soon.

filly A female horse less than 5 years old.

Final Four Final Four is a trademark of the NCAA and must be capitalized when referring to the remaining four teams in the NCAA Men's and Women's Division I basketball tournaments.

> Arkansas, Duke, Michigan, and North Carolina are in the Final Four.

Lowercase final four when referring to the final four teams in other tournaments.

> The high school team made it to the tournament's final four.

Finals Capitalize Finals as part of a proper name.

The NBA Finals begin this week.
Southern made it to the finals of the tournament.

firearm, firepower (n.)

Nomo has a firearm.
The Dodgers have firepower in their pitching lineup.

first base, first baseman (n.) No hyphen.

first-base (adj.)

Robert is the first-base coach.
Robbins hit the ball down the first-base line.
Do you know who will be tonight's first-base umpire?

first quarter (n.)

Iowa scored 21 points in the first quarter.

first-quarter (adj.)

Rutgers gave up 10 first-quarter points.

first round (n.)

Lyle was chosen in the first round.

first-round (adj.)

He was a first-round pick.

first string (n.)

Crews was selected for the first string.

first-string (adj.)

Kelly is the first-string quarterback.

first team (n.)

> Snow made the first team.

first-team (adj.)

> Keating is a first-team all-American.

fish (n.) Singular and plural; never fishes as a noun.

> He caught several fish during the BASS Masters Classic.

fish-tail (v.)

> The car fish-tailed on the wet pavement.

flagstick

> The flagstick was placed near the front of the green.

flea flicker In football, the flea flicker is a play in which a pass caught by the receiver is then lateralled to a trailing teammate, or a play that begins as a double reverse with the ball coming back to the quarterback, who then throws a long pass.

flèche Note the spelling of this running attack in fencing.

flip-flop Do not use as a synonym for handspring.

flipoff (n.) Lacrosse term is one word.

flip turn In swimming, a flip turn is made at the end of the pool.

floor exercise In gymnastics, the event is not floor exercises.

flume A high-tech water treadmill used to train swimmers.

fly-fishing Always hyphenate.

> Gust often goes fly-fishing.
> He is a fly-fishing expert.

flying rings This gymnastics event was discontinued in the 1950s. When referring to the remaining event (still rings) in the present, use rings.

Conner scored a 9.65 on the rings.

fly out (v.)

Goodwin flied out to left field.

flyweight Olympic boxing class is 107–112. IBF/WBA/WBC class is 109–112. *See* boxing.

follow through (v.)

Johnson followed through on his swing.

follow-through (n.)

Martin hit the ground on his follow-through.

follow up (v.)

Norton followed up on his promise.

follow-up (n., adj.)

Roger scored a basket on the follow-up.
Keller's progress will be evaluated during his follow-up visit.

foot fault (n.) Infraction in tennis occurs when a player steps on or over the baseline while serving.

Kennedy was called for a foot fault.

foot-fault (adj., v.)

He has been called for several foot-fault violations.
Thompson foot-faulted in the second match.

foothold

> The hikers were unable to find a foothold.

foot line Use two words for the curling boundary.

footwork (n.)

> Wes is known for his fancy footwork.

force out (v.)

> Jensen was forced out at home.

force-out (n.)

> The inning ended on a force-out.

fore Note spelling of this warning called after a golf drive.

forehand (n., adj.)

> Jenkins has improved her forehand.
> Heil won the point with a forehand shot down the line.

forfeit In baseball, record the final score as 9-0.

forgo Note spelling.

> Stackhouse will forgo his senior season.

forkball

> Curry's forkball was clocked at 65 mph.

49ers Do not spell out 49ers unless it appears at the beginning of a sentence.

> Forty-Niner fans liked the trade.
> Most 49ers fans are happy about the trade.

forward In soccer references, the forward primarily responsible for shooting the ball is the striker.

Fosbury flop Capitalize the name of this method of high jumping in which the athlete goes over the bar backward and headfirst, landing on his or her back.

foul line Free-throw line is preferred. Avoid using charity stripe.

foul start When a car leaves the starting line before the green light-start signal in drag racing, a foul start is called.
   In swimming and track, the term for an early start is false start.

four bagger Do not use this outdated term for a home run.

four-wheel drive Always hyphenate.

> Does your new truck have four-wheel drive?
> The race will feature four-wheel-drive vehicles.

fractions Spell out common amounts, or rewrite.

> About three-fifths of the team voted to go on strike.
> Six out of the eight team members rode the bus.
> The match lasted three and one half hours.

Quantities with both fractions and whole numbers should be expressed in numerals. Stack the fractions when possible.

> They played on a 90-by-50-yard field.
> She writes on 8½ x 11-inch paper.

fracture (n., v.) A breach in the continuity of a bone. There are several types and severity levels of fractures including simple, compound, comminuted, oblique, and stress.

> John suffered a fracture during the game against South.
> His femur is fractured.

frame (n.) Use frame in bowling stories. Avoid using it to mean inning, period, or quarter.

WRONG: Gibbs struck out two batters in the third frame.
RIGHT: Sackuvich bowled a strike in the 10th frame.

franchise player Under the NFL's Collective Bargaining Agreement, a franchise player is one whose team must offer a one-year contract at the average of the five highest-paid players at the franchise player's position or a 20 percent increase, whichever is greater. A transition player is one whose team must tender a one-year contract at the average of the 10 highest-paid players at the transition player's position or a 20 percent raise, whichever is greater.

Frank J. Selke Trophy *See* hockey, Part II.

free agent The NFL Collective Bargaining Agreement defines an unrestricted free agent as a player with four or more seasons of free agency experience. A restricted free agent is defined as a player with three seasons of free agency experience who is subject to compensation and/or right of first refusal.

Do not hyphenate free agent before a player's name or as a noun.

> The Reds picked up free agent Bob Lowden.
> Coldwell is an unrestricted free agent.

Hyphenate free-agent when it is used before a word other than a player's name.

> Dax wants to test the free-agent market.

free-lance, free-lancer

> Should we hire a free-lance writer for the game?
> Spicer is our new free-lancer.

free throw

> McCormick shot 10 free throws during the game.

free-throw line

> Shannon is five for 10 from the free-throw line.

freshwater (n., adj.) One word.

> Hoyne likes to fish in freshwater.
> Are trout freshwater fish?

Frisbee Capitalize this trademark name of flying disk.

from–to Always include *to* with *from* to show a span of time.

> He led the team in RBIs from 1968 to 1970.

frontcourt In basketball, the center and forwards make up the frontcourt.

front-runner

> Johnson is regarded as the front-runner in the race.

front zone Not hyphenated. In volleyball, this is the area between the center line and the attack line on either side of the net.

frostbite (n., adj.) One word. Refers to the freezing of part of the body, or sailing in cold weather.

> Butcher got frostbite on her thumb.
> Connor is a frostbite sailor.

fullback (n.) Use one word for the football or soccer position.

full-twisting (adj.)

> Hegarty did a full-twisting somersault.

fumble (n., v.) A fumble does not necessarily result in the ball being turned over to the opponent.

furlong One-eighth of a mile. Give race distances in furlongs through seven furlongs. For longer races, list distances in miles.

> Heintz won the one-mile race.
> Keyto won the race on the 1¼-mile track.

further An extension. *See* farther.

The committee will explore the issue further.

futurity Capitalize Futurity when it is part of a proper name.

Which horse do you think will win the All-American Futurity?

G

gain (n., v.)

Haley rushed for a 50-yard gain.
He gained 10 yards.

game, games Capitalize Game when it is part of the name of a specific game in a series.

The Blue Jays won World Series Game 3.
Tomorrow is Game 4 of the NBA Finals.

Lowercase game in other uses.

We lost the second game.
This is the 10th game of the tournament.

Capitalize Games as part of a proper name and in all references to the Olympic Games. *See* Olympics.

Hundreds will participate in the World University Games.
The United States won five medals at the Winter Games.

gamefish (n.) Use one word in reference to the salmon family of fish.

game high (n.)

Robin's 18 points were a game high.

game-high (adj.)

> Newman had a game-high 10 rebounds.

gamekeeper's thumb Tear of the ligament in the thumb joint, also called skier's thumb.

game winner (n.)

> Peterson was the game winner.

game-winning (adj.)

> Paulos hit the game-winning RBI.

gang-tackled (v.)

> The defense gang-tackled the receiver.

Gateway Football Conference Gateway Conference is acceptable in all references to this Division I-AA group. *See* college, Part II, for members.

Gatorade Capitalize this trademark name of sports drink.

Gator Bowl Refer to as the Outback Steakhouse Gator Bowl on first reference. *See* bowl games.

gel Gel is the incorrect word to denote a team's ability to work together. The correct spelling is jell.

> The team began to jell late in the season.

gender *See* men, women.

general manager Capitalize as a title before a name. GM is acceptable on second reference and in headlines.

> That is General Manager Carl Peterson.
> John Wagner, the general manager, was there.
> GM Frank Geryol always ran the show.

Style and Usage

giddyap Not giddyup.

girl Use until a female's 18th birthday. Do not refer to a female older than 18 as a girl.

> The woman is competing in her fifth collegiate race.

Never refer to a ship, car, or other inanimate object as someone's girl or with the pronoun *she* unless the sentence is contained within a quote.

> WRONG: The mechanic said she's running a little slow today.
> RIGHT: It's running slow.

The word *girls* does not require an apostrophe when used descriptively. *See* boys, women.

> She plays on the high school girls basketball team.

give-and-go

> Ryan scored on the give-and-go from Blum.

give away (v.)

> The A's will give away free tickets to their home games.

giveaway (n.)

> The Jets lead the league in giveaway-takeaway ratio.

globe-trotter Lowercase when referring to a person who travels around the world.

Globetrotter Capitalize when referring to a member of the Harlem Globetrotters.

glove Use glove in all references to the piece of baseball fielding equipment except in the case of the first baseman and catcher, who use mitts.

go-ahead (n., v.)

> Alex got the go-ahead from the coach.
> Sanders scored the go-ahead run.

goalie Acceptable in all references for goaltender or goalkeeper. Do not refer to the goalie as the netminder.

goal line (n.)

> The Bruins lined up on the goal line.

goal-line (adj.)

> The Chiefs had a strong goal-line stand.

goal post (n.)

> The Northwestern fans tore down the goal post.

goals against (n.) Goals allowed by a goaltender.

goals against average Calculate using the following formula:

> Total of goals against
> × 60 / number of minutes played

goaltending

> Our center frequently is called for goaltending.

Golden Gloves Capitalize the name of the amateur boxing tournament.

Gold Glove Capitalize the name of the major-league fielding award.

> Smith won the Gold Glove at shortstop.

golf The PGA and LPGA are the governing bodies for men's and women's professional golf.

Four events make up the men's major tournaments: The Masters, U.S. Open, British Open, and the PGA Championship.

The women's majors are the U.S. Women's Open, Nabisco Dinah Shore, LPGA Championship, and du Maurier Classic. *See* Part II.

Goodwill Games Athletic competition between the United States and Russia. Capitalize Games in all references. Competition takes place in the following events:

Archery	Gymnastics	Tae kwon do
Basketball	Handball (team)	Track and field
Boxing	Judo	Triathlon
Canoe/Kayak	Rhythmic gymnastics	Volleyball
Cycling	Rowing	Water polo
Diving	Short track speed skating	Weightlifting
Figure skating	Swimming	Wrestling
Football (soccer)	Synchronized swimming	Yachting

Gottlieb Award Award given to the NBA Rookie of the Year. *See* basketball, Part II.

Grand Prix Capitalize as part of an event's title.

Snethen will compete in the Malibu Grand Prix.

grand slam Lowercase in reference to a home run with the bases loaded. Do not use the redundant grand slam home run.

Grand Slam Capitalize Grand Slam when referring to the four major events of tennis. Do not hyphenate Grand Slam as a modifier under this use.

Sampras has won 10 Grand Slam events.
The Australian Open, French Open, Wimbledon, and U.S. Open are the four Grand Slam events.

Grapefruit League Use sparingly for the nickname of baseball spring training league in Florida. *See* Cactus League.

Greco-Roman wrestling (n., adj.) Always capitalized. Identify events by weight class.

Grey Cup The Canadian Football League's championship game is named for the trophy given to the winner. The trophy has been awarded since 1954. *See* football, Part II.

gridder, gridiron Avoid using these football cliches.

ground out (v.)

> Caceras grounded out to the third baseman.

ground-out (n.)

> The inning ended with a ground-out.

ground-rule (adj.)

> The umpire called the hit a ground-rule double when a fan touched the ball.

grounds crew No apostrophe.

groundskeeper (n.) One word.

ground stroke (n.)

> Musgrave has a powerful ground stroke.

Groza Award Award was first presented in 1987 to honor the top collegiate placekicker. Use Lou Groza Award on first reference.

gun down Do not use gun down to mean throw out.

> WRONG: The third baseman gunned down the runner.

gunwale Note the spelling of the upper edge of a canoe side.

gymnastics Gymnasts compete in events, not on apparatuses.

> WRONG: Retton placed first on the uneven parallel bars.
> RIGHT: Retton placed first in the uneven parallel bars.

Olympic all-around competition is made up of six events for men, four for women. Rhythmic gymnastics is not part of the all-around competition and does not count toward the team point totals.

Men's events	Women's events
floor exercise	floor exercise
rings	balance beam
vault	vault
parallel bars	uneven bars
pommel horse	
horizontal bar	

See Part II.

H

hack, hacker Avoid using these slang terms for a bad golfer.

halfback The halfback usually is smaller than the fullback.

halfcourt (n.)

> Austin made a shot from halfcourt.

half-court (adj.)

> Dean made a half-court shot to win the game.

half-hour

> Game time is a half-hour away.

half-mast

> Place the flags at half-mast.

half-mile pole In horse races, the pole marks the point that is one-half mile from the finish line.

half nelson Do not capitalize the name of this wrestling move.

half swing

> Garcia took a half swing at the pitch.

halftime (n., adj.)

> New Jersey had the lead at halftime.
> The cheerleaders put on a halftime performance.

half-way line Hyphenate the name of the line that runs the width of a rugby field, marking the middle.

Hall of Fame, Hall of Famer Capitalize.

Hall of Fame Game Capitalize when referring to the exhibition game in Cooperstown, N.Y.

hamstring Do not use hamstring as a verb to mean to disable. This category of muscles runs from the buttocks to the knee along the back of the thigh.

handball Games are won by the first player to score 21 points or, in a tie-breaker, 11 points. *See* team handball, Part II.

handicap (n., v.) Use figures in golf references.

> McGown has a 5 handicap.
> He has a handicap of 5 strokes.
> Carson is a 5-handicap golfer.
> Trace has a 5-stroke handicap.
> Who will handicap the race?

handlebars (n.)

> LeMond designed his own handlebars.

hand off (v.)

> Hagopian handed off the ball.

---

handoff (n.)

> Liginski took the handoff.

hands-on (adj.)

> Coach Sheridan insists on a hands-on approach.

hang a rope Do not use as a synonym for a line drive in baseball.

hard court (n.)

> McLain plays best on a hard court.

hard-court (adj.)

> Borden is a hard-court champion.

harness racing Races are trotted or paced.

Hart Memorial Trophy Award given to NHL's Most Valuable Player. *See* hockey, Part II.

hash mark On a football field, hash marks are the short lines that mark yard lines not divisible by 5.

hat Baseball players wear caps.

head (v.)

> Dupor headed the ball.
> He was able to head the ball into the net.
> He is working on heading the ball with more accuracy.

head coach It is not necessary to refer to someone as a head coach except to distinguish that person from others on a coaching staff.

> Joplin is the head coach, and Baxter is the assistant coach.

headfirst

The diver went into the water headfirst.

headgear

The wrestlers were provided with headgear.

head-on (adj., adv.)

Two cars were involved in the head-on crash.
Rosewell and Rockey collided head-on in the outfield.

headpin The No. 1 pin in bowling.

head start (n.)

Due gave the slower runners a head start.

heads-up play

Powers made a heads-up play.

head-to-head

They met in head-to-head competition.
Will the teams meet head-to-head?

hecht (n.) Gymnastics maneuver performed on the uneven parallel bars.

Shields performed a reverse hecht.

heavyweight Olympic boxing class is 179–201 pounds. IBF/WBA/WBC class is 191 pounds and up. *See* boxing.

heights Use figures.

The center is 6 feet 7 inches tall.
The scouting report said he was a 5-foot-10 guard. I think he is 5-8.
Kendell is a 7-footer.

Heisman Trophy This award, first presented in 1935, is given annually to the nation's outstanding college football player. It is presented at the Downtown Athletic Club in New York City and is named after John Heisman, who served as the Downtown Athletic Club's athletic director.

The Heisman Trophy winner is determined by a total vote by sportswriters who award three points to their first choice, two points to their second, and one to their third choice.

heptathlon The heptathlon, which replaced the pentathlon in track and field in 1988, is made up of seven events:

> 60-meter dash
> long jump
> shot put
> high jump
> 60-meter hurdles
> javelin
> 1,000-meter run

hidden-ball trick Baseball play designed to catch a runner off first base. The first baseman pretends to throw the ball to the pitcher, who then pretends to prepare to pitch. When the runner leads off from first, the first baseman tags him or her out.

high-five (n., v.)

> Wharton high-fived everyone on the team.
> Swanson got a high-five from her coach.

high jump (n.)

> Wayne won the high jump.

high-jump (v.)

> Spencer high-jumped over the bar and set a world record.

high school Do not hyphenate as a modifier.

> Grey is a high school athlete.

It is not necessary to write out High School with a school's name on first reference unless a school is named after a city and doing so would avoid confusion.

> WRONG: Kansas City is 0-1.
> RIGHT: Kansas City High School is 0-1.

high-sticking Carrying a hockey stick above shoulder level.

> Anderson was called for high-sticking.

Hill Trophy Award given to the Division II football Player of the Year. Use Harlon Hill Trophy on first reference.

hit and run (v.)

> The coach wanted Costo to hit and run.

hit-and-run (n., adj.)

> Shaw tried a hit-and-run.
> The Yankees are in a hit-and-run situation.

hockey *See* Part II.

hog line Use two words when referring to this curling line.

hole in one (n.) Three words, no hyphen.

home-court advantage (adj.)

home-field advantage (adj.)

home plate Do not hyphenate as a modifier.

> Britton argued with the home plate umpire.

home run (n., adj.) Do not hyphenate as a modifier.

> He is known as a home run hitter.

---

homestand

The Orioles began a seven-game homestand yesterday.

home stretch (n.) Use two words to refer to the final straight-away on a track.

hook In golf, a hook is a shot that curves to the left.

hoops Avoid using hoops as a synonym for basketball.

horsepower

The car is powered by a 400-horsepower engine.

horse racing A furlong is one-eighth of a mile. Race distances are given in furlongs up through seven. Use miles for distances greater than seven furlongs. *See* Part II.

hotshot (n.) The right fielder is a hotshot.

humerus (n., adj.) Not humorous. This bone in the upper arm runs from the shoulder to the elbow.

hunters' round Note the apostrophe in this archery tournament division.

hyperextend (n., v.)

Salaam suffered a hyperextension of his elbow.
He hyperextended it during the last game.

hyperventilate (v.) To take in an excess of air due to abnormally fast or deep breathing.

hypoxia Low oxygen content.

I

IAAF International Amateur Athletics Federation. Spell out on first reference to the international governing body of track and field.

I-back Capitalize the name of this football position.

ice dancing One of four Olympic figure skating events along with men's, women's, and pairs competitions.

IC4A Intercollegiate Association of Amateur Athletes of America. Spell out on first reference. IC4A may be used in headlines when space is limited or in phrases such as IC4A competition to avoid cumbersome leads. When this is done, spell out the full name later in the story.

Iditarod The 1,159-mile dog sled race from Anchorage to Nome, Alaska.

IFDIMF principle Acronym for aspects of anaerobic conditioning, Initial Fitness, Duration, Intensity, Mode, and Frequency.

IGFA Spell out International Game Fish Association.

illicit Means illegal. *See* elicit.

> Our best player was arrested for possession of illicit drugs.

IM Use on second reference for individual medley, a swimming event made up of butterfly, backstroke, breaststroke, and freestyle. *See* swimming.

inbound (v.)

> Jackson inbounded the ball.
> Paulsen will inbound the ball.

inbounds (n., adj.)

> Franklin received the inbounds pass.
> The wide receiver was inbounds when he caught the pass.

include Do not use include when referring to a complete list.

WRONG: The possible outcomes of the football game include wins, losses, and ties.
RIGHT: The outcomes include wins and losses.

Independence Bowl *See* bowl games.

Independents Collegiate teams not affiliated with a particular conference. *See* college, Part II.

in-depth

We had an in-depth conversation.
They really didn't go in-depth about the issue.

Indianapolis 500 Event is held every Memorial Day weekend at Indianapolis Motor Speedway. Racers complete 200 laps around the 2.5-mile track.

Spell out Indianapolis 500 on first reference, then Indy 500 or Indy.

indirect-free kick (n.) Note the hyphen in this soccer kick, which must be touched by two or more players before it is shot at the goal.

indoor (adj.)

Vlada's team won the indoor soccer championship.

indoors (n.)

When it rained, he went indoors.

IndyCar Note that there is no space between Indy and Car.

injured reserve Spell out on first reference. Avoid using IR, except in quotes. Injured-reserve list is redundant.

Early was placed on injured reserve.

injuries Injuries are sustained or suffered, not received.

> Cox suffered a broken arm.

inside-the-park home run (n.) Note the hyphens.

instep (n.) Inside area of the foot in line with the big toe toward the ankle.

insure Insure refers to insurance matters. *See* ensure.

Intercollegiate Association of Amateur Athletes of America Spell out first reference. IC4A tournament may be used in headlines when space is limited.

International Boxing Federation Spell out on first reference, then IBF. *See* boxing for weight classes.

International Hockey League Spell out on first reference, then IHL. *See* hockey, Part II.

International Olympic Committee Spell out on first reference, then IOC.

International Tennis Federation Spell out on first reference, then ITF.

intersquad Between squads.

intrasquad Within squads.

inward Note spelling for this dive in which the diver begins with his or her back to the water, jumps, and rotates toward the board or platform.

IR Spell out injured reserve in all references except in agate and when IR is contained in a quote.

Ironman Triathlon This triathlon, which takes place annually in Hawaii, consists of a 2.4-mile swim, 112-mile bike ride, and 26.2-mile run.

isometric training Muscle development through the exertion of force against an immovable object.

isotonic exercise Muscle development through the exertion of force against movable resistance.

it Always use in references to nations, ships, cars, and other inanimate objects. Do not refer to such objects as she.
Use it or its with a team, the team's school, state, or city.

> The team won its first game.
> Tampa Bay won its opener.
> North Carolina lost its starting center.

Use their as the pronoun for a team's nickname.

> The Tigers lost their first game.

Italian pursuit Capitalize Italian in the name of team pursuit race between cycling teams.

ITF Spell out International Tennis Federation on first reference, then ITF.

Ivy Group Athletic conference is not Ivy League. *See* college, Part II.

J

Jack Adams Award *See* hockey, Part II.

Jacob's ladder Note capitalization.

Jacuzzi Capitalize this trademarked brand name whirlpool bath.

jai alai Similar to handball, players catch and throw a small ball with a curved wicker basket called a cesta. Also called pelota.

jam (v.)

> The pitcher jammed the batter with an inside fastball.
> Wilkins jammed the basketball.

Dunk shot or slam dunk is preferred to jam as a noun.

> Stringer finished off the game with a slam dunk.

James Norris Memorial Trophy *See* hockey, Part II.

Japanese professional baseball There are two leagues, the Pacific and Central. *See* baseball, Part II, for teams.

Japanese set Capitalize Japanese in all references to this technique of setting a volleyball in which the ball gets just high enough to clear the top of the net.

jargon Special vocabulary used only among those in a field of interest. Do not ignore the casual reader by using words and phrases that only a knowledgeable sports fan might understand.

javelin (n.) The event and the long instrument thrown in track and field.

Jays Use Toronto Blue Jays or Blue Jays, not Jays alone.

jayvee JV is preferred in all cases for junior varsity.

jell (v.) Note spelling of word used to describe a team's ability to play together.

Jet Ski Capitalize the brand name of self-propelled water vehicle.

jib (n.) A triangular sail.

jibe (v.) To change course while sailing.

jig Type of artificial fishing lure.

jigging Fishing by jerking a jig or other bait up and down in the water.

jockette Do not use this word in reference to a female jockey.

jockstrap (n.) One word.

John R. Wooden Award Award given annually since 1977 to the nation's outstanding college basketball player. Wooden Award is acceptable on first reference.

journeyman Use this term when referring to an athlete who has performed consistently well for several teams.

    The key here is performed well. A journeyman is often a good player, but not a standout. A star player who has played for three or four teams is not a journeyman. For example, David Cone and Andre Dawson, who each have played for several teams and are well-known, are not considered journeymen.

Jr. Do not use a comma to separate Jr. from the name it follows.

> Ken Griffey Jr. broke his wrist.

To show possession, add an 's after the period.

> Michael Selick Jr.'s contribution helped the team succeed.

Spell out junior when referring to a high school or college student's year in school.

> Lou Nelson, a 6-5 junior, was chosen for the team.

juco Junior college is preferred on all references.

judo Do not capitalize the name of this form of jujitsu.

jujitsu An Oriental art of self-defense. Do not capitalize. *See* martial arts.

juke (v.) In football, to fake out an opponent in order to get past him or her. Do not use juke as a noun.

> WRONG: The receiver gave him a juke.
> RIGHT: The receiver juked the defender.

---

jump ball (n.) Two words. Method of putting the ball in play during a basketball game.

jumping events In track and field, jumping events are the pole vault, long jump, high jump, and triple jump. *See* track and field.

jumpmaster (n.) An instructor who supervises a group of skydivers.

junior Spell out junior when referring to a high school or college student's year in school or a person's first name.

> Jeff Hopkins, a 6-3 junior, was chosen for the team.
> Junior Seau is the team captain.

Abbreviate junior and do not use a comma to separate Jr. from the name it follows:

> Ken Griffey Jr. hit his second home run of the game.

junior bantamweight IBF/WBA/WBC boxing class is 113-115. *See* boxing.

junior college Capitalize when used as part of a proper name.

> Jackson attends Johnson Junior College.

junior featherweight IBF/WBA/WBC boxing class is 119-122 pounds. *See* boxing.

junior flyweight IBF/WBA/WBC boxing class is 106-108 pounds. *See* boxing.

junior heavyweight IBF/WBA/WBC boxing class is 176-190 pounds. *See* boxing.

junior lightweight IBF/WBA/WBC boxing class is 127-130 pounds. *See* boxing.

junior middleweight IBF/WBA/WBC boxing class is 148-154 pounds. *See* boxing.

junior varsity JV is acceptable on first reference.

junior welterweight IBF/WBA/WBC boxing class is 136–140 pounds. *See* boxing.

junkball Use sparingly in reference to a breaking ball.

JV Acceptable on first reference for junior varsity.

J valve There is no hyphen in the name of this valve on a diver's air tank that shuts off when pressure is reduced. It serves to warn the diver that his or her air is almost exhausted, but permits the diver to swim deeper if necessary.

K

k Use a lowercase k as an abbreviation for kilometer. Do not leave a space between a distance and the k. *See* kilometer.

> Benoit will run the 5k.

Spell out kilometer on first reference unless the official name of a race contains only the abbreviation k.

> Becca will run a 10-kilometer race.
> She ran the Victory Hospital 10k last year.

K Do not use K as a synonym for strikeout.

> WRONG: Abbott had six Ks.
> RIGHT: Abbott had six strikeouts.
> RIGHT: Abbott struck out six batters.

Kansas City Mo. or Kan. should be included in datelines. The Kansas City Royals and Chiefs are located in Kansas City, Mo.

karate Do not capitalize this martial art.

kart This miniature automobile is not spelled cart.

---

kayo Use knockout instead. Spell out on first reference, then KO.

kayaking *See* canoeing, Part II.

keel A fin under the hull of a boat or ship that provides stability.

keep-away (n.)

> The defense became frustrated as the offense played keep-away.

keeper Use goalkeeper, goaltender, or goalie instead.

kendo Do not capitalize this martial art.

Kentucky Derby Horse race for three-year-old thoroughbreds is 1¼ miles long. It is held at Churchill Downs in Louisville, Kent., on the first Saturday in May.
   The Derby, first run in 1875, is the first of the three races that make up the Triple Crown. *See* Preakness Stakes and Belmont Stakes.
   Capitalize the Derby on second reference.

key (n.) Do not use key as a verb when describing an element or player essential to winning.

> WRONG: Rodriguez keyed the victory.
> RIGHT: Rodriguez was the key to victory.

When referring to the key in basketball—the area at each end of the court made up of the free throw lane and restraining circle—do not use the dated reference, keyhole.

> Ritter shot from the top of the key.

key (v.) Use key as a verb in reference to an athlete's study of an opponent in anticipation of the upcoming play.

> The defender keyed on the running back.

kick boxer The term for one who participates in the sport of kick boxing is two words.

---

kicker (n.) In football, use kicker in reference to the place-kicker. Although the punter is a kicker as well, be specific and use punter to avoid confusing the reader. *See* punter.

kick off (v.)

> The Oilers-San Francisco game kicks off at 2 p.m.
> Steinhauser will kick off the ball.

kickoff (n., adj.)

> Kickoff is at 7 p.m.
> The Buccaneers lined up in kickoff formation.

kidney punch (n.) This blow to an opponent's lower back in boxing is illegal. Never use kidney punch as a verb. *See* rabbit punch.

> WRONG: Elrod kidney punched Michaels.
> RIGHT: Elrod hit Michaels with a kidney punch.

kilometer Spell out kilometer on first reference unless the first reference is the name of a race containing just the letter k.

> Parker won the Park City 10k.
> Parker won another 10-kilometer race. It is the fourth 10k she has won this summer.

A kilometer is 1,000 meters. To convert kilometers to miles, multiply by .62. *See* metric system.

Kingdome Note spelling of this Seattle stadium. *See* SkyDome.

kip (n.) Move done in gymnastics from a hanging position below the apparatus to a support position above it.

knee (n., v.)

> The runner was kicked in the knee.
> Popov kneed his opponent in the groin.
> Ross was penalized for kneeing the defender as they fought for the puck.

kneecap One word. The medical term is patella.

knee injuries *See* injuries.

knock down (v.)

> Frazier knocked down Ali.

knockdown (n., adj.) Do not use knockdown as a synonym for knockout in boxing references. A knockdown occurs when a boxer goes down, but is not necessarily knocked out.

> Ali dominated the fight after the knockdown.
> Cone threw a knockdown pitch.

knock out (v.)

> Morrison knocked out Moran.

knockout (n., adj.) A knockout occurs when a boxer is knocked out and unable to get back to his or her feet in a 10 count. Do not use as a synonym for knockdown.

> He won by a knockout.
> Louis delivered a knockout punch.

If a match ends early because a fighter can't continue, the winner stopped the loser. There is no such thing as a technical knockout.

knot A knot is one nautical mile (6,080 feet) per hour. Express knots with figures. Never use the redundant knots per hour.

> The wind was blowing at 5 knots.
> There is a 3-knot wind.

know-how (n.)

> Vukovich has the know-how to get the job done.

knuckleball (n., adj.) Use knuckleball to describe a pitch that has very little rotation and dives or moves suddenly near the plate.

Davidson threw a knuckleball.
He is a knuckleball pitcher.

KO, KO'd Acceptable in headlines when space is limited, but use knockout or knocked out on first reference in text, then KO or KO'd.

koshiwaza Note the spelling of this hip throw in judo.

Kovac Capitalize this move on the horizontal bar where the gymnast swings forward, does a back salto over the bar, and recatches the bar.

K-Swiss Always hyphenate the name of this athletic apparel company.

kudos (n.) Meaning credit or praise, kudos is singular. A person cannot receive one kudo.

kung fu No hyphen. *See* martial arts.

K valve Capitalize the K when referring to scuba diving valve without a reserve supply provision. *See* J valve.

L

lace (v.) Avoid using this slang term to describe the act of a batter hitting a line drive.

Walraff laced the ball into left field.

Lachman test Capitalize the name of this test for instability of the anterior cruciate ligament.

lackluster (adj.)

Arhibad put on a lackluster performance.

lacrosse There are 10 players from each team on the field during a game: one goalie, three defensemen, three midfielders, and three attackmen.

The field is 110 yards long. A match is made up of 15-minute periods. *See* Part II.

ladies' figure skating Do not hyphenate as a modifier. Note the apostrophe in ladies'. *See* skating, figure.

> Chen won the ladies' figure skating event.

Ladies Pro Bowlers Tour There is no apostrophe after Ladies. Spell out on first reference, then LPBT.

Ladies Professional Golf Association No apostrophe after Ladies. LPGA is acceptable in all references. *See* golf.

ladies' tee (n.) Note position of the apostrophe.

Lady Byng Memorial Trophy Award given to NHL player who exemplifies good conduct. *See* hockey, Part II.

laid-back (n., adj.)

> He is very laid-back.
> Jackson has a laid-back attitude.

lane When referring to a specific lane number, use figures. The same rule applies to row numbers, as in an automobile race.

> Van Asdale will start in Lane 3.
> She will swim in the third lane.
> Foyt began the race on the inside of Row 2.
> He started from the second row.

lanelines Use one word in reference to the lines that mark swimming lanes.

last, latest Use last to refer to something that is final. Latest refers to the most recent in a string of events. Do not use latest to imply finality.

The latest figures show the team is losing money.
The umpires are the latest ones to complain.
Suzanne finished last.
Who was the last one in the room?

last chance rule Do not hyphenate this boating rule that allows a driver to take whatever action is necessary to avoid a collision with another boat.

last minute (n.)

David scored six points in the last minute.

last-minute (adj.)

Jordan made a last-minute shot.

lateral (n., v.) A lateral is a pass, therefore, lateral pass is redundant. Unlike a forward pass, a lateral remains in play even if it is not caught.

Robertson threw a lateral.
He lateralled the ball to Johnson.

lateral water hazard On a golf course, a lateral water hazard runs almost parallel to the line of play. Do not hyphenate this term.

latest *See* last.

lay out (v.)

Who will lay out the sports section?

layout (n., adj.) An athlete, such as a diver or gymnast, performs a layout with a straight body, legs together, and a slight arch in his or her back.

He will perform the dive in layout position.
It will be his second layout.

lay up (v.)

> The golfer was worried about going over the green, so he decided to lay up instead.

lay-up (n.)

> Kaether scored with a lay-up.

lead Use lead only in present tense references. The past tense of lead is led.

> He leads the race.
> She is in the lead.
> He led the race for four miles.

lead off (v.)

> McDonnell will lead off the inning.

leadoff (n., adj.) The first batter in a lineup or an inning is the leadoff.

> He bats leadoff.
> Gregory is the leadoff hitter this inning.

leader board Two words, unlike scoreboard.

-leaguer

> Taylor is a major-leaguer.
> He was once a minor-leaguer.

led The past tense of lead.

> Crane led the race.

leeward (n.) Away from the wind.

left-center field Note hyphenation.

Belton hit the ball into left-center field.
The ball went over the left-center-field fence.

left field, left fielder (n.)

left hand (n.)

Mathison throws with his left hand.

Hyphenate left-handed and left-hander.

Sparks is a left-handed pitcher.
Hamlin didn't want to face the left-hander.

Avoid referring to a person as a lefty.

left wing (n.)

left-wing (adj.)

left-winger (n.)

lefty Use left-hander or left-handed instead.

LeMans There is no space in the name of this 24-hour automobile race in LeMans, France.

less Use less for collective quantities: distances, weights, periods of time, and sums of money. *See* fewer.

Their offensive line weighs less than ours.
I worked out for less than an hour.

let A serve, shot, or volley that is replayed in tennis or other racket sports.
In reference to a serve in tennis, a let occurs when the ball hits the net or strap and falls into the proper service court, or touches the receiver before hitting the ground. A let also occurs when the ball is served, but the receiver is not ready.
In reference to a point in tennis, a let point is decided by an official.

---

letterman Do not change letterman to letterwoman to reflect gender. To avoid an awkward sentence, use letterwinner, or use letter as a verb to indicate a female athlete's participation on a varsity team.

> Anna is a three-time letterwinner in swimming.
> She lettered in track this year.

letter of intent A letter signed by a high school athlete declaring his or her intent to attend a particular college or university. *See* college, Part II.

let up (v.)

> Maddux let up on his fastball in the fourth inning.

lie (n.) Note spelling of the word that describes the position of a golf ball after it has been hit and has landed.

> Waters found himself with a difficult lie.

lifeguard (n., adj.)

> Motley will be the lifeguard on duty.
> The triathlon will begin near the lifeguard stand.

lifetime Use lifetime or career in reference to an athlete's performance during his or her career.

> Korjenek is a lifetime .320 hitter.
> His brother is a career .290 hitter.

ligament This band of fibrous tissue connects bone to bone or bone to cartilage and supports joints.

> Harrison tore a ligament in his elbow.

lightweight Olympic boxing classification is 126–132 pounds. The IBF/WBA/WBC classification is 131–135 pounds. *See* boxing.

light flyweight Olympic boxing classification is 106 pounds and lower.

light heavyweight Olympic boxing classification is 166–178 pounds. IBF/WBA/WBC classification is 169–175. *See* boxing.

light middleweight Olympic boxing classification is 148–156 pounds. *See* boxing.

light welterweight Olympic boxing classification is 133–139 pounds. *See* boxing.

line (v.) To hit a line drive.

> He lined the ball into center field.

line drive Avoid slang terms for line drive such as clothesline and frozen rope. A line drive is a ball hit hard and straight, not far off the ground. *See* pop-up, loop.

linebacker One word. This football player lines up behind the defensive line.

line judge In football, the line judge operates on the side of the field opposite the head linesman. His responsibilities include timing the game, illegal motion, encroachment, watching for lateral passes, and counting the offensive players.

lineman A football player is a lineman; an official is a linesman. *See* linesman.

line of scrimmage (n.) An imaginary line that runs the width of a football field between the two teams as they line up over the ball at the start of a play.

line out (n., v.)

> The inning ended on a line out to first.
> Grey lined out to right field.

line score (n.) Two words for the summary of runs, hits, and errors of two baseball teams.

Atlanta   000 101 000   2   5   1
Pittsburgh 020 000 010   3   7   0

linesman (n.) In tennis, the linesman is an official who rules whether a ball is in play or out.

In football, a linesman's responsibilities include watching for illegal motion, players offside, encroachment, and actions at the line of scrimmage before the snap.

line up (v.)

Buffalo lined up in I-formation.

lineup (n.)

Cleveland announced its starting lineup.

Little Brown Jug Capitalize the name of the trophy played for each year by the Michigan and Minnesota college football teams.

Little League Capitalize Little League in reference to the youth summer baseball league.

The Little League World Series is held in my hometown.

Note that this capitalization rule applies in all references to Little League.

Thomas is a Little League player.

Little League shoulder is an injury that can occur in a young player throwing the ball too hard.

lob (n., v.) Use lob to refer to a soft throw or a high arching tennis shot.

Bell lobbed the ball.
He threw a lob to home plate.

---

locker room In baseball, it is usually referred to as the clubhouse.

lock out (v.)

> The owners voted to lock out the players.

lockout (n., adj.)

> Players are facing a lockout situation.
> The lockout lasted 42 days.

Lombardi Award Award is presented to the top collegiate lineman.

Lombardi Trophy Trophy is awarded to the winner of the Super Bowl.

long course A 50-meter pool is considered long course. Most major swimming competitions, including the Olympics, are held in long-course pools. A short-course pool is 25 meters.

long-course (adj.)

> He holds the long-course record in this event.

long distance (n.)

> Our coach made us run a long distance.

long-distance Hyphenate long-distance as a modifier and in all references to a phone call.

> Who is the fastest long-distance runner?
> Kris made several long-distance calls.
> She called long-distance.

long iron Avoid using this slang term in reference to a low-numbered iron with little loft.

long jump (n.) In the long jump, an athlete jumps from a running start. *See* track and field.

> Johnson will compete in the long jump.

long-jump (adj., v.)

> Evans holds the long-jump record.
> He long-jumped 20 feet.

long program In figure skating, the long program is four minutes and 30 seconds for men and four minutes for women.

long shot (n.) Use in reference to a competitor who is not expected to win. *See* dark horse.

long term (n.)

> Ingram will be serving a long term.

long-term (adj.)

> Lang has a long-term contract.

long-track speed skating Do not hyphenate speed skating even as a modifier. A long-track oval is 400 meters.

> Jansen won the long-track speed skating event.

loop (adj., v.) A high, shallow fly ball.

> Chamernik hit a loop single in the first inning.
> Burba looped the ball into center field.

loose ball (n.) A loose ball occurs when neither team has control of the ball.

> We fought over the loose ball.

loose-ball (adj.)

> Miller was called for the loose-ball foul.

Los Angeles Spell out on first reference. As a modifier on second reference, use L.A.

> Nomo plays for Los Angeles.
> He is an L.A. Dodger.

losers' bracket (n.) Place the apostrophe after the *s* as there is more than one loser in the bracket.

losing pitcher The losing pitcher in a major-league baseball game is:

the starting pitcher if that pitcher plays the entire game or is pulled from the game while his or her team is behind and the team remains behind;

the relief pitcher if that pitcher takes over during a tie or with the lead.

losing streak A losing streak can differ from a winless streak. A losing streak means there have been no victories or ties. In a winless streak, there are no victories, but there may have been ties.

loss of down In football, the penalty is not "loss of the down."

Lou Gehrig's disease The medical term is amyotrophic lateral sclerosis (ALS). ALS is a progressive neuromuscular disorder caused by degeneration of the motor nerves in the spinal cord that leads to atrophy of the muscles.

When referring to the disease as Lou Gehrig's disease on first reference, spell out the medical term later in the story, then ALS.

Louisiana Superdome The Superdome is acceptable on first reference.

Louisville Slugger Note spelling of athletic equipment company.

love When writing out a badminton or tennis score, do not spell out love, use 0.

WRONG: Meyers won 40-love.
RIGHT: Meyers won the game 40-0.

low board In diving references, use 1-meter board instead.

LPGA Acceptable on first reference for Ladies Professional Golf Association. *See* golf.

LPGA Championship LPGA event is played at Du Pont Country Club in Wilmington, Del. It is one of the four LPGA Major events. *See* golf.

LPGA Majors The four events that make up the LPGA Majors are the Dinah Shore, U.S. Women's Open, LPGA Championship, and du Maurier Classic. *See* golf.

luge (n.) A sled that moves on its two metal runners. One who competes in the luge is a luger.

Lutz Capitalize the name of this figure skating move in which a skater jumps from the outer edge of one foot, spins while in the air, and lands on the other foot. Use single, double, or triple to indicate the number of rotations in the air.

> May performed a double Lutz.

-ly Do not use a hyphen between -ly verbs and the adjectives they modify.

> Mackie had a fully financed education.

Lycra Capitalize the name of this expandable fabric used in athletic apparel, especially aerobic clothing and swimwear.

M

magazines *See* periodicals.

magic number Use to describe the number of games a team

must win in order to secure a title, place in a tournament, etc. The magic number is determined in the following manner:

> Number of games left to be played + 1 – number of
> games ahead of nearest opponent in the loss column

magnetic north On a compass, magnetic north is different from true north. Magnetic north is the middle of a Canadian ironfield, not the North Pole. It is magnetic north that attracts the compass needle.

magnetic resonance imaging An imaging procedure in which radio waves are used to establish a visual image for diagnostic purposes. Spell out on first reference, then MRI.

An MRI does not require the use of radiation and is not a synonym for X-ray or CT scan.

mainmast One word. The largest mast on a boat.

mainsail One word. The principal sail of a boat.

major, academic Do not capitalize the name of an academic major unless the name normally is capitalized.

> Hudson is an English major.
> He used to be a math major.

Major Indoor Soccer League Spell out on first reference, then MISL. League no longer exists.

major league (n.) Use major league as a generic reference to the American League and National League of Major League Baseball. *See* minor league.

> Oscar played in the major leagues during the 1960s.

major-league (adj.)

> Thomas plays at the major-league level.

Major League Baseball Capitalize when referring to the corporate entity.

> Peters is the public relations director for Major League Baseball.

Major League Baseball Players Association Use players association or the association on second reference to this union that represents major-league baseball players in work-related matters.

major-leaguer (n.)

> Alex is a major-leaguer.

Major League Soccer Spell out on first reference, then MLS.

Major League Umpires Association Spell out on first reference, then the association.

major penalty In hockey, any player but the goalie, who commits a major penalty is taken off the ice for five minutes during which time no substitute is permitted.

make do The term is not make due.

> He had to make do with seven players.

mallet Stick used to hit the ball in polo is made of bamboo.

man Do not change man to woman to reflect gender in phrases such as man-to-man defense, baseman, defenseman.

> Sue is our first baseman.

manager Capitalize Manager and General Manager when used as a title before a name.

> Manager Paul Hanson knew his players well.
> General Manager Peace made up the lineup.
> Boone is the general manager. He is the team's G.M.
> Alex is the equipment manager.

Manager of the Year Capitalize the name of this and similar awards such as Coach of the Year, Player of the Week. *See* awards.

man in motion (n.) A football player who changes position as the quarterback prepares to receive the snap at the beginning of a play is in motion.

> Christian was the man in motion.

mantel (n.) Note spelling when used in reference to a shelf.

> Trevor keeps his trophies on the mantel.

man-to-man Each defensive player on a team covers a different offensive player in a man-to-man defense. Do not change this expression to reflect gender in stories about women. *See* zone defense.

> The Lady Techsters used a man-to-man defense.
> They often play man-to-man.

marathon Capitalize marathon as part of an event's name. One who races in marathons is a marathoner. A marathon is 26.2 miles.

> Starbird finished first in the Chicago Marathon.
> He has run several marathons.

See track and field, Part II.

March Madness Capitalize the nickname of the month in which the NCAA men's and women's basketball tournaments are played.

mare A female horse 5 years and older.

martial arts Oriental arts of combat include aikido, judo, jujitsu, karate, kendo, kung fu, and tae kwon do.

mashie Do not use to refer to a 5 iron in golf. The same rule applies to mashie-iron (4 iron) or mashie-niblick (7 iron).

master of arts, master of science Use master's degree.

Masters, The The name of this golf event has no apostrophe. The tournament, first played in 1934, is held at Augusta (Ga.) National Golf Club.

Masterton Trophy *See* hockey, Part II.

masutemi waza Note the two-word spelling of this judo throw.

match play A method of scoring in golf where the number of holes won by a team is counted rather than the number of strokes. *See* medal play, scramble, golf.

match summary This summary is used in competitions with only two competitors or teams.

> Chris Evert def. Tracy Austin, 6-4, 5-7, 6-3.

See basic summary.

match up (v.)

> How do the teams match up?

matchup (n.)

> It should be a good matchup.

matinee Use matinee to refer to races, such as dog and horse races, run during the day as opposed to those run in the evening.

Mavs Acceptable in headlines when space is limited, but spell out Mavericks in other references.

Maxwell Award Award given to a collegiate football Player of the Year.

medal (n., adj.) Hyphenate medal as a modifier. Do not capitalize gold, silver, or bronze.

> Woodburn won a silver medal.
> That was a gold-medal performance.

Do not use medal as a verb.

> WRONG: He medaled in the 100-meter race.
> RIGHT: He won a first-place medal.

medal play Also called stroke play, this method of scoring in golf adds up the number of strokes to determine the winner, the golfer with the lowest score. *See* match play, scramble, and golf.

media (n.) Always plural. News media is preferred.

> The news media are blowing the situation out of proportion.

mediate (v.) To use reason to persuade two parties to agree. *See* arbitration.

medley relay Backstroke, breaststroke, butterfly, and freestyle, in that order, make up this swimming event.

men Unlike high school references in which *boys* does not require an apostrophe when used descriptively, *men,* because it is a plural noun that does not end in *s,* requires an apostrophe.

> The men's team plays at 7 p.m.
> The boys team played at 5 p.m.

Mendoza Line A batting average of .200 in baseball.

metacarpals The five long bones in the hand that run from the wrist to the fingers.

metatarsals The five long bones of the foot that run from the ankle to the toes.

metric system Some races and events are measured in both metric and standard measurements. Specify and spell out the measurement on first reference.

> The first race was the 50-yard freestyle. Staben swam the 50 in 24.23.
> Parker ran the 10-kilometer race. She won the 5k as well.

But do not spell out kilometer in the name of an event if it is not part of an event's official name.

The Shawnee Mission 10k was Sunday.

Temperatures should be written in Fahrenheit. If providing a metric equivalent, list Celsius temperature in parentheses.

It was 23 degrees (-5° C) when the Iditarod got under way.

Common metric conversions:

miles × 1.6 = kilometers
kilometers × .62 = miles
yards × .91 = meters
meters × 1.1 = yards
centimeters × .4 = inches
feet × 30 = centimeters
pounds × .37 = kilograms
kilograms × 2.2 = pounds
Fahrenheit × .55 = Celsius

Metro Atlantic Athletic Conference *See* college, Part II, for members of this Division I-AA football conference.

Metrodome Acceptable in all references to Hubert H. Humphrey Metrodome.

Mid-American Athletic Conference *See* college, Part II, for members.

midcourt (n., adj.) One word. The area on a basketball court near the midcourt line is referred to as midcourt.

middle distance In track and field, the 800-meter and 1,500-meter runs are considered middle distances. *See* track and field.

middleweight Olympic boxing class is 157-165. IBF/WBA/WBC class is 155-160 pounds. *See* boxing.

Mid-Eastern Athletic Conference *See* college, Part II, for members.

midfielder (n.) In soccer, a midfielder is one of three players who play near the middle of the field.

midseason (n., adj.)

> Atlanta had the lowest ERA at midseason.
> Seattle was in a midseason slump.

Midwestern Collegiate Conference *See* college, Part II, for members.

mile A mile is approximately equal to 1.6 kilometers. *See* metric system.

miles per gallon Use mpg in all references.

miles per hour Use mph in all references.

military pentathlon *See* modern pentathlon.

million Use figures when referring to a dollar amount.

> Bonds signed for $6 million.
> Majors negotiated a $2 million contract.
> June has a multi-million-dollar deal.
> He will make from $5 million to $6 million next year.

Milwaukee County Stadium County Stadium is acceptable in all references.

minicamp (n.)

> Most of the team participated in the minicamp.

mini-flyweight IBF boxing classification is 105 pounds and lower.

minimumweight WBA boxing classification is 105 pounds and lower.

minor league (n.) Use minor league in reference to Rookie, Class A, Double A, and Triple A baseball leagues. Teams in these leagues are associated with major-league teams.

Do not refer to players who compete in the minor leagues as amateurs. Use minor-leaguer.

minor-league baseball Major League Baseball's minor-league baseball system is made up of four levels: Rookie, Class A, Double A, and Triple A.

minor-leaguer (n.) *See* minor league.

minor penalty In hockey, any player but the goalie, who commits a minor penalty is taken off the ice for two minutes during which time no substitute is allowed. If a goalie is penalized, another player sits in the penalty box.

minute Spell out minutes on first reference.

> Sara won the race in two minutes, 23.5 seconds. Heather was second in 2:24.34.

miscue (n.) Do not use miscue as a verb.

misfire (v.) Avoid using misfire to indicate an errant throw.

> WRONG: The third baseman misfired his throw to first.
> RIGHT: The gun misfired.

MISL Acceptable on second reference to the Major Indoor Soccer League. League no longer exists.

mismatch (n., v.) In basketball, a mismatch indicates a situation in which a small player must guard a large player.

> A mismatch occurred when our guard had to defend their center. Barkley and Webb were mismatched.

misplay (v.)

Missouri Valley Conference *See* college, Part II, for members.

---

mitt Catchers and first basemen use mitts. When referring to players at all other positions, use glove.

> Fritz has a catcher's mitt, and Mark has a first baseman's mitt. Carter, the right fielder, got a new glove.

mixed Use mixed to describe a team made up of a man and a woman.

> We won the mixed-doubles competition.
> The American team won the mixed pairs skating event.

mix-up (n., adj.) Note the hyphen.

Mizuno Athletic equipment company.

MLS Acceptable on second reference for Major League Soccer. *See* Soccer, Part II, for teams.

modern pentathlon (n.) Pentathlon is acceptable in all references.

> The following five events make up the modern pentathlon: fencing, swimming, shooting, cross country running, and riding.

Monday morning quarterback Capitalize Monday and do not hyphenate this term for a fan who analyzes and comments on a game after it has been played.

Monday Night Football Capitalize the name of this ABC television program.

money-winner (n.)

> Hoover is the all-time leading money-winner.

monthlong (adj.)

> It is a monthlong tournament.
> The tournament is a month long.

Moore Capitalize this gymnastics move of performing circles on the pommel horse by bringing the hands together on one pommel and turning the body 180 degrees.

mop up (v.) Use sparingly in reference to a relief pitcher coming in to finish a game.

> With a three-run lead, Wettland came in to mop up for the Marlins.

Most Valuable Player Always capitalize and spell out on first reference. MVP is acceptable on second reference and in headlines when space is limited.

mother-in-law Do not refer to the 7-pin in bowling as the mother-in-law.

motocross (n., adj.) Note that there is no *r* in the name of this sport in which motorcyclists race on a closed course often made of dirt or mud.

motorcycle, motorcycling

motorsports (n.) Use motorsports when referring to automobile, airplane, powerboat, and motorcycle racing.

mpg Use in all references for miles per gallon.

mph Use in all references for miles per hour.

MRI Use magnetic resonance imaging on first reference, then MRI. *See* magnetic resonance imaging.

muff (n., v.) A muff occurs when a ball is touched by a player in an unsuccessful attempt to get possession of a loose ball.

> The punt returner fielded the muff.
> The kicker muffed the ball.

mulligan (n.) When a golfer hits a second ball and plays the better of the two, he or she has hit a mulligan.

---

multimillion

> Armstrong signed a multimillion-dollar agreement.
> King is a multimillionaire.

multiyear (adj.)

> Wesley has a multiyear contract with the team.

muscle-bound (adj.) Note the hyphen.

> Clark seemed more muscle-bound before he went to Arizona.

must win (v.)

> The Bullets must win to make the playoffs.

must-win (adj.)

> The team is in a must-win situation.

mutuel field Not mutual. In horse racing, a mutuel field is when two horses start in the same gate for betting interests.

MVP Spell out and capitalize Most Valuable Player on first reference. MVP is acceptable on second reference and in headlines when space is limited. *See* awards.

N

NAIA Spell out National Association of Intercollegiate Athletics on first reference, then NAIA.

nail Avoid using nail to mean to hit the mark.

> WRONG: He nailed the runner at home plate.
> WRONG: She nailed the dismount.

NASCAR Acceptable in all references for National Association for Stock Car Auto Racing.

natatorium Capitalize as part of the proper name of a building that houses a swimming pool.

>Southern competes at the Jackson-Haley Natatorium.
>The natatorium is located near the field house.

national anthem Capitalize Star-Spangled Banner, but lowercase national anthem.

National Association for Stock Car Auto Racing NASCAR is acceptable in all references.

National Association of Intercollegiate Athletics Spell out on first reference. Use NAIA in headlines when space is limited and on second reference.

National Association of Sportswriters and Broadcasters Spell out on first reference, then the association.

National Basketball Association NBA is acceptable in all references. *See* basketball, Part II.

national champion(s) (n., adj.) Lowercase even when used before a name. With a school's nickname, use the plural, national champions.

>The Cornhuskers were the 1994–1995 national champions.

With a school or individual's name, use national champion.

>The national champion Iowa Hawkeye wrestlers celebrated.
>Brands was the national champion two years in a row.

national championship Capitalize when National Championship is part of an event's official title.

>The team is going to the Sprint National Championships.
>Are the athletes going to the national championships?
>Who has qualified for nationals?

Style and Usage

National Collegiate Athletic Association NCAA is acceptable in all references. *See* college, Part II.

National Football Conference NFC is acceptable in all references. *See* football, Part II.

National Football League NFL is acceptable in all references. *See* football, Part II.

National Football League Properties NFL Properties is acceptable in all references.

National Hockey League NHL is acceptable in all references.

National Hot Rod Association Spell out on first reference, then NHRA. The four professional categories of NHRA competition are Top Fuel, Funny Car, Pro Stock, and Pro Stock Bike.

National In-Line Hockey Association Spell out on first reference, then NIHA.

National Invitation Tournament Spell out the name of this postseason tournament on first reference. NIT is acceptable in headlines and on second reference.
   Avoid using the redundant NIT tournament.

National Junior College Athletic Association Spell out on first reference, then NJCAA.

National League Spell out on first reference, then NL as a modifier on second reference. Avoid using NL as a noun. *See* baseball, Part II.

National Operating Committee on Standards for Athletic Equipment Organization conducts tests on athletic equipment. Spell out on first reference, then NOCSAE.

National Professional Soccer League Spell out on first reference, then NPSL. *See* Part II, for teams.

National Rifle Association Spell out on first reference, then NRA.

National Transplant Games Games are held annually for athletes who have received a transplant.

National Wheelchair Athletic Association Spell out on first reference, then the association.

nautical mile One nautical mile equals 6,080.20 feet.

Nautilus Capitalize this brand name of weightlifting equipment.

Naval Academy Navy is acceptable in all references to the school's athletic programs.

> Greene plays for Navy.

NBA Acceptable in all references to the National Basketball Association. *See* basketball, Part II.

NBA Finals Always capitalize Finals.

> The Bulls and Rockets will meet in the NBA Finals.
> The Bulls are ahead 2-1 in the Finals.
> Bulls and Knicks met in the Eastern Conference Finals.

NCAA National Collegiate Athletic Association does not need to be spelled out on first reference. *See* college, Part II.

near record One cannot set a near record. A person can, however, have a near-record performance or nearly break a record.

negative split In racing, a negative split occurs when a competitor completes the second half of a race faster than the first half.

nelson Do not capitalize the name of this wrestling move in which a wrestler places an arm under the arm of his or her opponent and with the same hand reaches up to push down against the back of the opponent's head. When used alone, nelson refers to a half nelson. Use reverse nelson, three-quarter nelson, or full nelson in other references.

---

nerve-racking (adj.) Not wracking.

netminder Do not use as a synonym for goalie, goalkeeper, or goaltender. *See* goalie.

new record This phrase is redundant.

> Lopez set a record.
> Rosenlof broke a record.

news conference Preferred to press conference.

newspapers *See* periodicals.

New York Spell out on first reference, then N.Y.

> The New York Yankees beat Boston.
> The N.Y. Mets are in third place.

Do not use the abbreviation N.Y. as a noun.

> WRONG: I am from N.Y.

New York Yankees Do not refer to the team as the Yanks.

NFC Acceptable in all references to National Football Conference. *See* football, Part II.

NFL Acceptable in all references for National Football League. *See* football, Part II.

NFL Combine Capitalize the name of this annual NFL event in which representatives from professional teams gather to assess the talent of college players hoping to be drafted.

NFL Properties Acceptable in all references to National Football League Properties.

NHL Acceptable in all references for National Hockey League. *See* hockey, Part II.

NHL Players Association No apostrophe in Players.

NHRA Spell out National Hot Rod Association on first reference to the motorsports sanctioning body. Four professional categories of NHRA competition are Top Fuel, Funny Car, Pro Stock, and Pro Stock Bike.

NHRA Winternationals Note spelling.

niblick Do not use this slang term for 9 iron.

nickel defense (n.) This football defense uses five defensive backs.

> The Eagles lined up in a nickel defense.

nickname Use on first reference and in headlines when the nickname is better known than the person's real name.

> Magic Johnson led the league in assists.

In the interest of clarity, when using a nickname on first reference or in a headline, it often is a good idea to identify the person by name early in the story.

> (headline) Shaq brings down the house
> (first reference) Shaquille O'Neal broke the backboard last
>   night in a game against New York.

When the nickname is not well-known, use quotation marks.

> Tommy "the Duke" Morrison will fight tonight.

When using a nickname derived from a team's name, use an apostrophe where letters are missing. Note the difference in the use of the apostrophe in the following examples.

> The Wildcats play tonight. It will be the second game in less
>   than a week for the 'Cats.
> The Buffaloes don't play Saturday. The Buffs will be well-rested
>   when they play Monday.

Nielsen ratings Acceptable on first reference for the television ratings system of A.C. Nielsen Co.

nightcap The second game of an evening doubleheader.

NIHA Spell out National In-Line Hockey Association on first reference, then NIHA.

NIT Use National Invitation Tournament on first reference, then NIT. Do not use the redundant NIT Tournament.

NL Spell out National League on first reference, then NL. Do not use NL as a noun.

NLCS Spell out National League Championship Series on first reference, then NL Championship Series of the series.

No. Use instead of *number* when referring to a rank or position.

> Stevens was the No. 1 qualifier.
> The Raiders are No. 2 in the poll.
> The No. 3 Huskies take on the No. 5 Devils.
> There were a number of former athletes present.

NOCSAE National Operating Committee on Standards for Athletic Equipment is the organization that conducts tests on athletic equipment in an attempt to establish safety standards. Spell out on first reference, then NOCSAE.

no decision

> No decision was reached in the matter.

no-decision A pitcher records a no-decision when he or she has not met the criteria to be considered the winning or losing pitcher. *See* losing pitcher.

> Waters has one victory, two losses, and four no-decisions.

no-hit (adj.) Do not use no-hit as a verb to indicate that a pitcher has not given up any base hits. *See* no-hitter.

WRONG: Glavine no-hit the Cardinals.
RIGHT: Ryan pitched his third no-hit game.

no-hitter (n.) A no-hitter occurs when a pitcher or pitchers do not allow the opposing team to get a hit. A no-hitter is not a perfect game. In a perfect game, no opposing batter is allowed to reach base. *See* perfect game, shutout.

> Simpson pitched his second no-hitter.
> Paige has a no-hitter going into the seventh inning.

no-huddle Use no-huddle to describe a style of play in which the offense does not use a huddle before coming to the line of scrimmage in a football game.

no-show (n.)

> Belle was a no-show.

non-conference (adj.) A competition between two teams that are not in the same conference.

> It is a non-conference game.

non-stop (adj.)

> The teams provided non-stop action.
> The action was non-stop.

Nordic skiing In Winter Olympic competition, men's events are ski jumping, 15k and 30k cross country skiing, 4 x 10k relay, 50k, 15k, and ski jump. Women's events are 5k and 10k cross country and 3 x 5k relay.

Norris Trophy *See* hockey, Part II.

North Atlantic Conference *See* college, Part II, for members.

Northeast Conference *See* college, Part II, for members.

nose guard (n.) This lineman, also referred to as the middle guard, plays between defensive tackles and opposite the opponent's center.

numbers Spell out numbers one through nine in most cases.

> Mullin had four rebounds.
> Ryan stole seven bases.

Use figures for numbers larger than nine and in the following cases:

Age

> I am 25 years old.
> She is a 5-year-old child.
> Darcy competed in the 9-and-under age group.

Betting Odds

> The odds are 3–1 Gerard will win.
> Meiners bet on the horse despite 5-to-1 odds.

Channel

> The game will be on Channel 12.

Draft Choice

> Jordan was the No. 3 pick in the draft.
> He was the third pick.

See No.

ERA

> Matt has a 4.60 ERA.

Golf Score, Club, and Handicap

> Price shot a 4 on No. 3.
> Lopez used a 5 iron on the par-3.
> Jasper has a 9 handicap.

Height

> King is 6 feet 2 inches tall.
> Johnson is a 6-foot-1 guard.

Wallace is 6-3.
Kansas signed a 7-footer.

Jersey
Daniel's number used to be 8. He now wears No. 6.

No.
Use instead of number when referring to a ranking or position.

Stevens was the No. 1 qualifier.
The Raiders are No. 2 in the poll.
The No. 3 Huskies take on the No. 5 Devils.
There were a number of former athletes present.
What is Sharifi's number? He wears No. 4.

Race Distance and Event Height
Scheiden won the 50-yard freestyle.
Baker ran the 100-meter hurdles in record time.
Wirth did a back dive off the 3-meter board.

Ratio
The bill passed by a 3–1 majority.

Record
Use figures for team and individual records.

Connecticut (20–4) will face O'Hara (18–6).

Score
Use a hyphen between the scores of the winner and loser.

The Dodgers won 9–7.
Lyons won the tennis match 6–3, 6–4.
Faldo had a 1-under-par 36.

Speed
Always use figures.

Richards averaged 171.103 kph (108.265 mph).
Cone throws in the 90s.

Salary
Use figures when referring to a person's salary.

Sandberg signed a $7.1 million contract.
Hopkins could make $1 million to $3 million.
She was paid $65,000 to coach the team.

Temperature
It was 3 degrees when the skiers started down the hill.

Time
Peterson finished the race in 3:45.23.
Iowa scored first with 5 minutes, 10 seconds remaining in the half.
Lynch fouled out with 3:30 left.

Weight
Use figures.

Hughes weighed in at 180 pounds, 7 ounces.

Yard Line
He caught the ball at the 4-yard line.
Jones fumbled on the Giants' 49-yard line.

O

oarsman (n.) Do not change oarsman to oarswoman to reflect gender when referring to a member of a rowing crew.

OB Spell out out-of-bounds.

O'Brien Award This award, named after former Texas Christian quarterback Davey O'Brien, is given to the outstanding collegiate quarterback. It was established in 1981. Use Davey O'Brien Award on first reference.

obscenities Refer to your publication's rules for handling words unsuitable for print. In general, avoid using offensive words. Replace offensive words in quotes with hyphens.

odds Use figures and a hyphen. *See* betting odds.

> The odds are 3-1 Gerard will win.
> He bet on the horse despite 5-to-1 odds.

odds-on favorite The backing of an odds-on favorite is so strong that profit to be made by the bettors is less than that wagered.

off-balance (adj.)

> Roy was off-balance when he crashed his bike.

off-day (n.) Use off-day to refer to a poor performance or a day on which an athlete is not competing.

> Joel had an off-day, giving up five hits in the first inning.
> Longo works out even on off-days.

off-road racing Racing that takes place over rugged terrain. Events feature motorcycles, cars, jeeps, and other off-road motor vehicles.

off-season (n., adj.) Use off-season to refer to the period of time during which an athlete is not competing.

> Vaughn was injured in the off-season.
> Wong did quite a bit of off-season training.

offshore (n., adj.)

offside Not offsides. A football player is offside if any part of his or her body is beyond the line of scrimmage when the ball is put in play.

> The lineman was offside.

off-speed (adj.) Use off-speed to describe a pitch thrown slower than normal.

> Jude threw an off-speed pitch.

off-track betting Spell out on first reference, then OTB if used as an adjective. Off-track betting is wagering that takes place at a facility other than the track at which the race is taking place.

Ohio Valley Conference *See* college, Part II, for members.

OK, OK'd Not okay or okay'd.

> Longo said he felt OK after being hit with the ball.
> Painter OK'd the trade.

old-timers' game Note apostrophe in timers'.

Olympics The four-year cycle of staging the Winter and Summer Games in the same year ended with the Olympics in Lillehammer, Norway, in 1994. The Winter and Summer Games now alternate every two years.

Always capitalize Olympic and Games in reference to the Olympics.

> The United States won 30 medals during the '84 Games.
> We went to the '84 Winter Olympics and the '88 Summer Olympics.

An Olympic-sized pool is 50m x 25m. Note the capitalization and hyphen.

> We swam in an Olympic-sized pool.

Capitalize Opening Ceremony in reference to the Winter and Summer Olympic Opening Ceremonies. Also capitalize Closing Ceremony. *See* Olympics, Part II.

on-base percentage Calculate by dividing the number of times a batter reaches base by the number of at-bats.

on-deck circle (n.) Note hyphenation. The on-deck circle is the area in which a batter prepares for his or her turn at bat.

one-and-one A free-throw situation in which the player shooting is awarded a bonus free throw if he or she makes the first one.

> Rebecca will shoot a one-and-one.

one bagger Avoid using to mean base hit.

one-hand (adj.)

> Dave made a one-handed catch.

one-on-one This style of play features one competitor facing one opponent. The term can also be used to describe an informal game between two players.

> Jordan and Johnson went one-on-one in the fourth period.
> Pittman and Minor played one-on-one at the park.

one-two punch (n.) Hyphenate and spell out this term for two quick punches in succession.

onside kick Not onsides. For the kicking team to take possession of the ball, it must travel at least 10 yards.

O-Pee-Chee Trading card line made by Topps.

Opening Ceremony Capitalize in reference to the Winter and Summer Olympic Opening Ceremonies. Also capitalize Closing Ceremony.

Opening Day Capitalize only when referring to the first day of the major-league baseball season.

opposite-field (adj.) Note the difference between an opposite-field hitter and a pull hitter. A right-handed batter who hits to right field consistently is an opposite-field hitter. A right-handed hitter who hits to left field consistently is a pull hitter.

> Boal scored on an opposite-field hit by Boone.

option (n., adj.) In football, the option allows the quarterback to run, pass, or hand the ball off after the snap. Do not use option as a verb in football references.

> WRONG: Fletter optioned the ball to the fullback.
> RIGHT: The quarterback confused the defense with an option play.

Option also can refer to a clause in a contract that allows a team to invoke terms of an expired contract one more season.

> An option clause in Starbuck's contract will keep him on the team one more year.

Orange Bowl Use Federal Express Orange Bowl on first reference.

orienteering Participants run cross country using a map and compass to find their way between checkpoints to the finish line.

Oriole Park at Camden Yards Use Camden Yards on second reference.

OTB Spell out off-track betting on first reference.

Outback Steakhouse Gator Bowl Use sponsor's name on first reference to the Gator Bowl. *See* bowl games.

outclass (v.)

> Lopez outclassed her opponents.

outcry (n.)

> There was public outcry over the decision.

outdistance (v.) One word.

> Silver outdistanced her opponents.

outdo (v.)

> Sanders was able to outdo the competition.
> He outdid his opponent.

outdoor (adj.) Note the difference between outdoor and outdoors. Outdoor is used to describe an object that is outside.

> The game will be played at the outdoor stadium.

outdoors (n.) Note the difference between outdoor and outdoors. Outdoors is a location.

> He loves the great outdoors.

outfield, outfielder One word.

outfight (v.)

> Holmes outfought his opponent.

outhit (v.)

> The Rockies outhit the Giants.

Outland Trophy This award is given to the outstanding NCAA Division I interior lineman.

out of bounds (adv.)

> The ball went out of bounds.

out-of-bounds (adj.)

> The Steelers were upset about the out-of-bounds tackle.

outperform (v.)

> Collins outperformed the competition.

outpoint (v.) In boxing and wrestling, the winner of a fight has outpointed his or her opponent, not outdecisioned.

outrebound (v.)

> Hardaway outrebounded Johnson 15–12.

overall (adj.)

> Waugh was the overall winner.

overhand serve Do not use overhand unless it is necessary to distinguish an overhand serve from an underhand serve.

overpower (v.)

> Graf overpowered her opponent.

overtime (n., adj.) Use overtime to describe the continuation of a game after regulation to break a tie. In baseball references, use extra innings, not overtime. In tennis, use tiebreaker.

> The Houston-Arizona game went into overtime.
> The Clippers began the overtime period by scoring five consecutive points.
> The Reds won the game in extra innings.
> Tied at 5-5 in the second game, Graf and Seles prepared to play a tiebreaker.

overthrow (n., v.)

> Rooney advanced to second base on the overthrow.
> Randle overthrew the second baseman.

over-under (n.)

owner Do not capitalize when used before a name.

> Hacket received a call from owner Ted White.
> Jay Esposito, the team's owner, fired the manager.

own goal In football, a team's own goal is the goal it is guarding.

P

pace car (n.) The car that leads a field of cars around the track at the start of a race and when caution is signaled.

pace line In biking, a pace line is a group of bikers that forms a line in which they take turns leading during a race.

pace-line (adj.)

> The riders got into pace-line formation.

pacesetter (n.) Use one word to describe an individual who leads the field in a race.

Pacific 10 Conference Spell out on first reference, then Pac-10. Note hyphenation. *See* college, Part II, for members.

Padres Do not abbreviate as Pads or Pods.

pairs skating (n.) *See* figure skating.

Pan American Games Competition between the nations of the Western Hemisphere has been held every four years since 1951. Capitalize Games in all references.

par, parred, parring Par is the number of strokes necessary to complete a hole as determined by the course. *See* golf.

> Watson shot 9 under par.
> Palmer shot a 7-under-par 60.
> Sheen parred the first hole.

parallel bars Note the spelling of this men's gymnastics apparatus.

Paralympic Games Capitalize the name of this event that features disabled athletes taking part in Olympic-style competition.

pari-mutuel betting System of betting in which all bets are pooled by the track or establishment and the winnings are distributed after operating expenses and state taxes have been deducted.

---

parlay To parlay a bet is to take a winning bet and its stake and bet it on a subsequent event.

parquet Type of wood floor used in some basketball arenas.

> The University of Iowa and Boston Gardens have parquet floors.

part-time (adj.)

> Pete is a part-time stadium worker.

passed ball (n.) Note the difference between passed ball and wild pitch. A passed ball is a pitch that passes the catcher but could have been stopped with reasonable effort. A wild pitch also gets by the catcher, but because it is so difficult to stop, it is blamed on the pitcher.

pastime (n.) Lowercase in phrases such as national pastime.

PAT Use point after or extra point instead.

> Grove missed the point after.

patella The kneecap.

Patrick Trophy *See* hockey, Part II.

payout

> The winner of this race can expect a $1.5 million payout.

pay per view (n.) Service offered on cable television gives viewers the option to pay for a program they would not otherwise receive.

> We watched the fight on pay per view.

pay-per-view (adj.) Note hyphenation.

> The fight was on the pay-per-view channel.

Payton Award Award given to the NCAA Division I-AA Player of the Year is voted on by Division I-AA sports information directors. It was established in 1987. Use Walter Payton Award on first reference.

PBA Use Professional Bowlers Association on first reference. PBA Tour is acceptable in headlines when space is limited and on first reference to avoid a cumbersome lead.

PBA Tournament of Champions Professional bowling event is held annually in Akron, Ohio.

peak To peak is to reach a high point.

> The team peaked last season when it finished 12-0.

To pique is to provoke or arouse.

> The book piqued his interest.

pedal (v.) To pedal is to operate a bicycle.

> Leon pedals his bike around the track.

peddle (v.) To peddle is to sell something.

> James peddles hot dogs from a cart in the parking lot.

penalty box Do not refer to the penalty box in any sport by a nickname, such as sin bin.

pennant (n., adj.) Pennant can be used as a synonym for championship when referring to the National League and American League titles.

> Boston will play Baltimore for the American League pennant.
> The Cubs and Phillies are in a pennant race.

percent Always spell out in text and use figures.

> He is shooting 47 percent from the free-throw line.
> She will get a 3.5 percent increase in her salary.

The team had a shooting percentage of .672. Their opponent shot 72 percent.

perfecta To win a perfecta, a bettor must pick the first- and second-place finishers.

perfect game In baseball, a perfect game occurs when a pitcher does not allow any opposing batters to reach first base.

During a no-hitter, a batter may reach first base, but not due to a hit.

In a shutout, the winning team does not allow the opposing team to score.

A perfect game cannot be broken up, but a bid for a perfect game can be.

periodicals Always italicize any reference to a periodical. After the first reference, the title may be shortened.

The *Boston Globe* reported an increase in city crime. According to the *Globe,* murders have increased by 50 percent.

petroleum jelly Lowercase petroleum jelly, but capitalize the trademark name Vaseline.

PGA Acceptable in all references to the Professional Golfers' Association. *See* golf.

PGA Championship Spell out on first reference, then the championship. *See* golf.

PGA Senior Players Championship Senior PGA event. *See* golf.

PGA Seniors' Championship Senior PGA event is played at PGA National Golf Course in Palm Springs Gardens, Fla.

PGA Tour Spell out on first reference, then the tour.

phase A temporary period of time. To faze is to disconcert.

Hugh is going through a phase.
White was not fazed by the accusations.

pick-and-roll (n., adj.) Hyphenate the name of this basketball move in which a player sets a pick, cuts away from the defender, and moves toward the basket to receive the pass.

pick off (v.)

> Kelly was able to pick off the runner.

pickoff (n., adj.) A quick throw made to catch a runner off base.

> Johnson attempted a pickoff.
> Hansen got caught on a pickoff play.

pigskin Avoid using as a synonym for football.

pike In diving or gymnastics, this is a position where the athlete bends at the waist with straight legs.

pinch hit (n., v.) To take a hitter's turn at bat.

> Liotta scored on a pinch hit by Abbott.
> Janike pinch hit for Darson.

pinch-hit (adj.)

> The Angels are in a pinch-hit situation.

pinch-hitter (n.) A player who hits for another player.

> Ireland is the pinch-hitter.

pinch-runner (n.) A player who runs for another player.

> Should we put in a pinch-runner?

Ping-Pong Tradename used as synonym for table tennis.

Pinnacle Note spelling of trading card company. Also the name of a manufacturer of golf equipment.

pipped Do not use this term without an explanation. The term refers to Wally Pipp, a Yankees first baseman who did not play in a game on June 1, 1925. Lou Gehrig took his place that day and went on to play 2,130 consecutive games.

If a person is "pipped," he or she is replaced after taking a day off.

pique (v.) To pique is to provoke or arouse. *See* peak.

> The book piqued his interest.
> She peaked last season.

Pirates Do not refer to any team named the Pirates as the Bucs.

pirouette Note the spelling of this gymnastics term, which is a twist in the handstand position.

pitch-and-run (n.) Chip shot can be used as a synonym. This golf shot is accomplished by hitting the ball low onto the green in order to allow it to roll toward the hole.

pitcher's mound In professional baseball, the mound is 18 feet in diameter, 60 feet, 6 inches from home plate.

pitch out (v.) *See* pitchout.

> Davis pitched the ball out to Simpson.

pitchout (n.) In baseball, use pitchout to describe an outside pitch thrown intentionally to allow the catcher to throw out a runner. In football, use pitchout to describe a lateral pass tossed underhand to a back.

> Rivera threw a pitchout.

pivotman (n.) In basketball, the pivotman is usually the center, who stands with his or her back to the basket.

place-kicker (n.) A football player who kicks the ball while it is stationary, such as during a kickoff or extra point.

---

planche Note the spelling of this gymnastics position where the gymnast balances on the hands with his or her body at an angle.

platform diving Olympic competition takes place from a 10-meter platform. Do not use high board or tower as a synonym for platform.

play-action (n., adj.) During play-action, a quarterback fakes a handoff to a back and then passes.

> The quarterback used play-action on second down.
> The Vikings fooled the defense with a play-action pass.

playbook (n.) Book containing a team's diagrams, plays, and signals.

play-by-play (n., adj.) A broadcast rendition of a game.

> Moyer does play-by-play for the Reds.
> Who will handle play-by-play duties for the Rangers?

Player of the . . . Capitalize. *See* awards.

> Stewart was voted Player of the Year.
> Moore is the Player of the Month.

players' union Lowercase and note the apostrophe. *See* Major League Baseball Players Association.

playmaker (n.) One word. Use to describe a team's driving force.

> Simms is the team's playmaker.

play off (v.) Holland and Mabry will play off for the title.

playoff (n., adj.)

> Fletter won the playoff.
> The Hawks and Stars met in the playoff game.

Plexiglas Capitalize this trademark name, but lowercase acrylic plastic.

p.m. Lowercase or specify small caps. Do not be redundant by using p.m. with evening or tonight.

> WRONG: The game is at 7 p.m. in the evening.
> WRONG: The game is at 7 p.m. tonight.
>   RIGHT: The game is at 7 p.m.

point after touchdown (n.) Use point after or extra point in all references. PAT is acceptable in agate.

point Spell out numbers one through nine. Use figures for numbers greater than nine.

> Brennan had eight points and four rebounds.
> Pat had 11 points.

Avoid using parentheses to set off point totals when they will break up the flow of a sentence.

> WRONG: Haley (10 points) led all scorers.
>   RIGHT: Haley led all scorers with 10 points.

When referring to final scores, always use figures.

> Seles won the tennis match 6-4, 6-2.
> The A's defeated the Yankees 5-3.

Do not refer to runs in baseball and softball, or goals in hockey and soccer as points.

> WRONG: The A's defeated the Yankees by two points.
>   RIGHT: The A's defeated the Yankees by two runs.
>   RIGHT: Columbia scored two goals against Brazil.

point after (n.) The kick attempted after a touchdown, also called the extra point, is worth one point. *See* point after touchdown.

Do not use redundant phrases such as missed the point after attempt.

> WRONG: Miller missed the point after attempt.
> RIGHT: Miller missed the point after.

points per game Spell out on first reference, then ppg.

poke check (n.) A stick check in hockey designed to knock the puck away from an opponent.

poke-check (adj., v.) Note hyphenation.

pole sitter (n.) The driver in an auto race who has earned the position on the inside of Row 1.

pole vault (n.) Field event in which competitor uses a long pole to vault over a horizontal bar.

> Tekampe won the pole vault.

pole-vault (adj., v.)

> O'Brien broke the pole-vault record.
> He pole-vaulted 17 feet.

pole vaulter Two words.

polo The playing field is 300 yards long and 160 yards wide (10 acres). The game is played in chukkers, or periods, of which there are six. There are four members on each team who use mallets in an attempt to hit the ball between the opponent's goal posts.

pommel horse The pommels are the two rounded hand grips on top of the apparatus used in gymnastics.

Pony League Always capitalized.

pop up (v.)

> Oliver popped up to right field.

---

pop-up (n.)

> Foster hit a pop-up.

Pop Warner Football Capitalize the name of this organization that creates youth football leagues.

port On a ship, when facing the bow, the left side is port. The right side is starboard.

possessives Use an apostrophe with a team's name when it is used as a possessive: the Saints' leading rusher, the Sooners' first game.

Use an apostrophe if a team name directly precedes a person's name.

> The Angels' Tim Salmon leads the league in base hits.

Be careful not to use an apostrophe incorrectly with a team's name.

> WRONG: The Angel's left fielder bats fifth.
> RIGHT: The Angels' left fielder bats fifth.

When used descriptively, a team name does not require an apostrophe.

> The award was given to Cowboys quarterback Troy Aikman.

posterior cruciate ligament This ligament of the knee provides stability and prevents displacement of the tibia backward within the knee joint. Spell out on first reference, then PCL. *See* anterior cruciate ligament.

postgame

> The coach argued with reporters during the postgame news conference.

postpone Do not use as a synonym for cancel. When a game is canceled, it isn't made up, but a postponed game is rescheduled.

postseason (n., adj.) No hyphen.

> The Vikings won five games in the postseason.
> They are 0-2 in the postseason tournament.

post-up (adj., v.) An offensive player takes a position near the free throw lane with his or her back to the basket.

> The Lakers' center ran a post-up play.
> He posted-up on his smaller opponent.

-pound Hyphenate pound when using it with a figure to describe a person's weight. Do not refer to a person as a -pounder.

> WRONG: The lineman is a 300-pounder.
> RIGHT: The 300-pound lineman was knocked down.

powerboat (n., adj.)

> The powerboat can go 150 mph.
> Spectators gathered to watch powerboat racing.

power play (n.) Use power play to describe a situation in which a hockey team has more players on the ice because of a penalty on an opposing player.

power-play (adj.)

> The Blackhawks scored a power-play goal.

PRCA Spell out Professional Rodeo Cowboys Association on first reference.

Preakness Stakes Thoroughbred race for three-year-olds held at Pimlico Race Course in Baltimore, Md. One of the three races that make up the Triple Crown. *See* Triple Crown.

---

pregame (adj.)

> Lang organized the pregame and postgame festivities.

preliminary (n., adj.) A qualifying heat run before the main race in sports such as swimming and track. Avoid using the abbreviation, prelims. Do not use the redundant preliminary trials

> DuPree hopes to do well in the preliminaries.
> Preliminary events will be held in the morning.

preseason No hyphen.

> The Bears won five games in the preseason.

Do not refer to major league baseball spring training games as preseason games. Use exhibition games instead. *See* exhibition.

president Capitalize President as a title before a name.

> League President Gene Budig agreed with the idea.
> Ron Sheppard, the president, had to make the final decision.

Always capitalize President in reference to the President of the United States.

> Bill Clinton is the President.

President's Cup Notice apostrophe in name of golf event in which players from the United States compete against an international team.

press conference Use news conference instead.

principal As an adjective, principal means chief. As a noun, it means person in charge.

> The storm is our principal concern.
> He asked his principal about the three-game suspension.

principle (n.) A principle is a standard.

> The team's concept is made up of three basic principles.

pro-am A best-ball competition in which professional and amateur golfers are paired. Capitalize as a part of a proper name.

> Griffen will play in the Pacific Pro-Am.

probation When a school or player is put on probation, they are not necessarily sanctioned. Do not use probation (a period of time in which a person is tested) as a synonym for sanctions (penalties).

Pro Bowl The NFL's all-star game.

pro bowler Do not refer to a football player as a Pro Bowler, but rather as a Pro Bowl player or a Pro Bowl selection.
Use pro bowler only when referring to a person who bowls professionally.

> Was Earl Anthony the best pro bowler of all time?

Pro Cap Capitalize the name of this piece of equipment used on the outside of a football helmet to provide extra protection from concussions.

profanity *See* obscenities.

professional A professional is paid for his or her participation in a sport. An amateur is not.
For example, along with players in the NHL, NBA, NFL and major leagues, minor-league baseball players, minor-league hockey players, and women who play for the Colorado Silver Bullets are considered professionals.

Professional Bowlers Association Note that there is no apostrophe in Bowlers. PBA and PBA Tour are acceptable in headlines when space is limited, but should be spelled out on first reference in the story.

Professional Golfers' Association Note apostrophe in Golfers'. PGA is acceptable on first reference. *See* golf.

prognosis Use prognosis when referring to the expected outcome of an injury's course. *See* diagnose.

> WRONG: The prognosis is a sprain.
> RIGHT: The doctor said his prognosis is good.

Proposition 48 Capitalize the name of the NCAA rule in all uses. *See* college, Part II.

Professional Rodeo Cowboys Association Spell out on first reference, then PRCA.

psych out (adj., v.) Use to describe a team or individual that is mentally unprepared for competition, or the act of intimidating an opponent.

> Graf is psyched out for the final match.
> Seles psyched out Graf.

psych up (adj., v.) Use this term when referring to a team or individual that is mentally prepared for competition.

> Our swim team is psyched up for the state meet.
> We psyched ourselves up by visualizing our events.

pull buoy This swimming aid allows a swimmer to pull in the water without kicking.

pull hitter Two words.

pull up (v.) To dribble, stop quickly and shoot. Hyphenate as a modifier.

> Hardaway pulled up for a jump shot.
> He hit a pull-up jumper in the fourth quarter.

pull-up (n.) Acceptable as a synonym for a chin-up.

> Young can do 50 pull-ups.

push-up (n.)

> He can do one push-up.

put out (v.)

putout (n.)

> Powter recorded the putout.

putt (n., v.) **putted, putting** (v.)

putter (n.) Use for both the name of the club and for the person putting the ball.

pylons Markers placed on the inside corners of the end zone in football.

Q

QB Spell out quarterback in all references. QB is acceptable in headlines when space is limited and in agate.

quadrangular This type of meet features four teams competing simultaneously, but each team is scored as if it were competing one-on-one with each of the other teams. Quad is acceptable in headlines when space is limited.

> The Lions won the volleyball quadrangular.

quadrennial Once every four years.

quadriceps Not quadricep. This muscle in the front thigh runs from the hip to the patella (kneecap). The four components of the quadriceps are the rectus femoris, vastus lateralis, vastus medialis, and vastus intermedius.

Spell with an *s* in both singular and plural references.

The starting quarterback injured the quadriceps in his left leg.

quality Quality requires a modifier such as high or low.

Radcliffe is a high-quality quarterback.

quarterback Do not abbreviate as QB except in headlines and agate.

quarterback sack Avoid using this redundant phrase. Only the quarterback can be sacked.

Thomas had nine sacks in 1994.

quarterfinals In an elimination tournament, the quarterfinals precede the semifinals, which precede the finals. Use quarterfinal as a modifier.

Larson advanced to the quarterfinals.
Tyler did well in his quarterfinal match.

quarter horse (n.) Two words.

quick kick (n.) A quick kick, which can take place on first, second, or third down in a football game, is designed to catch the defense off-guard. Hyphenate as a verb.

Deep in their own territory, the offense decided to attempt a quick kick.
The Wolverines quick-kicked the ball from the end zone.

quick pitch (n.) An illegal pitch thrown before the batter is ready.

McDonald was warned after he threw a quick pitch.

quick-pitch (v.)

Anderson quick-pitched the ball.

R

rabbit punch In boxing, an illegal punch delivered to the back of the neck or head. Never use as a verb.

> WRONG: Leonard rabbit punched Hagler.
> RIGHT: Leonard hit Hagler with a rabbit punch.

racecourse (n.) One word unless it is spelled differently as part of a proper name.

> We are going to the racecourse tonight.
> The Preakness Stakes is held at the Pimlico Race Course.

racehorse (n.) One word.

racer's edge The maximum speed at which an auto racer can negotiate a turn and maintain control.

racetrack (n.) Capitalize as part of a proper name.

raceway Capitalize as part of a proper name.

> The Slick 50 500 was held at the Phoenix International Raceway.

rack (v.) Rack can mean to arrange billiard balls for the break or to stress or strain. Avoid using rack to mean score, as in to rack up points.

> Good racked the billiard balls.
> Oscar racked his brain.

racket (n.) Not racquet.

> Conners needed a new racket.

racquetball Games are played to 21 points. The winner must win by one point.

Style and Usage

radio stations Use call letters with the dial position in parentheses.

> The game was broadcast on KHMA (980 AM).

rainout (n.) In baseball, a rainout may be postponed or canceled. If it is postponed, it is rescheduled. If it is canceled, it is not made up.

> We have to play two games Saturday because of yesterday's rainout.

rally (n., v.) Use rally to describe a series of points, runs, or goals scored by a team trying to come from behind.

> Dennis came back from a 6-2 deficit with a rally in the last set.
> The Mavericks scored 12 points during a third-quarter rally.
> Wong rallied to win the match.

A rally also is a long volley in tennis or badminton.

rally-point (adj.) Hyphenate the name of this point system in volleyball in which every serve results in a point.

ratios Use figures and a hyphen as in a ratio of 3-to-1, a 3-1 ratio.

Rawlings Note spelling of athletic equipment company.

razzle-dazzle (n.) Use this term to describe a trick or fancy footwork used to confuse a defender.

RBI, RBIs Acceptable in all references to run(s) batted in. Use an *s* to indicate more than one RBI.

> Gwynn had one RBI today.
> Sax has six RBIs.

rebound (n.,v.) Do not use board as a synonym for rebound.

> WRONG: Adams had five boards.
> RIGHT: Adams had five rebounds.

rebounds per game Use rpg in agate, but spell out rebounds per game in all other uses.

record (n.) Do not use the redundant new record or old record.

> He broke the record.
> She set a record.

Be specific when it is necessary to indicate the type of record set to avoid confusion.

> Evans set an Olympic record.
> She was less than two seconds off the world record.

Many publications use parentheses when including an individual or team record in a story. Follow your publication's rule for using parentheses, as some prefer to set off records with commas.

> The Bears (8-1) take on the Packers (5-4) tonight.

record holder (n.) Lewis is the record holder in this event.

red card (n.) Never a verb, as in red carded. In volleyball, a red card is given for unsportsmanlike conduct. In soccer, a red card is given for violent conduct, foul play or language, or a second cautionable offense after receiving a caution.

red line Hockey term for the line that runs the width of the rink and divides it in half is two words.

redshirt, redshirted, redshirting As a general rule, a collegiate athlete is allowed to redshirt for one year and still maintain four years of athletic eligibility. *See* college, Part II.

> Matt is a redshirt freshman.
> He will redshirt this year.
> Thome redshirted as a sophomore.
> He plans on redshirting next season.

Redskins Do not refer to the team as the Skins or Tribe. *See* derogatory terms.

redundancy The following are some common examples of redundancy found in sportswriting.

> REDUNDANT: Chandler will attempt to kick a field goal.
> BETTER: Chandler will attempt a field goal.

In football, all field goals are kicked.

> REDUNDANT: The city plans to build a new stadium.
> BETTER: The city plans to build a stadium.

It's given that the stadium will be new.

> REDUNDANT: The fans sat in close proximity to the court.
> BETTER: The fans sat close to the court.

Close is an expression of proximity.

> REDUNDANT: Rodman was ejected from the game in the third period.
> BETTER: Rodman was ejected in the third period.

It can be assumed that he was in the game.

> REDUNDANT: Sutter is favored to win.
> BETTER: Sutter is favored.

He would not be favored to lose.

> REDUNDANT: San Diego was unable to score on first down and goal-to-go.
> BETTER: San Diego was unable to score on first-and-goal.

Down is implied.

> REDUNDANT: Lynn held the charity game for the benefit of Little League baseball.
> BETTER: Lynn held the charity game for Little League Baseball.

REDUNDANT: The game was played for the benefit of the kids.
BETTER: The game was played to benefit the kids.

"For the benefit of" is unnecessary, particularly if charity is stated.

REDUNDANT: Vaughn fumbled the ball on the 9-yard line.
BETTER: Vaughn fumbled on the 9-yard line.

What else would he have fumbled?

REDUNDANT: DeThorne scouted future prospects at the college.
BETTER: DeThorne scouted prospects at the college.

The word *prospects* implies future.

REDUNDANT: What are the team's future plans for the rookie?
BETTER: What are the team's plans for the rookie?

The team would not be making past plans, so future is implied.

REDUNDANT: Pikalek hit a grand slam home run.
BETTER: Pikalek hit a grand slam.

A grand slam is always a home run.

REDUNDANT: Drury was called for icing the puck.
BETTER: Drury was called for icing.

Only a puck can be iced.

REDUNDANT: Wisconsin scored with two minutes remaining to go in the game.
BETTER: Wisconsin scored with two minutes remaining.

Unless a story is confusing chronologically, the reader will not assume you mean in the half, or in the quarter.

REDUNDANT: Wes set a new record.
BETTER: Wes set a record.

A record set is always new.

> REDUNDANT: He broke the old record set by Sullivan in 1985.
> BETTER: He broke the record set by Sullivan in 1985.

Old is unnecessary.

> REDUNDANT: The NIT tournament begins this week.
> BETTER: The NIT begins this week.

The word *tournament* is already present in the acronym.

> REDUNDANT: Anthony bowled a perfect 300 game.
> BETTER: Anthony bowled a perfect game.

A 300 game is always perfect.

> REDUNDANT: Dent has 10 quarterback sacks this season.
> BETTER: Dent has 10 sacks this season.

Only a quarterback can be sacked.

> REDUNDANT: Their stadium is small in size compared to the
> SkyDome.
> BETTER: Their stadium is small compared to the
> SkyDome.

Small implies size.

> REDUNDANT: Howe recorded a three-goal hat trick.
> BETTER: Howe recorded a hat trick.

A hat trick by definition is three goals in a game.

reel Piece of equipment used for fishing is not spelled real.

referee's crease Note apostrophe. In hockey, the referee's crease is the semicircle located in front of the penalty timekeeper's seat.

refuse to comment Avoid using refuse unless a person actually says he or she will not comment. Use decline to comment or could not be reached for comment if more appropriate.

regatta A race or series of races in which a large number of boats participate.

rehabilitation (n., v., adj.) Avoid using the slang term *rehab.*

> WRONG: Nixon is on a rehab assignment in the minors.
> RIGHT: Nixon is playing in the minors while rehabilitating.

relief pitcher General term describes a pitcher who replaces another pitcher during a game. Use reliever on second reference.

> Langer has been a relief pitcher most of his career. He is a reliever for the Cardinals.

When a pitcher's job is more specific, use a more descriptive term.

> Evans is a middle reliever.
> Montgomery is the team's closer.

representative Capitalize only as a congressman or congresswoman's formal title.

> The game was attended by Representative Jan Meyers.
> Royals player representative Jeff Montgomery spoke out.

re-sign (v.) To sign again.

> Cummingham re-signed with the Raiders.

resign (v.) To leave a position.

> Homan resigned his position with the club.

restricted free agent The NFL Collective Bargaining Agreement defines this player as one with three seasons of free agency expe-

---

Style and Usage

rience who is subject to compensation and/or right of first refusal. Do not hyphenate.

> Watters is a restricted free agent.

revolutions per minute Spell out on first reference, then rpm.

RFK Stadium RFK is acceptable on first reference for Robert Fitzgerald Kennedy Stadium.

rhythmic gymnastics Events are performed using a rope, hoop, ribbon and stick, ball, or clubs. Participants are different from those competing in gymnastics, and scores are not part of a gymnastics all-around competition.

ricochet, ricocheted (v.)

> The ball ricocheted off the post.

right field, right fielder Use two words for the position and the player.

riffle Small rapids in a river or stream.

rifle (n.) Distinguish rifles by their cartridge size.

> Brandon fired the .22-caliber rifle at the target.

Use sparingly as a synonym for throwing hard.

> Chavez rifled the ball over to first.

right-center (adj.)

> Dutch plays right-center field.
> He is the right-center fielder.
> He hit the ball over the right-center-field fence.

right hand (n.)

> She injured her right hand.

Hyphenate adjective form right-handed and noun form right-hander.

> Shoemaker is right-handed.
> He made a right-handed throw.

Avoid using righty in reference to a right-handed person.

ringside

> Rogers sat ringside. He had a ringside seat.

Robert Fitzgerald Kennedy Stadium RFK is acceptable on first reference.

rodeo *See* Part II.

Rollerblade Capitalize this trademark name for in-line skates.

roller-blading (v.) Do not use roller-blading as a synonym for in-line skating.

roller hockey Acceptable synonym for in-line hockey.

roller skates (n.) Do not use as a synonym for in-line skates.

roller-skate (v.)

> Harmon doesn't roller-skate down the big hills.

Roman Capitalize in phrases such as Roman cross, Greco-Roman wrestling.

Roman numerals Use Roman numerals when part of an event's formal title.

> The Chicago Bears won Super Bowl XX.
> Did you attend the XIII Olympics?

Rookie of the . . . Capitalize the name of this award. *See* awards.

> He was voted Rookie of the Month and Rookie of the Year.

---

rosin bag Preferred to resin bag. A rosin bag is used by pitchers to gain a better grip on the ball.

Ross Trophy *See* hockey, Part II.

rotator cuff This area is made up of four muscles encircling and supporting the shoulder: the supraspinatus, infra-spinatus, teres minor, and subscapularis.

Rotisserie League baseball Capitalize the name of the fantasy baseball league named after a restaurant called La Rotisserie Francaise.

round Capitalize when referring to a specific round in a boxing match and use figures.

> McGraw won Round 4.
> Ali won the third round.

roundballer Do not use roundballer as a synonym for basketball player.

roundhouse (n., adj.) One word in reference to a karate kick or boxing punch.

round-robin tournament In this type of tournament, every competitor meets every other competitor and win-loss records determine the winner. Note the difference between round-robin and elimination tournaments. In an elimination tournament, competitors play until they lose a specific number of times. For example, in a double-elimination tournament, a team is out after losing twice.

> Bernardi will play in a round-robin tennis tournament.
> The girls team won a round-robin softball tournament.

Row Capitalize Row when it used with a figure to describe a driver's position at the start of an auto race.

> Mears will start on the inside of Row 2.
> Hampton will start in the second row.

rowing Scoring is in minutes, seconds, and tenths of a second. Events include single sculls, double sculls, coxless pair, coxed pair, coxless four, quadruple sculls, coxed four, and eight-oars. *See* Part II.

Royal and Ancient Golf Club of St. Andrews R & A acceptable after first reference.

Rozelle Award This award is given to the Most Valuable Player in the Super Bowl. Use Pete Rozelle Award on first reference.

rpg Always spell out rebounds per game except in agate.

rpm Spell out revolutions per minute on first reference, then rpm.

rugby *See* Part II.

run and gun (n.) This style of play in basketball emphasizes speed, not defense. Hyphenate as a modifier.

> The Wildcats have trouble against the run and gun.
> Arkansas plans to use a run-and-gun offense.

run and shoot (n.)

runaround (n.) An evasive tactic used to avoid a final decision.

> The players accused the owners of giving them the runaround during negotiations.

runback (n.) The return after a kickoff, punt, or interception.

> Danan gained 30 yards on the runback.

run batted in RBI (RBIs) is acceptable in all references.

> Gwinn had one RBI.
> He has 35 RBIs this season.

run-down (adj.)

> She was feeling run-down.

---

rundown (n.) A situation in which a player is caught between the bases.

> Hendersen got caught in a rundown.

Run for the Roses Capitalize this nickname for the Kentucky Derby.

Runner's World Note apostrophe in the name of this magazine. Always italicize periodical titles.

runner-up (n.) Second place. For more than one second-place finisher, use runners-up.

Do not use runner-up in reference to a second-place finish at the Olympics. Use silver medalist.

> New York was the runner-up in the Eastern Division.
> Kile and Darwin were the runners-up.
> Kerrigan was the silver medalist.

running 40 Method of measuring an athlete's speed in the 40-yard dash that begins with a running start. The athlete runs 50 yards, but his or her time is determined by subtracting the first 10 yards.

> Kaether ran the 40-yard dash in 4.94.
> He did the running 40 in 4:31.

running back Two words. This offensive back carries the ball on running plays.

rush (n., v.) Note the different meanings. Rush, in reference to the offense, means to gain yards.

> Smith rushed for 110 yards.

In reference to the defense, rush means to key on the quarterback.

> New England came at the quarterback with a four-man rush.
> They rushed the quarterback several times during the game.

Russian Capitalize in references to the gymnastics maneuver performed on the pommel horse, the Russian, and in phrases such as the Russian split jump.

Ryder Cup First played in 1927, the Ryder Cup is a golf competition held every odd year between teams from the United States and Great Britain. *See* golf.

S

saber One of three classes of fencing. *See* fencing.

sacrifice (adj.) Do not use sacrifice as a verb when referring to a ball hit in such a way as to advance the runner.

> WRONG: Thomas sacrificed the runner to third.
> RIGHT: Thomas hit a sacrifice fly.

said (v.) Said is most often the best way to attribute a quote. Do not use words such as admitted, claimed, or declared as synonyms for said.

Do not use refused to comment or would not comment to mean could not be reached for comment.

salaries Use figures. *See* dollar amounts.

> He will make $4.2 million this year.
> He will get $5 million to $6 million next year.

Salchow Capitalize the name of this figure skating move in which a skater jumps from the inner back edge of his or her foot, turns in the air, and returns to the outer edge of the other foot. Use single, double, or triple to indicate the number of rotations in the air.

> Lupika landed his triple Salchow perfectly.

saltwater (adj.) He is a saltwater fisherman.

salto In gymnastics, this is a flip with the body rotating at the waist.

sanctions When a school or player is put on probation, they are not necessarily sanctioned. Do not use probation (a period of time in which a person is tested) as a synonym for sanctioned (penalized).

sandlot (n., adj.) Use sandlot to describe an informal area used to play baseball, such as an empty city lot.

San Francisco Do not refer to the city as Frisco. Capitalize Bay Area. *See* '49ers.

save (n.) A pitcher is awarded a save under all of the following conditions:

- He must be the finishing pitcher in a game won by his team.
- He is not considered the winning pitcher.
- He enters the game with a lead of no more than three runs and pitches for at least one inning, or he enters the game with the potential tying run either on base, at bat, or on deck; or he pitches effectively for at least three innings.

score Use figures.

> The Cubs defeated the Cardinals 5-2.
> Colbert won the match in three sets 6-2,4-6,7-6.

Use a comma when listing scores in this format: Raiders 10, Chargers 0.
Do not use commas with essential clauses. *See* numbers.

> The Hornets' 112-96 victory put them in first place.

Avoid overusing the following phrases, in each case, the word scored can be substituted:

> WORDY: Kennedy got on the scoreboard.
> WORDY: Kennedy put points on the board.
> WORDY: Kennedy dented the scoring column.

scoreboard One word, unlike leader board.

scorecard The card on which scores are kept in sports such as golf and boxing.

scorekeeper One word.

scorers' table (n.) Note apostrophe.

Scouting Combine Capitalize the name of this NFL event in which professional teams gather to assess the talent of college players hoping to be drafted.

scramble A method of play in golf in which each member of a team shoots, then plays the ball with the best lie. *See* match play, medal play, golf.

screwball (n.) This pitch is thrown with so much spin on it that it swerves. A screwball thrown by a right-handed pitcher swerves to the right.

scull Note the spelling of this rowing shell with staggered oars.

season For sports that are played in a season that overlaps years, such as professional football, hockey, and college basketball, refer to both years.

> Lohrer's best season was 1994–95.

season opener Lowercase the name of the first game of the season in sports such as baseball and football.

> The Cubs won the season opener.
> The Bulls play their season opener in Chicago.
> They lost last year's season-opening game.

season ticket (n.) Hyphenate as a modifier.

> Do you have season tickets at Arrowhead Stadium?
> Mike is a season-ticket holder.

seasoned veteran Avoid this overused cliché.

---

second base, second baseman (n.) Hyphenate second base as a modifier.

> Ryan plays second base.
> Aubran is the second-base umpire.

second-guess (v.)

> Don't second-guess the coach.

second-rate (adj.) Inferior.

> Coach Guy called Miller a second-rate running back.

second string, second-stringer Hyphenate the term for a player who is not a starter.

> Anderson plays on the second string.
> He is a second-stringer.

seconds *See* numbers, time.

seed Not seat, in reference to a player's rank before a competition based on previous performances.

> Kris is the first seed.
> She is seeded first.

seeing-eye single Use sparingly in reference to a base hit that seems to find a narrow gap between infielders.

Selke Trophy *See* hockey, Part II.

sell out (v.)

> Do you expect the game to sell out?

sellout (n.) A sellout occurs when all tickets to an event have been sold. Use caution when using sellout as a synonym for capacity crowd. In some cases, all the tickets for a game may be sold, but everyone with a ticket may not be in attendance. For example,

---

tickets held by season-ticket holders count as tickets sold whether or not the person is in attendance.

> Was the game a sellout?

semifinals (n.) Not semis.

senior Spell out and lowercase senior when referring to a high school student's year in school.

> Sharifi is a senior in college.

Use Sr. as part of a person's name. Do not use a comma to separate the name from Sr.

> Allen Marshall Sr. owns the team.

Senior PGA Majors The four events that make up the Senior PGA Majors are the Tradition, PGA Senior Players Championship, PGA Seniors' Championship, and the U.S. Senior Open.

series Capitalize on second reference to the World Series. Lowercase series on second reference to other events.

> Cleveland and Los Angeles could meet in the World Series. It
> has been decades since the Indians won the Series.
> Texas and Tai Pei met in the championship game of the Little
> League World Series. Tai Pei won the series.

series opener Acceptable in reference to the first game of a series, but opening game is preferred.

> The Mets will play a three-game series with the Marlins. The se-
> ries opener is tonight.
> The opening game of the World Series is just days away.

served as Use in reference to a temporary position.

> He served as manager while Herk was sick.

---

set-up man Avoid using this slang term for relief pitcher.

> Conklin has spent his career as a relief pitcher.
> Burdett is a middle reliever.

seventh-inning stretch Short break that takes place before the home team bats in the seventh inning of a baseball game.

shake up (v.)

> Bertels was shaken up after the collision.

share In reference to television ratings, a share measures the viewing percentage among homes where a television is in use.

shell This is the term for the boat in rowing. *See* scull.

shinguard (n.) Use one word in reference to the protective plates soccer players wear on their shins.

shinsplints An injury in which pain occurs between the shin bone and calf muscles.

shoestring catch Use to describe a running catch made by reaching forward just before the ball hits the ground.

shoo-in (n.)

> Douglas is a shoo-in to win the award.

shoot around (v.)

> Armstrong shot around before the game.

shoot-around (n.)

> The team had a shoot-around.

shooting Some shooting events are three-position rifle, running-game target, rapid fire pistol, free rifle, air pistol, air rifle, free pistol, and sport pistol.

When indicating the type of pistol or rifle, use caliber.

> Peterson owns a .22-caliber rifle.

shootout (n.)

short-arm (v.) To throw without fully extending the throwing arm.

> Gerben short-armed the throw.

short-course pool A swimming pool 25 yards or 25 meters in length. Most major swimming events, including those at the Olympics, are long course. Long-course pools are 50 meters in length.

short-handed (n.)

> With eight players, the softball team was short-handed.

short-handed goal A goal scored by a hockey team with fewer players on the ice than its opponent.

short hop (n.)

> The ball took a short hop.

short-hop (v.)

> The third baseman short-hopped the ball over to first base.

short program In figure skating, the short program for men and women is two minutes, 40 seconds. *See* long program.

shortstop (n.) One word in reference to the position and the athlete who plays the position in baseball and softball.

shot-blocker (n.)

shotgun (n., adj.)

> The hunters carried shotguns.
> The Eagles lined up in shotgun formation.

shot put International rules require women to throw an 8-pound, 13-ounce shot put. Men throw a 16-pound shot put. Do not hyphenate shot put as a modifier.

> Kerry threw the shot put.
> He won the shot put event at the track and field meet.

shot-put (v.) Taylor shot-putted his throw over to first base.

shot-putter

> Wilkinson is a shot-putter.

show off (v.) Hyphenate as a noun.

> Don't show off during an important game.
> Meyers is a show-off.

shut out (v.) To not allow an opponent to score.

> The Tigers shut out the Rangers.

shutout (n., adj.) Do not use the redundant complete-game shutout.

> Carter pitched a shutout.

Only refer to the length of a shutout if it is less than a complete game.

> Smoltz pitched six shutout innings.

shuttlecock Bird is acceptable for the badminton shuttle.

sidearm Use sidearm to describe a throw made with the hand and forearm parallel to the ground. Do not use sidearm as a verb.

> WRONG: Hanks sidearmed the throw to first.
> RIGHT: Hanks made a sidearm throw to first.
> RIGHT: He throws sidearm.

---

sideboards The boards that run along the sidelines of a hockey rink or polo field.

side judge In football, the side judge is responsible for eligible receivers on his side of the field and for counting the number of defensive players.

sideline, sidelines One coach or team cannot be on more than one sideline.

> Ditka stood on the sideline.
> The team's players paced the sideline.
> The coaches of the Bears and Redskins paced the sidelines.

sidestep (v.)

> Matti was able to sidestep the defender.

sidestroke The swimming stroke is not one of the four competitive strokes: backstroke, breaststroke, butterfly, and freestyle.

signal caller Avoid using as a synonym for quarterback.

Silver Bullets The women's professional baseball team is sponsored by Coors. Do not refer to players on the team as amateurs.

simulcast Do not use as a synonym for broadcast. A simulcast is a program that is simultaneously broadcast over radio and TV, or AM and FM radio.

since, because Use since when referring to a span of time. Use because to denote a cause-effect relationship.

> Clements left because of the controversy.
> Williams hasn't been back since the surgery.

Single A Use Class A when referring to the minor-league baseball classification.

> How long has he been playing in Class A?
> Vasquez plays for a Class-A team in the Midwest.

---

single-elimination tournament A team playing in this type of tournament may only lose once before being eliminated. *See* double-elimination, round-robin.

We will be playing in a single-elimination tournament.

single-handedly Be careful when using this term. It is unlikely that a team member could single-handedly win or lose a game.

sink Do not use as a synonym for make in golf and basketball stories.

WRONG: Robert sank a 20-foot putt.
RIGHT: Robert made a 20-foot putt.

sinker (n.) Pitch that drops as it nears the plate.

sire (n., v.) Use only in reference to animals.

Secretariat sired that colt.
Holy Bull is the sire of Bullintheheather.

sit spin (n.) Use two words in reference to this figure skating spin where the skater squats close to the ice.

sit up (v.)

Garrick sat up on his bed.

sit-up (n.) Use a hyphen in reference to the abdominal exercise.

Teague can do 60 sit-ups in a minute.

skateboard (n., v.)

Langstrom owns a skateboard.
He is learning how to skateboard.
Gordan will take part in the skateboarding exhibition at the park.

skating, figure *See* figure skating.

---

skating, speed *See* speed skating.

skeptic, skeptical Note the spelling of a person who is doubtful.

ski, skis (n., v.)

> Brett hopes to ski in the Winter Olympics.
> Amber skied the steepest hill on the mountain.
> She skis better than she did last year.
> Skiing will be impossible unless we get more snow.

Olympic competition is divided into two categories, Alpine skiing and Nordic skiing.

Alpine (Men and Women)
downhill
super giant slalom (Super-G)
giant slalom
slalom
combined

Cross Country (Men)
10k classical
15k freestyle pursuit
30k freestyle
50k classical
4 x 10k mixed relay

Cross Country (Women)
5k classical
10k freestyle pursuit
15k freestyle
30k classical
4 x 5 mixed relay

Ski Jumping (Men)
ski jumping (normal hill)
ski jumping (large hill)
team ski jumping

skier's thumb Note the apostrophe in this hand injury.

ski jump (n., adj.) Competitors jump twice and are scored on the distance and style of their jump.

> Wright won the ski jump.
> He is the ski jump champion.

Skins Game Capitalize the name of the PGA, LPGA, and Senior skins events. The Skins Game for each association is a shootout between four golfers playing 18 holes. Each hole counts as a skin. The player with the lowest score on each hole wins a skin and a predetermined amount of prize money. If players finish in a tie on a hole, the prize money is added to the next hole.

sky box (n.)

SkyDome Do not precede the name of Toronto's ball park with The.

> The Blue Jays play tonight at SkyDome.

slalom Note the spelling of this course where competitors must weave in and out of gates.

slam dunk (n., v.) Dunk is acceptable in all references.

slang terms Many of the sports editors who contributed to this book suggested the following words be avoided because the words are either outdated, trendy, or not widely recognized. Next to each word in parentheses is a better choice.

bucket	(basket)
cagers	(basketball players)
clothesliner	(line drive)
dinger	(home run)
frozen rope	(line drive)
grapplers	(wrestlers)
gridders	(football players)
gridiron	(football field)
harriers	(cross-country runners)
hoopsters	(basketball players)
ink, as in "to ink an agreement"	(sign)

mashie	(4 iron)
mother-in-law	(7 pin in bowling)
pigskin	(football)
southpaw	(left-hander)
tater	(home run)
trey	(three-pointer)

slap shot (n.) Use two words to describe this hockey shot where the blade of the stick slaps the floor before it hits the puck.

slice (n., v.) A golf shot that curves to the right. A slight curve to the right is a fade.

> Montgomery almost hit another golfer with a slice.
> Bell sliced the ball.

sloop rig Use two words to describe a boat with a mainsail and a jib.

slug fest Avoid this term for an intense boxing match or a particularly rough game.

slugger Avoid using this term for a strong baseball hitter or a boxer.

Smith & Wesson Note ampersand in the name of this gunmaker.

Smythe Trophy *See* hockey, Part II.

snatch In weightlifting, the lifter raises the weight above the head with only a slight pause at the chest.

snowboard (n., v.) Avoid using board as a synonym.

> Wright bought a new snowboard.
> She will snowboard down the mountain.

Soap Box Derby *See* All-American Soap Box Derby.

Solheim Cup First presented in 1990, the Solheim Cup is given to the winner of a golf competition between professional women golfers from the United States and Europe.

somersault (n., v.)

south Capitalize when referring to a specific region or the name of an area.

> Stolarick went to school in the South.
> Hawkins grew up on the South Side of Chicago.
> O'Brien lives south of the city.

southeast, southwest Capitalize when referring to part of a conference name or a specific region.

> The Donahey family lives in the Southeast.
> Is Houston a member of the Southwest Conference?

Southeastern Conference Spell out on first reference, then SEC. *See* college, Part II, for members.

Southern Conference *See* college, Part II, for members.

Southland Conference *See* college, Part II, for members.

southpaw Avoid using as a synonym for left-hander.

Southwestern Athletic Conference *See* college, Part II, for members.

spearing In hockey, stabbing an opponent with the point of the stick blade. *See* butt-ending.

Special Olympics Capitalize in all references.

special teams (n.) Teams used on kickoffs, punts, and field-goal situations in football. Hyphenate as a modifier.

> Hughes plays on special teams.
> Sheanan is the special-teams coach.

speed Use figures. Spell out hours, minutes, and seconds on first reference.

Scott finished the race in 1 hour, 36 minutes, and 25 seconds.
Kevin finished second in 1:37.46.

speed skating Long-track oval is 400 meters. The short-track oval is 111 meters.

Races are run counterclockwise around the track.

Do not hyphenate speed skating when used as a modifier.

Blair set several speed skating records.
Jansen won the event in 1:12.43.

Men's Olympic Events	Women's Olympic Events
500 meters	500 meters
1,000	1,000
1,500	1,500
5,000	3,000
10,000	5,000

spinnaker Note the spelling of this large, billowing sail.

spitball (n.) Use this term to describe a ball moistened by the pitcher.

split-fingered fastball Not split-finger.

split second (n.)

split-second (adj.)

split-squad (adj.)

The team played a split-squad game.

sponsorship When a sponsor's name is part of an event's official name, use the sponsor's name on first reference.

Northwestern went to the Thrifty Car Rental Holiday Bowl.
    They won the Holiday Bowl.
Nebraska will play in the Federal Express Orange Bowl.

sportfishing (n.) Rod and reel fishing for fish such as bass, pike, salmon, and trout.

Sportflics Trading card line owned by Pinnacle.

Sporting News, The Always italicize periodicals.

Sports Broadcasters Association Spell out on first reference.

sportscaster One word.

SportsCenter Do not use a space in the name of this ESPN news program. Always italicize TV or radio programs.

SportsChannel America, SportsChannel Chicago (or other city) Note spelling of this television channel devoted to sports.

sports editor Do not capitalize.

> All editorial decisions are made by sports editor Joe Elliot.
> If you have a sports-related question, ask Harold Turner, sports editor.

Sports Illustrated Always italicize periodicals.

Sports Information Director Capitalize when used as a formal title before a name.

> Sports Information Director Josh Miller gave us the statistics.
> Josh Miller, Southern's sports information director, gave us the statistics.

sportsmanship (n.) Do not change sportsmanship to reflect gender.

> Stephanie exhibits good sportsmanship when she plays.

sportswriter One word for the person.

sportswriting One word.

sprain (n., v.) Injury in which a joint is partially, temporarily dislocated at the time of an injury and supporting ligaments are stretched or torn.

springboard (n.) Board is acceptable after the first reference. When referring to a springboard diving competition, use figures.

> The U.S. diver dominated his competition on the 1-meter board and 3-meter board.

spring training (n.)

> The team finished spring training.

Avoid referring to baseball spring training games as preseason games. Use spring-training game or exhibition game.

> The Padres won their first spring-training game.

square-out (n.) A football pass route run straight downfield with a 90-degree break toward the sideline.

> Moody ran a square-out.

squash *See* Part II.

squeeze bunt (n.) A general term for a bunt with a runner on third whose purpose it is to score on the play.
Bunt is not necessary in making a more specific reference to the kind of squeeze bunt being used.
A safety squeeze occurs when the runner waits to see if the batter makes contact with the ball before running.
A suicide squeeze occurs when the runner takes off as soon as the pitch is released.

stadium Capitalize Stadium as part of a proper name.

> The Royals play at Kauffman Stadium.
> What time did they go to the stadium?

stair-climbing machine *See* StairMaster.

StairMaster Capitalize the brand name of exercise equipment. When referring to this piece of equipment in general terms, use stair climber or stair stepper.

stallion A male horse kept for breeding.

standoff (n.) One word.

stand out (v.) To be prominent.

> O'Neal stands out from the crowd.

standout (n., adj.) An exceptional performer or performance.

> Lobo is a standout in women's basketball.

stand-up (adj.) In baseball references, use stand-up to describe a hit in which a batter reaches second or third base without having to slide.

> Dawber hit a stand-up double.

Stanley Cup Award given to the winner of the NHL playoffs was first presented in 1893.

stanza (n.) Do not use as a synonym for inning or period.

starboard Not starbird. The right side of a boat. The left side is port.

Star-Spangled Banner, The Capitalize *The Star-Spangled Banner,* but lowercase national anthem.

starting block (n.) Use two words in reference to the device used by sprinters to help them push off at the start.

state Do not abbreviate state names when used alone.

> WRONG: Phillips played tennis in Neb.
> RIGHT: He played tennis in Nebraska.

When a state is part of a team's name, such as in the case of the New Jersey Devils or Arizona Cardinals, use the pronoun *its* when using the state name alone.

> WRONG: New Jersey won their last game.
> RIGHT: New Jersey won its last game.

When abbreviating state names, use these abbreviations:

Ala.	Md.	N.D.
Ariz.	Mass.	Okla.
Ark.	Mich.	Ore.
Calif.	Minn.	Pa.
Colo.	Miss.	R.I.
Conn.	Mo.	S.C.
Del.	Mont.	S.D.
Fla.	Neb.	Tenn.
Ga.	Nev.	Vt.
Ill.	N.H.	Va.
Ind.	N.J.	Wash.
Kan.	N.M.	W.Va.
Ky.	N.Y.	Wis.
La.	N.C.	Wyo.

Do not abbreviate the following state names:

Alaska	Maine
Hawaii	Ohio
Idaho	Texas
Iowa	Utah

stationary To be stationary is to be standing still.

stationery Stationery is material for writing.

statistics Always spell out statistics. Do not use the abbreviation, stats.

Statue of Liberty play Capitalize the name of this football play in which an offensive player raises his or her arm as if to pass, allowing the ball to be taken by a teammate.

Style and Usage

steeplechase (n.) Use one word for this track and field event where athletes race over obstacles such as hurdles and water.

stern (n.) The rear end of a boat. The front end is the bow.

steroids Chemical substances composed of hormones, vitamins, body constituents, and drugs. Many are banned from use by athletes in competition.

stickball (n.)

stiff-arm (v.) To attempt to elude a defender by extending and locking an arm and putting the palm of the hand on a defender's body.

> Payton stiff-armed the defender.

stimulants Drugs that excite, cause rapid heart rate, and increase blood pressure.

stirrup (n.)

Stockli Capitalize when referring to the gymnastics move performed on the pommel horse.

stolen-base percentage Calculate by dividing the number of successful stolen bases by the number of attempted steals.

stop-and-go (n.)

straight-arm *See* stiff-arm.

strain A strain is a stretch or tear of muscle or tendon tissue. This is different from a sprain, an injury in which a joint is partially, temporarily dislocated at the time of an injury and supporting ligaments are stretched or torn.

straightaway (n., adj.)

> The cars bumped as they came down the straightaway.
> Renner hit a ball to straightaway center field.

strawweight WBC boxing class is 105 pounds and lower.

streamlined (adj.)

> Indurain's new helmet has a streamlined design.

Street & Smith's Use ampersand when referring to the company that publishes sports-related magazines.

stress fracture Injury occurs when a bone is subjected to frequent, repeated stress.

strikeout Do not use the slang term K, as in "Morris has 10 K's." Strike out is two words as a verb.

> Lavris recorded six strikeouts.
> Planter was the last strikeout victim.
> Powers didn't strike out.
> Roscoe struck out twice yesterday.

striker The center-forward or attacking player in soccer whose primary duty is to score goals.

strike zone (n.) Area between a batter's knees and armpits.

stroke play In golf, golfers play a predetermined number of holes. The player with the lowest total wins. *See* golf.

strong side (n.) Use to describe the side of a football field where most of the players are. Hyphenate as a modifier.

> The fullback ran to the strong side.
> Kubrick is a strong-side linebacker.

struck out (v.) Use as the past tense of strike out.

> The leadoff hitter struck out.

student-athlete Hyphenate in all uses.

---

stutter step (n.) An irregular foot movement designed to cause a defender to change his or her timing. Hyphenate as a verb.

Stutz Capitalize the name of this gymnastic maneuver performed on the parallel bars.

subpar (adj.)

> Knudson delivered a subpar performance.

sudden death (n.) An extra period that takes place after regulation to break a tie. Note that sudden death is not a synonym for overtime in basketball and football references, nor a synonym for extra innings in baseball references. Hyphenate as a modifier.

> The football game went into sudden-death overtime.

Sugar Bowl Use USF&G Sugar Bowl on first reference.

Sullivan Award Award given annually to an athlete who "by his or her performance, example and influence as an amateur, has done the most during the year to advance the cause of sportsmanship."
Use James E. Sullivan Memorial Trophy on first reference, then Sullivan Award.

Summer Games Capitalize in reference to the Summer Olympics.

Summer Olympics Spell out on first reference, then use Summer Games, or the Games.
Capitalize Winter Games, the Olympics, Opening Ceremony, and Closing Ceremony as well.

summer rules In golf, players follow summer rules when they play by regular rules. This means they are not allowed to improve the lie of the ball. *See* winter rules.

Sun Belt Conference *See* college, Part II, for members.

Super Bowl Capitalize the name of the NFL championship game.

Do not hyphenate as a modifier. Use Roman numerals.

> Miami defeated Washington in Super Bowl VII.

Superdome Acceptable in all references to the Louisiana Superdome.

super-G Acceptable for super-giant slalom in all uses. *See* skiing.

super heavyweight Olympic boxing classification is 202 pounds and higher.

super middleweight IBF/WBA/WBC classification is 161–168 pounds.

sweatshirt One word.

swimmer's ear Note the apostrophe.

swimming Events can take place in a short-course or long-course pool measured in yards or meters. Specify race distances on first reference.

> The girls won the 200-yard medley relay. They will compete in the 400 freestyle relay later.

The four competitive strokes are backstroke, breaststroke, butterfly, and freestyle.

Scoring is in minutes, seconds, tenths and hundredths of a second.

> Daehler won the 200 freestyle in 2:09.16.

Olympic events are the same for men and women except as noted.

50-meter freestyle	200 breaststroke
100 freestyle	100 butterfly
200 freestyle	200 butterfly
400 freestyle	200 individual medley
800 freestyle (women)	400 individual medley
1,500 freestyle (men)	4 x 100 medley relay

100 backstroke	4 x 100 free relay
200 backstroke	4 x 200 free relay
100 breaststroke	

swingman One word.

switch-hit To hit from either side of the plate in baseball.

McRenolds is planning to switch-hit during the season.

switch-hitter

Maxwell is a switch-hitter.

switch-hitting (adj.) Thomas is a switch-hitting first baseman.

sync Acceptable abbreviation for synchronization.

The team is in sync tonight.

synchronized swimming Olympic events are solo and duet. Basic positions include the ballet leg, ballet leg double, bent knee, knight or castle, vertical, tuck, front pike, back pike, and split.

T

table tennis Lowercase table tennis, but capitalize the trademark name, Ping-Pong.

tack (n., v.) Sailing maneuver in which a boat turns into the wind. When the wind is from the right, a boat is on a starboard tack. When the wind is from the left, the boat is on a port tack.

tae kwon do (n.) Use three words in reference to this martial art.

tailback Running back lined up farthest from the line of scrimmage.

takeaway (n.) In football, a takeaway occurs any time the defense takes the ball from the offense, by intercepting the ball or recovering a fumble, for example. Giveaways occur when, while on offense, a team gives up the ball to the defense. The giveaway-takeaway statistic is the net difference between the two numbers.

takedown (n.) To force an opponent to the mat in wrestling. Two words as a verb.

> Handy recorded the takedown.
> Dawson took down his opponent.

Talladega Superspeedway Note spelling of this racetrack in Alabama.

TD Use touchdown in all references, except in headlines when space is limited and in agate.

team Spell out a team's full name on first reference.

> The Jacksonville Jaguars play their first game today. The Jaguars won 14-0.

Always capitalize a team's city and name: Boston Red Sox, Calgary Flames.
When referring to a team by its city, use which or its.

> Chicago, which has lost only one game, is in the lead.
> Chicago lost its second game.

When referring to a team by its nickname, use who or their.

> The Royals, who are in first place, play tonight.
> The Royals won their opener.

Use an apostrophe when using a team's name as a possessive.

> This is the Tigers' opening day roster.
> The Padres' ace left-hander is Lisec.

Do not add an apostrophe to a word ending in *s* when the word is used descriptively.

Jenkins is a Cincinnati Reds outfielder.
His brother is a Cougars linebacker.

Do not remove the *s* from a team's name when using the name as a modifier.

> WRONG: Cub pitcher Neil Jones won the award.
> RIGHT: Cubs pitcher Neil Jones won the award.

CAUTION: Be careful not to use an apostrophe before the *s* when a word normally ends in *s.*

> WRONG: Show us the Falcon's lineup.
> RIGHT: He made up the Falcons' lineup.

When referring to two competing teams, use a hyphen.

> The Bulls-Knicks game begins at 7:05.

Do not refer to teams with an Indian mascot as the Skins, Tribe, or other word that might be offensive.

Spell out Red Sox and White Sox. Do not use BoSox or ChiSox.

teammate One word.

team records Use parentheses when referring to a team's record in a story. This rule varies. Check your publication's rule as some prefer to set off scores with commas. *See* records.

> The Sharks (11-1) take on the Flyers (9-2) tonight.

TeamTennis, World Note spelling of professional tennis league. The league would prefer to have TEAMTENNIS written in capital letters, but TeamTennis (one word) is acceptable.

teamwork

technical knockout There is no such thing in boxing. If a fighter cannot continue a match, he or she has been stopped by the opponent.

tee off (v.)

> Daly will tee off first.
> Bell threw his driver after he teed off on the ninth hole.

teen-age, teen-ager Note hyphen.

television TV is acceptable in all references.
Capitalize the word *Channel* when referring to one particular channel.

> The game will be broadcast on Channel 2.

Do not capitalize when referring to two or more channels or in general reference.

> Watch channels 7 and 9.
> What channel is the game on?

tendinitis (n.) Inflammation of a tendon.

tennis Scoring is in points, games, sets, and matches.
Use commas when showing scores in a story.

> Dean won the set 6-3.
> Keough won the match 6-0, 4-6, 6-3.

tenpin bowling *See* bowling.

tewaza Note the spelling of this judo throw using the hands.

Texas leaguer Baseball term refers to a short fly ball that falls between the outfielders and infielders.

T formation Offensive formation in football in which backs line up in a T behind the quarterback. *See* I formation.

> An example of a basic T formation:

```
E  T  G  C  G  T  E
        QB
   HB         HB
        FB
```

their, they Use with team nicknames.

> The Buccaneers won their first game.
> They are in second place.

Use *it* as the pronoun for a team's school, state, or city.

> Central will play its first game tonight.
> Tampa Bay won its first game.
> North Carolina lost its starting center.

The Masters Do not use an apostrophe in the name of this golf tournament. Tournament is held at Augusta (Ga.) National Golf Course. *See* golf.

third base, third baseman (n.) Hyphenate as a modifier.

> Meyers plays third base.
> Kamdon hit the ball down the third-base line.

thoroughbred (n.)

Thorpe Award Award given by the Jim Thorpe Athletic Club of Oklahoma City to the outstanding NCAA Division I defensive back was established in 1986. Use Jim Thorpe Award on first reference.

three-base hit Use triple instead.

300 game Twelve strikes in a game in bowling. A 300 game is a synonym for perfect game. Do not use the redundant "perfect 300 game."

three-on-one

> The Rockets had a three-on-one break.

three-point line Note the hyphen.

three-point shot

three-point stance Football position in which a player, usually a lineman, puts one hand and both feet on the ground while leaning forward in preparation for the start of a play.

3-putt (n., v.)

throw in (v.) To put a ball in play from out of bounds. Hyphenate as a modifier.

> Matthews threw in the ball.
> Lalas completed the throw-in.

tibia The main lower leg bone.

TicketMaster Ticket agency responsible for distributing tickets to many athletic events.

ticky-tack foul Use sparingly as a synonym for questionable foul.

tiebreaker Note that some sports, such as tennis, use a tiebreaker. Use overtime in football and basketball references or extra innings in baseball references for the additional time used to break a tie.

ties When an event is tied, do not use the redundant, tied at 35-35, or tied at 35 all. Use tied at 35.

tight end Offensive football player lines up just outside the tackle.

tiller This stick is attached to a boat's rudder to control steering.

time Spell out minutes and seconds on first reference.

> Howard finished the race in 2 minutes, 14.1 seconds.
> Jackson was second in 2:17.3.

Always use figures. Use a colon to separate hours, minutes, and seconds. Use a period to indicate decimal expression for fractions of seconds.

> Mackie ran the race in 2:30:21.65.

time-day-place Use this order when indicating when and where an event will occur.

> The tennis match will be held at 2 p.m. Tuesday at the high school.

time elements Use the day of the week if it is within seven days of the current date. For example, if today is Sunday, the game is Tuesday (not next Tuesday or last Tuesday).

timeout (n.)

time remaining, time of game Use figures in reference to the game clock.

> Kelly shot the ball with 3 seconds remaining.
> Battle hit a two-point shot with .27 left in the half.
> Minor scored at the 7:36 mark in the second period.

tip in (v.) Howard tipped in the ball.

tip-in (n.) Vincent scored on the tip-in.

tip-off (n.) The start of a basketball game.

> What time is the tip-off for the Bulls-Hornets game?

Tkatchev Capitalize this gymnastics maneuver, which consists of a backward straddle release to a hang on the bar.

toe loop Do not use the redundant toe loop jump. Hyphenate when using a number to indicate rotations. A toe loop is performed by a figure skater who jumps from one foot, turns in the air, and returns to the same foot.

> Baiul performed a triple-toe loop.

tonight To avoid redundancy, do not use tonight and p.m. together.

> WRONG: The game is at 8 p.m. tonight.
> RIGHT: The game is at 8 p.m. or at 8 tonight.

top Hyphenate when used as a modifier. Capitalize Top when referring to a specific collegiate or high school poll.

> Duke is ranked No. 3 in the AP Top 25 and the Kansas City
> Star's Top 10.
> Indiana has the potential to break into the top 25.
> Michigan is a top-10 team.

Top-Flite Athletic equipment company.

Top Fuel Capitalize the name of this type of drag racing car.

Topps Note spelling of this trading card company.

Top Rank boxing Not top-ranked.

top-ranked (adj.)

> The top-ranked Cougars play the Tigers tonight.

topspin (n.)

total bases Calculate by adding the total number of bases reached by a team or individual.

touchback (n.) A touchback occurs when a player downs the ball in his or her own end zone after a punt or kickoff. The ball is brought out to the 20-yard line to start the next play.

touchdown (n.)

touchline The line running the full length of the field on each side of a soccer field.

Tour de France Four-week long cycling race in France consists of 21 stages that take place in various areas in and around France and covers 2,490 miles.

tournament Do not capitalize tournament when used after the name of a tournament's organizing body.

> The NCAA tournament and the Big Eight tournament are two weeks apart.
> Waukegan West won the high school tournament.

Capitalize tournament as part of a tournament's official name, as in Tournament of Champions.

toward The word is not towards.

> Holland moved toward the line.

track and field Events are measured in distance or by time. When a meet includes races measured in feet and meters, make sure the measurement is expressed on first reference.

> Griffen won the men's 100-meter dash.
> The women's 880-yard run is about to begin (first reference).
> She won the 880 (second reference).

Spell out minutes and seconds on first reference.

> The record is 3 minutes, 11.2 seconds.
> Thompson finished in 3:14.27.

For a marathon, include hours.

> 2 hours, 9 minutes, 3.18 seconds
> 2:10:3.10

Do not use a colon before times given only in seconds and tenths.

> 8.21 seconds
> 9.6

For field events, use fraction.

> Howard jumped 18½.
> Gordon leaped 22-10½.

Events for men (m), women (w), or both (m, w) are:

Sprints
100 meters (m, w)
200 meters (m, w)
400 meters (m, w)

Hurdles
100-meter hurdles (w)
110-meter hurdles (m)
400-meter hurdles (m, w)

Middle Distances
800 meters (m, w)
1,500 meters (m, w)

Relays
4 x 100 meter relay (m, w)
4 x 400 meter relay (m, w)

Long Distances
3,000 meters (w)
5,000 meters (m)
10,000 meters (m, w)

Throwing Events
discus throw (m, w)
hammer throw (m)
shot put (m, w)
javelin (m, w)

Jumping Events
triple jump (m)
high jump (m, w)
long jump (m, w)
pole vault (m)

Road Races
20 km walk (m)
50 km walk (m)
3,000-meter steeplechase (m)
marathon (m, w)

Combined Events
heptathlon (w)
decathlon (m)

trademark names Most dictionaries indicate trademark names, which should be capitalized.

In running text, it is not necessary to include the ™ or ® symbol next to a trademark name.

> Cameron used petroleum jelly.
> Cameron used Vaseline.
> Jane skated in her Rollerblade in-line skates.

Tradition, The Senior PGA event is played at Desert Mountain Cochise Course in Scottsdale, Ariz. The Tradition, along with the PGA Senior Players Championship, PGA Seniors' Championship, and U.S. Senior Open, make up the Senior PGA Majors.

tranquilizers A group of drugs designed to calm a person without affecting consciousness.

Trans America Conference *See* college, Part II, for members.

transition player Under the NFL's collective bargaining agreement a transition player is one whose team must tender a one-year contract at the average of the 10 highest-paid players at the transition player's position or a 20 percent raise, whichever is greater. A franchise player is one whose team must offer a one-year contract at the average of the five highest-paid players at the franchise player's position or a 20 percent increase, whichever is greater.

travel, traveled, traveling One el.

trey Do not use as a synonym for three-point shot

trials Capitalize as part of a proper name. Do not use the redundant preliminary trials.

Evans will compete at the U.S. Olympic Trials.

triangular (n.) Spell out in all references. Never use tri.

triathlon Event features competitors swimming, cycling, and running, in that order. One who competes is a triathlete.
Triathlons vary in distance. A sprint triathlon may be a $^3/_{10}$-mile swim, nine-mile bike ride, and three-mile run. The Ironman Triathlon, held annually in Hawaii, is a 2.4-mile swim, 112-mile bike ride, and 26.2-mile run.

trifecta To win a trifecta in horse or greyhound racing, a bettor must pick three race entrants that finish first, second, and third.

Triple A Use instead of Class AAA when referring to the minor-league baseball classification.

> Wilkinson excelled in Triple A.
> He played Triple-A baseball in New York.

triple axel (n.) Figure skating move features three rotations in the air. *See* axel.

triple bogey (n.)

> Yang had a triple bogey on the eighth hole.

triple-bogey (v.)

> He also triple-bogeyed the 10th.

Triple Crown The Triple Crown in thoroughbred racing is made up of the Kentucky Derby, Preakness Stakes, and Belmont Stakes.

In baseball, a player who wins the Batting Triple Crown finishes the season with the most home runs, the most RBIs, and the best batting average.

The Pitching Triple Crown is won by the pitcher who finishes the season with the most victories, the most strikeouts, and the lowest ERA.

triple double In basketball, a triple double occurs when a player records double figures in three categories.

> Stackhouse had a triple double with 20 points, 15 rebounds, and 11 assists.

triple jump (n., v.) Use two words for this track and field event where the competitors run to a hop, step, and leap into the pit.

triple play (n.)

true north True North is different from magnetic north. On a compass, magnetic north attracts the compass needle. True north refers to the North Pole, while magnetic north is in the middle of a Canadian ironfield.

Style and Usage

T-shirt (n.) Always capitalize *T.*

try out (v.) Two words for the act of auditioning.

tryout (n.) One word for the event.

tuck In diving and gymnastics, this position features the body bent at the waist, with the legs bent and drawn to the chest.

turn Capitalize when referring to a specific turn on a racetrack and use figures.

> He passed the leader in Turn 4.

Do not capitalize general references to a turn.

> The two cars collided near the third turn.
> The dogs are coming around the far turn.

turn over (v.)

> Anderson has turned over the ball four times.

turnover (n.) Any time a team loses possession.

> Waddle has one turnover tonight.

TV TV is acceptable in all references for television.

> The team discussed the next play during a TV timeout.

Capitalize the word *Channel* when referring to one particular channel.

> The game will be broadcast on Channel 2.

Do not capitalize channel when referring to two or more channels or in general references.

> Watch channels 7 and 9.
> What channel is the game on?

24 Hours of Daytona Endurance race is held on the 3.56-mile course at Daytona International Speedway.

Spell out 24 only at the beginning of a sentence.

24 Hours of Le Mans First held in 1923, the race takes place over an 8.451-mile circuit in Le Mans, France. The official name of this race is the Le Mans Grand Prix d'Endurance, but 24 Hours of Le Mans is acceptable on first reference as well.

.22 Use .22 when referring to a type of gun.

> Walters used a .22-caliber rifle when he went hunting.

twi-night doubleheader Notice spelling. It is not twi-light.

Twin Cities Capitalize the nickname of Minneapolis and St. Paul, Minnesota.

two-point conversion In football, an opportunity to score two points after a touchdown by running or throwing the ball into the end zone.

Twin Spires Capitalize this registered trademark of Churchill Downs.

two-base hit Use double instead.

two-handed (adj.)

> He made a two-handed catch.

two-minute warning Signal given to notify participants that there are two minutes remaining in a game.

two-on-one, two-on-two (n., adj.)

> The kids played a game of two-on-two.
> The Nuggets had a two-on-one break.

2-putt (v.)

> Higgins 2-putted on the first hole.

tying Note spelling, the word is not tieing.

> We ended up tying another team for first place.

U

UConn University of Connecticut on first reference, then UConn.

ultimate Frisbee Capitalize Frisbee in all uses.

ultrasound A method of therapy in which sound waves are transmitted through an applicator into the skin, often to relax injured tissue or to disperse fluids.

UMass University of Massachusetts on first reference, then UMass.

Umbro Note spelling of athletic apparel company.

umpire Spell out on first reference. Do not capitalize umpire as a title before a name.

> Our manager argued with umpire Pikalek.

umpire-in-chief Also the plate umpire.

unanswered points Use consecutive or straight points instead when a team scores several points in a row without allowing its opponent to score.

> The Tar Heels scored 10 straight points.

unassisted double play, unassisted triple play (n.) No hyphenation.

unbeaten streak An unbeaten streak can be different from a winning streak. An unbeaten streak can include victories as well as ties. A winning streak does not include ties.

under (n.) Betting term means that the point total of two competing teams is less than a predetermined number.

> Woodsen bet the under, hoping the teams would not score
> more than 42 points.

Do not use under when referring to quantities.

> WRONG: Under 2,000 people were at the game.
> RIGHT: Fewer than 2,000 people were at the game.

undercard Use to describe boxing matches that take place before the main fight.

> Morrison and Fry are fighting on the undercard.

underclassmen Use when referring to freshmen and sophomores in high school or college.

underdog (n.) A competitor who is not expected to win. Also dark horse, long shot.

underhand serve Use underhand only to distinguish from an overhand serve if a tennis player uses both methods.

under way Two words.

> Let's get the game under way.

uneven bars Use two words for this gymnastics apparatus.

Unified Team Capitalize name of 1992 Olympic team made up of Belarus, Kazakhstan, Ukraine, Russia, and Uzbekistan.

Unitas Award Award is given to the top senior college quarterback. Spell out Johnny Unitas Award on first reference.

United States Always spell out as a noun.

> We live in the United States.

The abbreviation is acceptable as a modifier.

> Can anyone beat the U.S. team?

United States Olympic Committee Spell out on first reference, then USOC.

university Capitalize when part of a proper name.

> I attended the University of Iowa.
> Did you visit the university?

With a few exceptions, spell out the full name, and then use the acronym.

> Schwarz attends the University of Nevada-Las Vegas. UNLV has been 18-5 since he arrived last year.

unsportsmanlike conduct (n.) Conduct deemed inappropriate by a game's officials that results in a penalty.

upcourt

> Swoopes saw her teammate upcourt.

upfield

> O'Donnell threw to his receiver upfield.

upperclassmen Refer to juniors and seniors in high school or college as upperclassmen.

uppercut (n., v.) A short punch directed upward at an opponent.

Upper Deck Trading card company.

up-tempo (n., adj.)

U.S. Always spell out United States as a noun. U.S. is acceptable as a modifier.

We live in the United States.
The U.S. team is favored.

USA Today/CNN Coaches Poll The poll is based on the votes of 60 Division I-A head coaches. Spell out USA Today/CNN Coaches Poll on first reference, then the poll or the Coaches Poll. Do not refer to the poll only as the Coaches Poll on first reference.

USA Today/Hall of Fame Poll The poll is based on the votes of 72 members of the National Football Foundation and College Hall of Fame. Spell out on first reference, then the poll.

USA Volleyball National governing body of indoor and outdoor volleyball.

U.S.F.L. Use on second reference for United States Football League.

U.S. Naval Academy Navy is acceptable on first reference.

U.S. Open Spell out on first reference to the golf event played at a different course each year, then the Open.
Spell out on first reference to the tennis championships held at Flushing Meadows, N.Y., then the Open.

U.S. Senior Open Senior PGA event is played at Pinehurst Country Club in Pinehurst, N.C. The U.S. Senior Open, along with the PGA Senior Players Championship, PGA Seniors' Championship, and The Tradition, make up the Senior PGA Majors.

USTA Spell out United States Tennis Association on first reference, then USTA.

USTA Spell out United States Trotting Association on first reference to avoid confusion with the United States Tennis Association.

U.S. Women's Open LPGA event is played at Indianwood Golf Course in Lake Orion, Mich. It is one of four events that make up the LPGA Majors. *See* golf.

utility infielder A baseball player who plays a variety of positions in the infield.

Style and Usage

utility player A baseball player who plays a variety of positions for a team.

V

Valdez Capitalize this gymnastics backward walkover from a seated position.

Vardon Trophy Award given to the PGA Tour player with the best scoring average.

Vare Trophy Award given to the LPGA player with the best scoring average.

Vaseline Capitalize this brand name of petroleum jelly.

vault (n.,v.) Can be used in gymnastics or track and field.

> Retton scored a 10.0 on the vault.
> Martin vaulted over the bar.

verb Try to keep verbs together whenever possible, but not if doing so makes the sentence awkward.

> WRONG: She had always planned to play.
> RIGHT: She always had planned to play.

verbal commitment Be specific when referring to an athlete's intention to attend a school. A verbal commitment means an athlete intends to attend the school but can change his or her mind. *See* letter of intent.

Versa Climber Capitalize the trademark name of this exercise equipment.

versus Use vs. in all references.

Vezina Trophy Award given to best NHL goaltender. *See* hockey, Part II.

vice president Capitalize as a title before a name.

> Giants Vice President John Smith called the manager.

vice versa Two words.

victory Don't assume a victory is easy by looking at the final score. For example, a game that ends in a 10-point margin of victory may have been been tied until the last two minutes.

> WRONG: Minnesota recorded an easy 100-80 victory over Cincinnati.
> RIGHT: Minnesota recorded a 100-80 victory over Cincinnati.

videotape (n., v.)

> Arlan watched the game on videotape.
> Our team manager videotaped the game.

vie, vied, vying (v.) Competing.

> Cincinnati is vying for the championship.

volleyball Games are won by the first team to score 15 points. The winner must win by two points.

vs. Use in all references for versus.

W

waders (n.) Clothing used by fishermen to keep clothes dry while walking in water.

Walker Award Award given to top Division I-A junior or senior running back for achievements on the field, in the classroom, and in the community was first presented in 1990. Use Doak Walker Award on first reference.

Walker Cup First presented in 1922, the Walker Cup is a men's amateur golf competition between teams from the United States and Great Britain held every other year.

walk-on (n., adj.) Use to describe a player who was not recruited for a team.

> Powell is a walk-on.
> The team plans to allow 15 walk-on players to participate.

walkout (n.) A situation in which workers, such as players, go on strike.

> The baseball players are in the middle of a walkout.
> They walked out last month.

wall (n.) Use to describe the line formed by soccer defenders to deflect a kick.

wallyball Volleyball game played in a racquetball court.

war Avoid using war references in sports stories.

> WRONG: He was the trigger man.
> WRONG: She landed a bomb.
> WRONG: The Kings launched an attack.

Other words to avoid include *annihilate, destroy, kill, maim.*

warm up (v.)

> When will the team begin to warm up?

warm-up (n., adj.)

> Cincinnati began warm-up 30 minutes before the game.
> Hughes took some warm-up shots.

Washington Redskins Avoid referring to the team as the Skins.

water polo (n.) *See* Part II.

water skiing (n.) Use two words.

WBA Spell out World Boxing Association on first reference.

WBC Spell out World Boxing Council on first reference.

WBO Spell out World Boxing Organization on first reference.

weak side (n.) In football, the weak side is that side of the field on which there are fewer players. *See* strong side. Hyphenate as a modifier.

> Jeremy lined up on the weak side.
> Lincoln is the weak-side linebacker.

week's rest, weeks' rest

> Kramer had one week's rest.
> O'Donnell had three weeks' rest.

weigh in (v.)

> The fighters are about to weigh in.

weigh-in (n.) Events attended before a boxing match to determine whether fighters are within regulation weight limits.

> The weigh-in will take place at 1 p.m.

weight Use figures and spell out on first reference.

> The fighter weighed in at 150 pounds, 6 ounces.
> The other fighter is 148-5.

weightlifter

weightlifting Events should be identified by weight class. Olympic classifications are:

115 pounds	182 pounds
123 pounds	198 pounds
132 pounds	220 pounds
149 pounds	243 pounds
165 pounds	244+ pounds

well (adv.) Always use well as an adverb.

> WRONG: Givens played good.
> RIGHT: Jordan played well.

welterweight Olympic boxing classification is 140–147 pounds. IBF/WBA/WBC classification is 141–147 pounds.

West Coast Conference *See* college, Part II, for members.

Western Athletic Conference Spell out on first reference, then WAC. *See* college, Part II, for members.

whetstone (n.) Stone device used to sharpen knives.

whiff Do not use as a synonym for strikeout.

WIBC Spell out Women's International Bowling Congress on first reference.

WIBC Queens Spell out Women's International Bowling Congress Queens on first reference. The Queens is a double elimination, match play tournament.

wide open Hyphenate as a modifier.

> He was wide open.
> He passed to a wide-open receiver.

wide-out Wide receiver is preferred.

wide receiver (n.) Offensive football player whose purpose is to catch passes.

Wiffle ball Capitalize the trademark name of plastic ball.

---

wild-card berth (n.) Opportunity to participate in postseason play.

> The Patriots have a shot at a wild-card berth.

Wimbledon Not Wimbleton. Tennis tournament is played at the All England Lawn Tennis and Croquet Club in Wimbledon, a London suburb.

win Avoid using as a noun. Use victory, triumph, or other synonym. Win should be reserved for verb usage.

> WRONG: Nomo got the win.
> RIGHT: Nomo won the game.

wind up (v.)

> The referee will wind up his stopwatch before the game.

wind-up (n.) Also wind-out. In cycling, this is a gradual acceleration that grows into a sprint, usually with more than one lap to go.

windup (n.) A method of pitching used primarily when there are no runners on base. *See* stretch.

> Mitchell, the team's pitcher, has a strange windup.

winless streak A winless streak can differ from a losing streak. A winless streak refers to consecutive games without a victory, though there may have been a tie. A losing streak means there were no ties or victories.

win-loss record Not won-lost.

winners' bracket Note apostrophe. There is more than one winner in the bracket.

winner's circle (n.) Note apostrophe. There is only one winner.

winning streak A winning streak can differ from an unbeaten

---

216   *Style and Usage*

streak. A winning streak refers to consecutive games without a loss or a tie, while an unbeaten streak means there may have been a tie.

Winter Olympics Capitalize and spell out on first reference, then use Winter Games or the Games.

Capitalize Opening Ceremony and Closing Ceremony.

Events are:

Alpine Skiing	Ice Hockey
Biathlon	Luge
Bobsled	Nordic Combined
Cross Country Skiing	Speed Skating
Figure Skating	Ski Jumping
Freestyle Skiing	

winter rules Winter rules are played when a golf course is not in satisfactory condition. Golfers are allowed to improve the lie of their ball. *See* summer rules.

wishbone (adj.)

The Jets lined up in a wishbone formation.

women's Unlike high school references in which girls does not require an apostrophe when used descriptively, women's does. *See* girls, men's.

The women's team plays at 7 p.m.

Women's Tennis Association Spell out on first reference, then WTA.

work out (v.)

The team works out every day at 5 p.m.

workout (n.)

Montross wasn't looking forward to the afternoon workout.

World Boxing Association Spell out on first reference, then WBA.

World Boxing Council Spell out on first reference, then WBC.

World Boxing Organization Spell out on first reference, then WBO.

world championship (n.) Lowercase unless part of a proper name.

> Foster participated in the IAAF Track and Field World Championships.

world-class (adj.)

> Decker is a world-class runner.

World Cup Soccer's quadrennial championship features 24 national teams, each made up of 22 players.

world record (n.) Synonym for all-time record. Hyphenate as a modifier.

> Lewis set the world record at last year's meet.
> His world-record performance stunned his critics.

World Series Spell out on first reference, then the Series.
When referring to a World Series game by number, always use figures.

> The Royals need to win Game 4 of the Series to have a chance.
> The fourth game is Tuesday.

wrack (v.) Wrack means to damage. *See* rack.

wrestling Identify events as freestyle or Greco-Roman. Olympic weight classes are:

109 pounds	163 pounds
115 pounds	181 pounds
126 pounds	198 pounds
137 pounds	220 pounds
150 pounds	286 pounds

Style and Usage

WTA Tour Players Association Spell out Women's Tennis Association on first reference, then WTA.

X

x Use in relay events to represent the word *by*.

> Kansas won the 4 x 100-yard relay.

X-ray Electromagnetic radiation used in diagnostic procedures. Not a synonym for MRI, magnetic resonance imaging.

X's and 0's Note apostrophe. Letters are used to indicate the defense and offense, respectively, in diagrams of plays.

Y

yachting Identify Olympic events by class, which include:

> | | |
> |---|---|
> | Soling | Flying Dutchman |
> | Star | Europe |
> | Tornado | Men's 470 |
> | Finn | Women's 470 |

Yankee Conference *See* college, Part II, for members.

yard *See* metric system for conversions.

yard lines Use figures for clarity when indicating a position on a football field and distance traveled: 10-yard line, the 50-yard line, but 32 yards, 4 yards. Yard lines come in multiples of five.

> The ball is on the 5-yard line.
> Keiser ran to the 10-yard line. On the next play, he gained 7 yards.

year Use figures without commas.

> Cruise graduated in 1994.
> The Scouts finished second in '92.

Use an *s* without an apostrophe to show spans of time.

> He was the best pitcher in the 1900s.

Use figures for years even when used to start a sentence: 1982 was the team's best season.

When a season covers more than one year, do not use year as a synonym for season.

yearling One-year-old horse.

yellow card First offense in soccer and volleyball.

yo-yo Always hyphenate.

YMCA Acceptable in all references for Young Men's Christian Association.

YWCA Acceptable in all references for Young Women's Christian Association.

Z

Zamboni Capitalize name of the ice-resurfacing machine.

zig zag Hyphenate as a modifier.

> Walker zig zagged across the field.
> McConnell ran in a zig-zag motion.

Punctuation in Sports Writing

Following are rules for punctuation as they apply specifically to sports writing.

Apostrophe

Use an apostrophe when numbers are omitted.

> She led the team to three titles in the '70s.

Do not use an apostrophe if no numbers are omitted.

> What team was the most dominant in the early 1900s?

Use an apostrophe when letters are omitted.

> He listens to rock 'n' roll before he pitches.

Use an apostrophe with a team's name to show possession.

> Love is the Saints' leading rusher.
> Today is the Sooners' first game.

When used descriptively, a team's name does not require an apostrophe.

> He is an Expos outfielder.
> Anderson is a Bears running back.

When using boys and girls descriptively, do not use an apostrophe.

> The boys basketball program is successful.
> The girls team is in first place.

Because men and women are plural nouns that do not end in *s*, each requires an *'s* when used descriptively.

> The women's team won the tournament.
> The men's volleyball team advanced to the finals.

To show possession, use an apostrophe without an *s* when a plural proper name represents a singular object or organization.

> The Bulls' defense is the best in the league.

To show possession, use an apostrophe without adding an *s* when a word already is plural.

> The horses' times were slow on the muddy track.

Use an apostrophe when creating a plural out of a single letter.

> The coach used X's and O's to represent the defense and offense.
> The A's have a seven-game homestand.

Use an apostrophe with a pronoun when a contraction is needed.

> It's time for the strike to end.
> The team traded in its old uniforms.

Note the position of the apostrophe when indicating spans of time.

> Ventura will not get a day's rest before having to play again.
> Appier will pitch on five days' rest.
> Jeff will be ready to play after a week's rest.
> Kris is considered the decade's best hitter.

Colon

Use a colon to introduce a list.

> There will be three awards given: first place, runner-up, and Most Improved Player.

Capitalize the first word after a colon if it begins a complete sentence.

> Coach Clemens told his team this: The game will make or break the season.

Use a colon when indicating hours, minutes, and seconds.

> Kickoff is set for 7:05 p.m.
> Saroka swam the 100-yard backstroke in 1:01.15.
> Fredrickson finished the race in 2:20:19.5.

Use a colon with question and answer interviews.

> Q: How did the players react to the announcement?
> A: They were very distraught.

Comma

Use commas to separate scores.

> Stickels won the match 6-2, 4-6, 6-3.

Although reference style requires a comma in a series before a conjunction, in journalism it is acceptable to omit a comma before the conjunction.

> Solie played baseball, basketball and football.

Use a comma in a number when the number is greater than 999.

> Hansen will run the 1,500-meter race.

Do not use a comma in a number when referring to a year, street address, room number, or telephone number.

> Wong played tennis in 1990.
> The stadium is located at 1100 Stadium Drive.
> You can reach the public relations director at 555-1987.

Set off nonessential clauses with commas. A nonessential clause can be taken out of a sentence without changing the meaning of that sentence.

> The team, which was delayed, arrived at 6:00.

Do not use commas with essential clauses. An essential clause cannot be taken out of a sentence without changing its meaning.

> Williams will attend Northwestern if he can improve his grades this semester.
> The man who sang the national anthem was hired yesterday.

Use a comma between two independent clauses connected by and, but, or or.

> I have my tickets for the game, and Tracy said he will pick his up later.

Use a comma between a city and state.

> The Bullets will play a game in Edina, Minn.

Use a comma when introducing a direct quote but not before an indirect or partial quote.

> Coach Reeves said, "The starters are not doing the job."
> Callahan said the team was "not living up to expectations."

Dash

Use a dash when a phrase that would normally be set off by commas contains a series of words that must be separated by commas.

> A team of four seniors—Scheiden, Baker, Peterson and Swan—broke the school record.

Use a dash to show an abrupt change in a sentence.

> The offensive line—bigger than the last year—has given the quarterback time to throw.

Use a dash in datelines.

> CHICAGO—The Cubs released two pitchers.

Style and Usage

Exclamation Point

Avoid overuse. Use an exclamation point to express surprise or emotion. Do not use a comma after an exclamation point.

"I'm going to Disneyland!" he exclaimed.

Hyphen

Do not hyphenate the name of a sport that is not usually hyphenated even when using it as a modifier.

Gardner won the figure skating competition.
Blair set several speed skating records.

Use hyphens in phrases such as day-to-day, down-and-out, first-and-10, goal-to-go.

Use a hyphen when a compound modifier precedes a noun, but do not use a hyphen when a compound modifier ends in -ly.

Coaching is a full-time job.
Wylie scored a third-period goal.
The game has fairly easy rules.

Use a hyphen to separate figures in odds.

The team is favored 3-1.

Use a hyphen to separate figures in scores.

The Clippers won 99-97.

Use a hyphen to separate opposing teams.

The Pacers-Heat game is tonight.

Include a space when using suspended hyphenation.

He may have a 5- to 10-year contract by the end of the day.

See individual entries for specific uses of hyphens.

Parentheses

Follow the style rules established by your publication. Be consistent. If your publication uses parentheses when scores are inserted in a story, use them every time. Do not use commas on one occasion, parentheses on others.

> West (4-1) plays South (5-0).
> West, 4-1, plays South, 5-0.

Use parentheses sparingly in quotes. If there are several needed, it often is better to paraphrase.

Use parentheses when inserting a state name into a proper name.

> The Waukegan (Ill.) Raiders won the championship.

Avoid breaking up the flow of a quotation with words in parentheses whenever possible.

> WRONG: "He (East coach Jim Clemson) had a fine season and ought to be proud of their record (7-1) after their (2-6) performance in 1992," O'Brien said.
>
> RIGHT: O'Brien said East coach Jim Clemson should be pleased with the team's 7-1 record after finishing the season 2-6 last year.
>
> "He had a fine season and ought to be proud of their record after their performance in 1992," O'Brien said.

Do not change quotes to reflect proper word usage. A great deal can be determined about sports personalities through their use of language. Therefore, changes should only be made to avoid obscenities.

Semicolon

Use semicolons to separate elements in a series.

> Swim Meet Results
> 50-yard freestyle—Kim Mackie, Greenwood, 25.5; Jody Baronovic, North, 25.67; Kim Dean, West, 26.1.

PART II

INTRODUCTION

Part II is arranged by sport. There is an entry for every major sport covered by American newspapers, consisting of a list of common terms, the addresses, phone numbers, and functions of the major professional and amateur governing bodies, as well as information on how to summarize game and match results. If a sport has a professional league, each team and its division is listed.

Major sports such as baseball, basketball, college sports, football, golf, hockey, the Olympics, and tennis also have information on special scoring conventions, minor league teams, stadium information, usage, abbreviations, numbers, and other unique elements.

Individual and Team Sports

Aikido *See* martial arts.

Archery

Terms

arrow
barebow
bolt
bow freestyle
bull's eye
FITA: Fédération Internationale de Tir à l'Arc.
field round
Grand FITA
hunters' round
match crossbow
target

Governing Bodies

National Archery Association of the United States
One Olympic Plaza
Colorado Springs, CO 80909
(719) 578-4576
Conducts national tournaments; selects national team

Fédération Internationale de Tir à l'Arc (FITA on second reference)
Via Cervo 30
Milan 20122 Italy
+39 +2/796 038
International governing body

Scoring

Scoring is in points. Use the basic summary.

EXAMPLE:

> (After 3 of 5 distances) 1, Garrick Beil, Chicago, 937 points. 2, Martin Monahan, Kansas City, Mo., 890. 3, etc.

Auto Racing

Terms

balaclava
bank (v.)
chicane
circuit
Formula One
horsepower
IndyCar
LeMans
NASCAR
National Hot Rod Association (NHRA)
pace car
pole sitter (n.)
racer's edge
24 Hours of Daytona
24 Hours of LeMans

Usage

Speeds are listed in miles per hour.

> A. J. Foyt set a record going 123.474 mph.

Turns are banked in degrees not percentages. Use figures in the names of specific turns.

> He crashed on Turn 2.
> He took the lead near the third turn.

Use figures in the names of specific row names.

Mears will start on the inside of Row 3.
He will start in the fifth row.

Governing Bodies

Championship Auto Racing Teams/IndyCar
390 Enterprise Court
Bloomfield Hills, MI 48302
(810) 334-8500
Conducts races for IndyCars

National Association for Stock Car Auto Racing (NASCAR)
1801 W. International Speedway Blvd.
Daytona Beach, FL 32114
(904) 253-0611
Conducts NASCAR races

National Hot Rod Association (NHRA on second reference)
2035 Financial Way
Glendora, CA 91741-4602
(818) 914-4761
Conducts Hot Rod Races

Scoring

Use the basic summary. Use the following forms for all major auto races.

EXAMPLES:

Qualifying:
1. Renato Umali, Italy, Ferrari, 171.103 kph (108.265 mph).
2. Hadji Williams, Canada, Ferrari, 170.297 kph (107.919 mph).
3. etc. for the entire starting grid.

Race:
1. Renato Umali, Italy, Ferrari, 44 laps, 164.297 kph (101.823 mph).
2. Alain Prost, France, Ferrari, 44.

3. etc. for entire starting grid, adding all non-finishers as follows:
23. Bernhard Bergen, Austria, McLaren-Honda, 12, broken axle.
After the final driver, add:
Time of race: 1:43:16
Margin of victory: 2.3 seconds
Caution flags: No full-course yellows
Lead changes: 3 between 3 drivers
Lap leaders: Umali 1-34, Williams 35-36, Prost 37-40, Umali 41-44.

For point leaders:
World Driver Leaders
(Points on 9-6-4-3-2-1 basis)
1. Nicki Lauda, Austria, 47 points. 2. Emerson Fittipaldi, Brazil,
 53.3, etc.

Badminton

Terms

bird
shuttlecock

Governing Body

United States Badminton Association
One Olympic Plaza
Colorado Springs, CO 80909
(719) 578-4808
Selects national team

Scoring

The first player to score 15 points with a two-point spread wins a
game. A match usually consists of three games. In one-game tournaments, competitors often play to 21.

Use a match summary. *See* racquetball for an example.

Baseball

Terms

at-bat (n.)
backstop
ballclub
ballgame
ballpark
ballplayer
base line
base on balls
base path
base runner
base running (n.)
base-running (adj.)
Basic Agreement
battery
beanball
brushback (n., adj.)
bullpen
center field
center fielder
change-up
checked swing
checked-swing
  (adj.)
coach's box
comebacker
curveball
designated hitter
doubleheader
double play (n.)
double-play (adj.)
ERA
exhibition game
extra-base hit
extra-inning game
fair ball
fastball
fielder's choice
first-base line

first baseman
fly out (v.)
fly-out (n.)
force out (v.)
force-out (n.)
forkball
foul ball
foul line
foul tip
grand slam
ground out (v.)
ground-out (n.)
ground-rule double
hidden-ball trick
hit-and-run (n.,
  adj.)
hit batsman
home plate
home run
home-run hitter
home stand
inside-the-park
  home run
knuckleball
lead off (v.)
lead-off (adj.)
leadoff (n.)
left-center field
left-center-field
  fence
left-handed
left-hander
line drive (n.)
line-drive (adj.)
line out (v.)
lineout (n.)
line up (v.)
lineup (n.)

major league
major-leaguer
minor league
minor-leaguer
no-hitter
on-deck circle
on-base percentage
outfielder
passed ball
pinch hit (n., v.)
pinch-hit (adj.)
pinch hitter
pinch runner
pine tar
pitchout
playoff (n., adj.)
pop out (v.)
pop-up (n.)
put out (v.)
putout (n.)
RBI (singular)
RBIs (plural)
right-center field
right field
right-handed
rosin bag
run down (v.)
rundown (n.)
sacrifice (n., adj.)
screwball
second baseman
second-base
  umpire
short-arm (v.)
short hop (n.)
short-hop (v.)
series opener
Series, the

set-up man	strike out (v.)	third-base line
shut out (v.)	strikeout (n., adj.)	third baseman
shutout (n., adj.)	strike zone	twi-night double-
split-fingered fast-	struck out (v.)	header
ball	switch-hitter	wind up (v.)
squeeze bunt	Texas leaguer	windup (n.)
stand-up double	third-base coach	World Series

Usage

AL Spell out American League on first reference, then AL.

All-Star Capitalize.

> When is the All-Star Game?
> Five players from the Royals made the All-Star team.
> Dawson is an All-Star.
> Hugh worked on his hitting during the All-Star break

Baseball Writers' Association of America Spell out in first reference, then BBWAA.

Class A Use Class A, Class AA, and Class AAA when referring to minor-league baseball classifications. Hyphenate as a modifier.

complete game A pitcher must start and finish a game to record a complete game.

Cy Young Award Do not refer to this award, which goes to the major league pitcher of the year, as the Young Award.

designated hitter Avoid using DH except in agate and when necessary for space reasons in headlines.

ERA Acceptable in all references for earned-run average.

forfeit In baseball, record the final score as 9-0.

Gold Glove Capitalize both words for this award, which goes to an outstanding major league fielder.

Little League Capitalize when referring to the youth summer baseball league.

Major League Baseball Capitalize when referring to the corporate entity. Use the League on second reference; avoid using MLB.

Major League Players Association Use the association or the players' association on second reference.

Major League Umpires Association Spell out on first reference, then the association.

Mendoza line Term refers to a batting average of .200

mitt Catcher and first basemen use mitts. When referring to players at all other positions, use glove.

NL Spell out National League on first reference, then NL.

names Team names: Capitalize team names and associations.

> The Chicago White Sox played the A's.

Avoid using nicknames, such as Bucs for Pirates, Cubbies for Cubs, BoSox for Boston, etc.

Personal names: Use a player's full name on first reference, and the last name afterward.
Use a player's nickname only when the nickname is more well-known than the real name.

> Frank Thomas showed the Yankees why he is called "the Big Hurt."

numbers Always use figures for scores, ball and strike counts, ERA, and records. Some sample uses of numbers:

> The Mariners beat the Indians 5-4.
> Pasqual has a 3.24 ERA.
> He swung on a 3-0 pitch.
> The pitcher's record is 7-1.

Spell out numbers under 10 in other references.

> It's time for the seventh-inning stretch.
> The game went into the 10th inning.
> He has one RBI today, 10 RBIs this season.
> Joyner had two hits last week.
> The Blue Jays are in first place.
> Parker stole second base.
> Pichelman went eight for 10.
> Cone pitched a seven-hitter.

Professional Baseball Hall of Fame Baseball's Hall of Fame is located in Cooperstown, N.Y. Hall of Fame is acceptable as a second reference.

RBI, RBIs Use an s to denote multiple RBIs.

World Series Capitalize Series on second reference.

Governing Bodies

USA Baseball
2160 Greenwood Ave.
Trenton, NJ 08609
(609) 586-2381
Selects and trains national amateur team

Major League Baseball
350 Park Ave.
New York, NY 10022
(212) 339-7900
Governs the national professional league teams

Leagues and Teams

This alignment went into effect at the start of the 1994 season.

AMERICAN LEAGUE WEST
California Angels
Oakland Athletics
Seattle Mariners
Texas Rangers

AL CENTRAL
Chicago White Sox
Cleveland Indians
Kansas City Royals
Milwaukee Brewers
Minnesota Twins

AL EAST
Baltimore Orioles
Boston Red Sox
Detroit Tigers
N.Y. Yankees

NATIONAL LEAGUE WEST
Colorado Rockies
Los Angeles Dodgers
San Diego Padres
San Francisco Giants

NL CENTRAL
Chicago Cubs
Cincinnati Reds
Houston Astros
Pittsburgh Pirates
St. Louis Cardinals

NL EAST
Atlanta Braves
Florida Marlins
Montreal Expos
N.Y. Mets
Philadelphia
  Phillies

Minor-league affiliations: Following are the major-league teams, their Class-A, Double-A, and Triple-A affiliations, and the leagues.

ATLANTA BRAVES

Triple A	Richmond Braves (International)
Double A	Greenville Braves (Southern)
Class A	Durham Bulls (Carolina)
Class A	Macon Braves (South Atlanta)
Short A	Eugene Emeralds (Northwest League)
Adv. Rookie	Danville Braves (Appalachian)
Rookie	Gulf Coast Braves (Gulf Coast)

BALTIMORE ORIOLES

Triple A	Rochester, N.Y. Red Wings (International)
Double A	Bowie, Md. Baysox (Eastern)
Class A	Frederick, Md. Keys (Carolina)
Class A	High Desert Mavericks (California)
Adv. Rookie	Bluefield Orioles (Appalachian)
Rookie	Gulf Coast Orioles (Gulf Coast League)

BOSTON RED SOX

Triple A	Pawtucket, R.I. Red Sox (International)
Double A	Trenton Thunder (Eastern)

Class A	Michigan Battle Cats (Midwest)
Class A	Sarasota Red Sox (Florida State)
Short A	Utica, N.Y. Blue Sox (New York-Penn)

CALIFORNIA ANGELS

Triple A	Vancouver, B.C. Canadiens (Pacific Coast)
Double A	Midland, Texas Angels (Texas)
Class A	Cedar Rapids, Iowa Kernels (Midwest)
Class A	Lake Elsinore Storm (California)
Short A	Boise, Idaho Hawks (Northwest)
Rookie	Mesa, Ariz. Angels (Arizona)

CHICAGO CUBS

Triple A	Iowa Cubs (American Association)
Double A	Orlando Cubs (Southern)
Class A	Daytona Cubs (Florida State)
Class A	Rockford Cubbies (Midwest)
Short A	Williamsport Cubs (New York-Penn)
Rookie	Gulf Coast Cubs (Gulf Coast League)

CHICAGO WHITE SOX

Triple A	Nashville Sounds (American Association)
Double A	Birmingham Barons (Southern)
Class A	Prince William Cannons (Carolina)
Class A	South Bend, Ind. Silver Hawks (Midwest)
Class A	Hickory, N.C. Crawdads (South Atlantic)
Adv. Rookie	Bristol White Sox (Appalachian)
Rookie	Sarasota, Fla. (Gulf Coast)

CINCINNATI REDS

Triple A	Indianapolis Indians (American Association)
Double A	Chattanooga Lookouts (Southern)
Class A	Winston-Salem Warthogs (Carolina)
Class A	Charleston (W.V.) Alleycats (South Atlantic)
Adv. Rookie	Billings Mustangs (Pioneer)
Adv. Rookie	Princeton (W.V.) Reds (Appalachian)

CLEVELAND INDIANS

Triple A	Buffalo Bison (American)
Double A	Canton-Akron Indians (Eastern)
Class A	Kinston (N.C.) Indians (Carolina)

Class A	Columbus (Ga.) Redstixx (South Atlantic)
Short A	Watertown (Ga.) Indians (New York-Penn)
Adv. Rookie	Burlington Indians (Appalachian)

COLORADO ROCKIES

Triple A	Colorado Springs Sky Sox (Pacific Coast)
Double A	New Haven Ravens (Eastern)
Class A	Asheville Tourists (South Atlantic)
Class A	Salem Avalanche (Carolina)
Short A	Portland Rockies (Northwest)
Rookie	Arizona Rockies (Arizona)

DETROIT TIGERS

Triple A	Toledo (Ohio) Mud Hens (International)
Double A	Jacksonville Suns (Southern)
Class A	Lakeland (Fla.) Tigers (Florida State)
Class A	Fayetteville (N.C.) Generals (South Atlantic)
Short A	Jamestown Jammers (New York-Penn)
Rookie	Gulf Coast Tigers (Gulf Coast)

FLORIDA MARLINS

Triple A	Charlotte Knights (International)
Double A	Portland Sea Dogs (Eastern)
Class A	Brevard County Manatees (Florida State)
Class A	Kane County Cougars (Midwest)
Short A	Elmira Pioneers (New York-Penn)

HOUSTON ASTROS

Triple A	Tucson Toros (Pacific Coast)
Double A	Jackson Generals (Texas)
Class A	Kissimmee Cobras (Florida State)
Class A	Quad City River Bandits (Midwest)
Rookie	Auburn Astros (New York-Penn)
Rookie	Gulf Coast Astros (Gulf Coast)

KANSAS CITY ROYALS

Triple A	Omaha Royals (American Association)
Double A	Wichita Wranglers (Texas)
Class A	Wilmington (Del.) Blue Rocks (Carolina)
Class A	Springfield Indians (Midwest)
Short A	Spokane Indians (Northwest)
Rookie	Gulf Coast Royals, Fla. (Gulf Coast)

LOS ANGELES DODGERS

Triple A	Albuquerque Dukes (Pacific Coast)
Double A	San Antonio Missions (Texas)
Class A	San Bernardino Spirit (California)
Class A	Vero Beach Dodgers (Florida State)
Short A	Yakima (Wash.) Bear (Northwest)
Adv. Rookie	Great Falls Dodgers (Pioneer)

MILWAUKEE BREWERS

Triple A	New Orleans Zephyrs (American Association)
Double A	El Paso Diablos (Texas)
Class A	Stockton (Calif.) Ports (California)
Class A	Beloit (Wis.) Snappers (Midwest)
Adv. Rookie	Helena (Mt.) Brewers (Pioneer)
Rookie	Chandler (Ariz.) Brewers (Arizona)

MINNESOTA TWINS

Triple A	Salt Lake Buzz (Pacific Coast)
Double A	New Britain Rock Cats (Eastern)
Class A	Fort Myers (Fl.) Miracle (Florida State)
Class A	Fort Wayne (Ind.) Wizards (Midwest)
Adv. Rookie	Elizabethton (Tenn.) Twins (Appalachian)
Rookie	Gulf Coast Twins (Gulf Coast)

MONTREAL EXPOS

Triple A	Ottawa Lynx (International)
Double A	Harrisburg Senators (Eastern)
Class A	West Palm Beach Expos (Florida State)
Class A	Albany Polecats (South Atlantic)
Short A	Vermont Expos (New York-Penn)
Rookie	Gulf Coast Expos (Gulf Coast)

NEW YORK METS

Triple A	Norfolk (Va.) Tides (International)
Double A	Binghamton Mets (Eastern)
Class A	St. Lucie Mets (Florida State)
Class A	Columbia Bombers (South Atlantic)
Short A	Pittsfield Mets (New York-Penn)
Adv. Rookie	Kingsport Mets (Appalachian)

NEW YORK YANKEES

Triple A	Columbus (Ohio) Clippers (International)
Double A	Norwich Navigators (Eastern)
Class A	Tampa Yankees (Florida State)
Class A	Greensboro Bats (South Atlantic)
Short A	Oneonta Yankees (New York-Penn)
Rookie	Gulf Coast Yankees (Gulf Coast)

OAKLAND ATHLETICS

Triple A	Edmonton Trappers (Pacific Coast)
Double A	Huntsville (Ala.) Stars (Southern)
Class A	Modesto A's (California)
Class A	West Michigan White Caps (Midwest)
Short A	Southern Oregon Athletics (Northwest)
Rookie	Arizona Athletics (Arizona)

PHILADELPHIA PHILLIES

Triple A	Scranton/Wilkes-Barre Barons (International)
Double A	Reading Phillies (Eastern)
Class A	Clearwater Phillies (Florida State)
Class A	Piedmont Phillies (South Atlantic)
Short A	Batavia Clippers (New York-Penn)
Rookie	Martinsville Phillies (Appalachian)

PITTSBURGH PIRATES

Triple A	Calgary Cannons (Pacific Coast)
Double A	Carolina Mudcats (Southern)
Class A	Lynchburg Hillcats (Carolina)
Class A	Augusta Greenjackets (South Atlantic)
Short A	Erie Seawolves (New York-Penn)
Rookie	Gulf Coast Pirates (Gulf Coast)

ST. LOUIS CARDINALS

Triple A	Louisville Redbirds (American Association)
Double A	Arkansas Travelers (Texas)
Class A	St. Petersburg Cardinals (Florida State)
Class A	Savannah Cardinals (South Atlantic)
Class A	Peoria Chiefs (Midwest)
Short A	New Jersey Cardinals (New York-Penn)
Adv. Rookie	Johnson City Cardinals (Appalachian)

SAN DIEGO PADRES

Triple A	Las Vegas Stars (Pacific Coast)
Double A	Memphis Chicks (Southern)
Class A	Rancho Cucamonga Quakes (California)
Class A	Clinton Lumber Kings (Midwest)
Adv. Rookie	Idaho Falls Braves (Pioneer)
Rookie	Arizona Padres (Arizona)

SAN FRANCISCO GIANTS

Triple A	Phoenix Firebirds (Pacific Coast)
Double A	Shreveport Captains (Texas)
Class A	San Jose Giants (California)
Class A	Burlington Bees (Midwest)
Short A	Bellingham Giants (Northwest)

SEATTLE MARINERS

Triple A	Tacoma Rainiers (Pacific Coast)
Double A	Port City Roosters (Southern)
Class A	Riverside Pilots (California)
Class A	Wisconsin Timber Rattlers (Midwest)
Short A	Everett Aquasox (Northwest)
Rookie	Arizona Mariners (Arizona)

TEXAS RANGERS

Triple A	Oklahoma City 89ers (American Association)
Double A	Tulsa Drillers (Texas)
Class A	Charlotte (Fla.) Rangers (Florida State)
Class A	Charleston (S.C.) Riverdogs (South Atlantic)
Short A	Hudson Valley Renegades (New York-Penn)
Rookie	Gulf Coast Rangers (Gulf Coast)

TORONTO BLUE JAYS

Triple A	Syracuse (N.Y.) Chiefs (International)
Double A	Knoxville (Tenn.) Smokies (Southern)
Class A	Dunedin Blue Jays (Florida State)
Class A	Hagerstown (Md.) Suns (South Atlantic)
Short A	St. Catharines (Ont.) Stompers (New York-Penn)
Rookie	Medicine Hat (Alta.) Blue Jays (Pioneer)
Rookie	Gulf Coast Blue Jays (Gulf Coast)

Independent Leagues

Duluth-Superior Dukes
Sioux City Explorers
Sioux Falls Canaries
St. Paul Saints
Thunder Bay Whiskey Jacks
Winnipeg Goldeyes

TEXAS-L.A. LEAGUE
North Division:
   Abilene Prairie Dogs
   Amarillo Dillas
   Lubbock Crickets
   Tyler Wildcatters
South Division:
   Alexandria Aces
   Corpus Christi Barracudas
   Mobile Baysharks
   Rio Grande Valley Whitewings

FRONTIER LEAGUE
Chillicothe Paints
Evansville Otters
Johnstown Steel
Newark Buffaloes
Ohio Valley Redcoats
Portsmouth Explorers
Richmond Roosters
Zanesville Greys

WESTERN LEAGUE
North Division:
   Bends Bandits
   Grays Harbor Gulls
   Surrey Glaciers
   Tri-City Posse
South Division:
   Long Beach Barracudas
   Palm Springs Suns
   Salinas Peppers
   Sonoma County Crushers

The following independent teams play in leagues with affiliated teams:

Class A	Visalia Oaks (California League)
Class A	Bakersfield Blaze (California)
Adv. Rookie	Huntington Rumblers (Appalachian League)
Adv. Rookie	Lethbridge Mounties (Pioneer League)
Adv. Rookie	Ogden Raptors (Pioneer)
Adv. Rookie	Butte Copper Kings (Pioneer)

Japanese Professional Baseball

PACIFIC	CENTRAL
Chiba Lotte Orions	Chunichi Dragons
Fukuoka Daiei Hawks	Hanshin Tigers
Kintetsu Buffaloes	Hiroshima Toyo Carp
Nippon Ham Fighters	Yakult Swallows
Orix Blue Wave	Yokohama Taiyo Whales
Seibu Lions	Yomiuri Giants

Scoring

Box Score:

Kansas City 3, Florida 2

KANSAS CITY

	ab	r	h	bi	ave.
Miller 3b	3	1	3	0	.345
Tucker lf	2	0	1	0	.220
McRae cf	1	1	0	0	.246
Hiatt rf . . .					
Totals	3	2	3	7	

FLORIDA

	ab	r	h	bi	ave.
Browne cf	3	1	1	1	.219
Barberie 2b	1	0	0	0	.310
Magadan 3b	2	1	1	0	.254
Sheffield rf . . .					
	3	3	3	2	9 2

Kansas City	010 101 000 - 3	7 0
Florida	000 020 000 - 2	9 1

DP-Kansas City 2. LOB-Kansas City 5, Florida 7. E-Alvarez (2). 2B-Crane (4), Rosenlof (3). 3B-Lopez (1). HR-Scheiden (11). SB-Rigoni (11), Campbell (4), Jerikian (6). S-Steinhauser. SF-O'Brien.

	IP	H	R	ER	BB	SO	NP	ERA
Kansas City								
Appier	6 1/3	4	5	5	5	1	91	3.69
Magnante	2 2/3	2	1	1	1	3	32	1.97
Florida								
Bowen	5	4	4	4	2	3	85	3.80
Aquino	4	2	0	0	0	2	58	2.25

HBP - Hiatt (by Aquino). WP-Appier

Umpires - HP, Palermo; 1B, Hirschbeck; 2B, Poncino; 3B, West.

T - 2:15. A - 15,560

Stadiums

TEAM	BALLPARK	PERMANENT SEATING CAPACITY
Atlanta Braves (404) 522-7630	Atlanta-Fulton County Stadium PO Box 6907 Lakewood Station Atlanta, GA 30315 (404) 522-1967	52,710
Baltimore Orioles (410) 685-9800	Oriole Park at Camden Yards 555 Russell St. Ste. A Baltimore, MD 21230 (410) 576-0300	48,262
Boston Red Sox (617) 267-9440	Fenway Park 4 Yawkey Way Boston, MA 02215 (617) 267-9440	33,871
California Angels (714) 937-7200	Anaheim Stadium 2000 Gene Autry Way Anaheim, CA 92806 (714) 254-3100	64,593

Chicago White Sox (312) 924-1000	Comiskey Park 333 W. 35th St. Chicago, IL 60616 (312) 924-1000	44,321
Cincinnati Reds (513) 421-4510	Riverfront Stadium 201 E. Pete Rose Way Cincinnati, OH 45202 (513) 352-5400	52,952
Cleveland Indians (216) 864-1200	Jacobs Field 2401 Ontario St. Cleveland, OH 44115 (216) 420-4200	42,400
Chicago Cubs (312) 404-2827	Wrigley Field 1060 W. Addison St. Chicago, IL 60613 (312) 404-2827	38,765
Colorado Rockies (303) 292-0200	Coors Field 2001 Blake St. Denver, CO 80205-2000 (303) 292-0200	50,100
Detroit Tigers (313) 962-4000	Tiger Stadium 2121 Trumbull Ave. Detroit, MI 48216 (313) 862-4000	52,416
Florida Marlins (305) 626-7400	Joe Robbie Stadium 2269 N.W. 199th St. Miami, FL 33056 (305) 626-7400	46,662
Houston Astros (713) 799-9500	The Astrodome 8400 Kirby Drive Houston, TX 77054 (713) 799-9500	54,313

Individual and Team Sports

Kansas City Royals (816) 921-2200	Ewing Kauffman Stadium 1 Royal Way Kansas City, MO 64129 (816) 921-2200	40,625
Los Angeles Dodgers (213) 224-1500	Dodger Stadium 1000 Elysian Park Ave. Los Angeles, CA 90012 (213) 224-1351	56,000
Milwaukee Brewers (414) 933-1818	Milwaukee County Stadium 201 S. 46th St. Milwaukee, WI 53214 (414) 933-4114	53,192
Minnesota Twins (612) 375-1366	Hubert H. Humphrey Metrodome 900 S. Fifth St. Minneapolis, MN 55415 (612) 332-0386	53,192
Montreal Expos (514) 253-3434	Olympic Stadium 4141 Pierre De Coubertin Ave. Montreal, PQ H1V 3N7 (514) 252-4636	46,500
New York Mets (718) 507-6387	Shea Stadium Flushing, NY 11368 (718) 507-METS	55,601
New York Yankees (718) 293-4300	Yankee Stadium 161st St. & River Ave. Bronx, NY 10451 (718) 293-4300	57,545
Oakland Athletics (510) 638-4900	Oakland-Alameda County Stadium 7000 Coliseum Way Oakland, CA 94621 (510) 569-2121	47,313

Philadelphia Phillies (215) 463-6000	Veterans Stadium Broad St. & Pattison Ave. Philadelphia, PA 19148 (215) 685-1500	62,530
Pittsburgh Pirates (412) 323-5000	Three Rivers Stadium 400 Stadium Circle Pittsburgh, PA 15212 (412) 321-0650	47,972
St. Louis Cardinals (314) 421-3060	Busch Stadium 300 Stadium Plaza St. Louis, MO 63102 (314) 241-3900	57,076
San Diego Padres (619) 283-4494	San Diego Jack Murphy Stadium 9449 Friars Road San Diego, CA 92108 (619) 525-8266	46,510
San Francisco Giants (415) 468-3700	3 Com Park Giants Dr. and Gilman Ave. San Francisco, CA 94124 (415) 467-1994	60,000
Seattle Mariners (206) 628-3555	The Kingdome 201 S. King St. Seattle, WA 98104 (206) 296-3663	59,166
Texas Rangers (817) 273-5222	The Ball Park at Arlington 2401 E. Airport Freeway Irving, TX 75062 (214) 438-7676	49,292
Toronto Blue Jays (416) 341-1000	Skydome 1 Blue Jays Way, Ste. 3000 Toronto, ON M5V 1J3 Canada (416) 341-3663	53,169

Basketball

Terms

alley-oop	front court	playoff (n., adj.)
backboard	full-court press	pull up (v.)
backcourt	halfcourt	pull-up (adj.)
backcourtman	half-court press	run-and-gun
baseline	halftime	scorers' table
box-and-one	hook shot	shot-block
coaches' box	jump ball	shot-blocker
crossover dribble	jump shot	technical foul
double dribble (n.)	lay-up	10-second count
double-dribble (v.)	loose ball (n.)	timeout
downcourt	loose-ball (adj.)	tip in (v.)
dunk	man-to-man (n., adj.)	tip-in (n.)
end line	midcourt	three-pointer
fadeaway	one-and-one	three-point line
fast break	1-2-1 zone	three-point shot
field goal (n.)	outlet pass	three-second rule
field-goal (adj.)	out-of-bounds (n., adj.)	throw in (v.)
foul line		throw-in (n., adj.)
foul shot	over and back	triple double
four-corner defense	pick-and-roll	turn over (v.)
	pivotman	turnover (n.)
free throw	player control foul	24-second violation
free throw line	play off (v.)	2-3 zone

Usage

ABA Acceptable on second reference to the American Basketball Association.

Eddie Gottlieb Trophy Trophy awarded to the NBA Rookie of the Year, selected by a pool of writers and broadcasters.
Gottlieb Trophy is acceptable on the second reference.

Larry O'Brien Trophy Team award given to the National Championship winners. O'Brien Trophy is acceptable on the second reference.

Maurice Podoloff Trophy Award given to the regular season NBA Most Valuable Player selected by players and a panel of writers and broadcasters. This trophy is named after the first commissioner of the NBA. Podoloff Trophy is acceptable on the second reference.

names Team names: Use full name on first reference, and city or team name following.

EXAMPLE:

> The Chicago Bulls beat the Orlando Magic 110-102 last night. Chicago came back from a 16-point hole to defeat Orlando in overtime.

Personal names: Use a player's full name, then the last name. Avoid using nicknames unless the player is better known by the nickname.

EXAMPLE:

> Magic Johnson

A nickname may be used in a headline, but follow with the player's full name in the story.

> Headline: Shaq stuffs Charlotte
> Lead sentence: Shaquille O'Neal scored 36 points last night to defeat the Charlotte Hornets 111-94.

NBA Acceptable in all references to the National Basketball Association.

NBA Finals Capitalize Finals.

NBA Slam Dunk Competition

numbers Always use figures for scores, heights, and references to the game clock.

> Our team won the pick-up game 41-7.
> King is a 6-foot-6 guard.

She is 5-11.
They scored with one minute, 33 seconds remaining, but Ritter made a three-pointer with 1.08 to go.

Spell out numbers one through nine in other references. Some sample uses of numbers:

The Sonics beat the Jazz 105-94.
Rosenlof had seven points, three rebounds and one assist.
Fitzgerald was eight for 10.
Phelps was two for two from the free throw line.
Taylor hit his fifth three-pointer.

Red Auerbach Trophy Named after Arnold "Red" Auerbach, this award is given to the NBA Coach of the Year. Auerbach Trophy is acceptable on second reference.

three-on-three Type of basketball played in Iowa with six-player teams: three on defense, three on offense. Each set of three plays on an opposite end of the court, so only three players on a team play at a given moment.

Governing Bodies

Continental Basketball Association
701 Market Street Suite 140
St. Louis, MO 63101
(314) 621-7222
Governing body of national professional league

NBA
645 5th Ave. 15th Floor
New York, NY 10022
(212) 826-7000
Governing body of national professional basketball league

USA Basketball
5465 Mark Dabling Blvd.
Colorado Springs, CO 80918-3842
(719) 590-4800
Selects and trains national team

Leagues and Teams

Past professional leagues:

> American Basketball League (ABL): 1925–32, 1934–46, 1961–63.
> National Basketball League (NBL): 1937–49, 1950–51.
> Basketball Association of America (BAA): 1946–49.
> American Basketball Association (ABA): 1967–76.

The NBL and BAA combined in 1949 to form the NBA.

Current Professional Leagues:

National Basketball Association. NBA is acceptable in all references. The league, founded in 1949, is made up of four divisions in two conferences.

EASTERN CONFERENCE

Atlantic Division

Boston Celtics
Miami Heat
New Jersey Nets
New York Knicks
Orlando Magic
Philadelphia 76ers
Washington Bullets

Central Division

Atlanta Hawks
Charlotte Hornets
Chicago Bulls
Cleveland Cavaliers
Detroit Pistons
Indiana Pacers
Milwaukee Bucks
Toronto Raptors

WESTERN CONFERENCE

Midwest Division

Dallas Mavericks
Denver Nuggets
Houston Rockets
Minnesota Timberwolves
San Antonio Spurs
Utah Jazz
Vancouver Grizzlies

Pacific Division

Golden State Warriors
L.A. Clippers
L.A. Lakers
Phoenix Suns
Portland Trailblazers
Sacramento Kings
Seattle Sonics

Individual and Team Sports

Continental Basketball Association.

Spell out on first reference, then CBA. The league is made up of four divisions in two conferences.

Eastern Division

Fort Wayne Fury
Harrisburg Hammerheads
Pittsburgh Piranhas
Hartford Hellcats

Midwestern Division

Quad City Thunder
Chicago Rockers
Grand Rapids Mackers
Rockford Lightning

NATIONAL CONFERENCE

Eastern Division

Sioux Falls Skyforce
Yakima Sun Kings
Tri-City Chinook
Rapid City Thrillers

Midwestern Division

Oklahoma City Cavalry
Omaha Racers
Mexico City Aztecs
Shreveport Crawdads

Scoring

Box Score:

Nuggets 98, Magic 89

Orlando: Avent 2-7 2-2 6, Scott 2-9 3-4 7, O'Neal 9-23 4-10 22, Hardaway 9-21 4-6 23, Anderson 4-12 1-2 10, Krystkowiak 4-10 1-2 9, Bowie 1-3 0-0 2, Royal 1-2 5-6 7, Skiles 1-4 1-1 3, Rollins 0-0 0-0 0. Totals 33-91 21-33 89.

Denver: Ellis 5-16 8-10 18, R. Williams 8-14 2-2 20, Mutombo 3-6 3-6 9, Abdul-Rauf 1-9 3-4 6, Smith 5-10 0-0 1, Pack 3-9 1-2 7, Rogers 5-12 4-4 15, B. Williams 3-6 2-2 8, Hammonds 2-2 1-2 5. Totals 35-84 24-32 98.

| Orlando | 15 | 28 | 23 | 23 | — | 89 |
| Denver | 18 | 17 | 35 | 28 | — | 98 |

Three-point goals—Orlando 2-8 (Anderson 1-2, Hardaway 1-4, Scott 0-2). Denver 4-11(R. Williams 2-4, Abdul-Rauf 1-2, Rogers

---

Individual and Team Sports

253

1-5). Fouled out—none. Rebounds—Orlando 61 (O'Neal 16), Denver 66 (Mutombo 10). Assists—Orlando 11 (Anderson 4), Denver 20 (Abdul-Rauf, Pack 6). Total fouls—Orlando 26, Denver 22. Technicals—Pack. Announced attendance—17,171.

LEAGUE STANDINGS

(Professional) Atlantic Division

	W	L	PCT	GB
New York	38	9	.667	—
Orlando	34	22	.607	3 1/2
Miami	31	25	.554	6 1/2

Arenas

The following is a list of each NBA team, its phone number, home arena, the arena's seating capacity, and its phone number.

TEAM	BALLPARK	PERMANENT SEATING CAPACITY
Atlanta Hawks (404) 827-3800	The Omni 100 Techwood Drive, N.W. Atlanta, GA 30303 (404) 681-2100	16,416
Boston Celtics (617) 523-6050	FleetCenter One FleetCenter Boston, MA 02114 (617) 624-1050	14,890
Charlotte Hornets (704) 357-0252	Charlotte Coliseum 100 Paul Buck Blvd. Charlotte, NC 28266-9247 (704) 357-4700	23,901
Chicago Bulls (312) 455-4000	United Center 1901 W. Madison Chicago, IL 60612 (312) 455-4000	21,500

Cleveland Cavaliers (216) 420-2000	Gund Arena 100 Gateway Plaza Cleveland, OH 44115 (216) 420-2000	20,592
Dallas Mavericks (214) 988-0117	Reunion Arena 777 Sports St. Dallas, TX 75207 (214) 939-2770	17,502
Denver Nuggets (303) 893-6700	McNichols Sports Arena 1635 Bryant St. Denver, CO 80204-1743 (303) 640-7300	17,022
Detroit Pistons (313) 377-0100	The Palace at Auburn Hills 2 Championship Drive Auburn Hills, MI 48326 (810) 377-8200	21,454
Golden State Warriors (510) 638-6300	Oakland-Alameda County Arena 7000 Coliseum Way Oakland, CA 94621 (510) 569-2121	25,000
Houston Rockets (713) 627-0600	The Summit 10 Greenway Plaza Houston, TX 77046 (713) 627-9470	16,279
Indiana Pacers (317) 263-2100	Market Square Arena 300 E. Market St. Indianapolis, IN 46204 (317) 639-6411	16,530

Los Angeles Clippers (213) 748-8000	Los Angeles Memorial Sports Arena 3939 S. Figueroa St. Los Angeles, CA 90037 (213) 748-6136	16,500
(7 games)	Arrowhead Pond of Anaheim 2695 E. Katella Ave. Anaheim, CA 92806 (714) 704-2400	19,400
Los Angeles Lakers (310) 419-3100	Great Western Forum 3900 W. Manchester Blvd. Inglewood, CA 90306 (310) 419-3100	17,505
Miami Heat (305) 577-4328	Miami Arena 701 Arena Blvd. Miami, FL 33136 (305) 530-4400	16,500
Milwaukee Bucks (414) 227-0500	Bradley Center 1001 N. Fourth St. Milwaukee, WI 53203 (414) 227-0400	18,633
Minnesota Timberwolves (612) 673-1600	Target Center 600 First Avenue North Minneapolis, MN 55403 (612) 673-1600	19,006
New Jersey Nets (201) 935-8888	Brendan Byrne Arena 50 Route 120 E. Rutherford, NJ 07073 (201) 460-4296	20,029

New York Knicks (212) 465-6499	Madison Square Garden 4 Penn Plaza New York, NY 10001 (212) 465-6000	19,763
Orlando Magic (407) 649-3200	Orlando Arena 600 W. Amelia St. Orlando, FL 32801 (407) 849-2000	15,291
Philadelphia 76ers (215) 339-7600	CoreStates Spectrum Broad & Pattison Ave. Philadelphia, PA 19148 (215) 336-3600	18,168
Phoenix Suns (602) 379-7900	America West Arena 201 E. Jefferson St. Phoenix, AZ 85004 (602) 379-2000	19,023
Portland Trail Blazers (503) 234-9291	Rose Garden 1 Center Court Portland, OR 97227 (503) 234-9291	20,340
Sacramento Kings (916) 928-0000	ARCO Arena 1 Sports Pkwy Sacramento, CA 95834 (916) 928-0000	17,317
San Antonio Spurs (210) 554-7700	Alamodome 100 Montana San Antonio, TX 78203 (210) 207-3663	20,500
Seattle Sonics (206) 281-5800	Seattle Center 305 Harrison St. Seattle, WA 98109 (206) 684-7202	17,800

Toronto Raptors (416) 214-2255	SkyDome 1 Blue Jays Way Toronto, ON M5V 1J3 (416) 341-3663	20,000
Utah Jazz (801) 325-2500	Delta Center 301 W. South Temple Salt Lake City, UT 84101 (801) 325-2000	19,911
Vancouver Grizzlies (604) 899-4666	General Motors Place 780 Beatty St. Vancouver, BC V6B 2M1 (604) 681-2280	20,000
Washington Bullets (301) 773-2255	USAir Arena 1 Harry S. Truman Drive Landover, MD 20785 (301) 350-3400	18,756

Biathlon

Governing Body

U.S. Biathlon Association
421 Old Military Rd.
Lake Placid, NY 12946
(518) 523-3836
National governing body; coordinates national team

Scoring

Include individual events and final standings. *See* decathlon in track and field for format.

Billiards

Governing Bodies

Pro Billiards Tour Association
4311 Lee Rd.
Spring Hill, FL 34608-3853
(904) 688-5837
Organizes professional billiards and pool tournaments

Billiards Congress of America
1700 First Ave. S. #25A
Iowa City, IA 52240
(319) 351-2112
National governing body

Scoring

Scoring is in points. Use a match summary.

EXAMPLE:

Minnesota Fats, St. Paul, Minn., def. Pool Hall Duke, 150-141.

Boating

Terms

aft	commodore	reaching
America's Cup	Europe	rudder
ballast	Finn	running
beam	Flying Dutchman	sloop rig
beating	genoa	Soling
boatswain	hull	spinnaker
boom	jib	Star
bow	keel	starboard
breakwater	knot	stern
catamaran	legs	tack
cat rig	mast	tiller
centerboard	nautical mile	Tornado
centerline	port	

Governing Bodies

U.S. Sailing Association
P.O. Box 209
Newport, RI 02840
(401) 849-5200
National governing body

International Yacht Racing Union
60 Knightsbridge
London SW1X 7JX
England
+44 +71/235 6221
International governing body

American Power Boat Association
17640 E. Nine Mile Rd.
Eastpointe, MI 48021
(810) 773-6490
National governing body for motorboat racing

Union Internationale Motor Boating
Union Internationale Motonautique
Stade Louis II
Monte Carlo, 98000
Monaco
+33 +93 50 12 60
International governing body

Scoring

Use the basic summary format, identifying by classes for scoring yacht racing.

Scoring for motorboat races may be posted in laps, miles per hour, or points depending on the competition. In general, use the basic summary format. *See* auto racing for examples.

Bobsledding/Luge

Terms

brakeman
driver
four-man
pushers
two-man

Governing Bodies

United States Bobsled and Skeleton Federation
P.O. Box 828
Lake Placid, NY 12946
(518) 523-9491
Selects and trains national bobsledding team

Federation Internationale de Bobsleigh et de Tobogganing
Via Piranesi 4416
Milan, 20137
Italy
+39 +2/757 3319
International governing body

U.S. Luge Association
35 Church St.
Lake Placid, NY 12946
(518) 523-2071
Selects and trains national luge team

Fédération Internationale de Luge de Course
56, Vallon de Toulouse
Marseille, 13009
France
+33 +91/74 21 50
International governing body

Scoring

Scoring is measured in minutes, seconds, and tenths of a second. Extend to hundredths if this information is available.

Identify the events for bobsled as two-man or four-man, and for luge as men's luge or women's luge.

Use a basic summary:

Bobsled—Two-Man
1. Great Britain (I), 4:21.90, Anthony Nash, Robin Dixon; 2. Italy (II), 4:22.02, Sergio Zardidni, Romano Bonagura; 3. etc.

Luge—Men's Singles
1. Jens Mueller, Germany, 3:05.548; 2. Georg Hackl, Germany, 3:05.916; 3. etc.

Bowling

Terms

American Bowling Congress (ABC)
frame
Ladies Pro Bowlers Tour (LPBT)
Professional Bowlers Association (PBA)
perfect game
spare
split
strike
300 game
Women's International Bowling Congress (WIBC)

Governing Bodies

Professional Bowlers Association
1720 Merriman Rd.
Akron, OH 44313
(216) 836-5568
Conducts men's professional tournaments

Ladies Professional Bowlers Tour
7171 Cherryvale Blvd.
Rockford, IL 61112
(815) 332-5756
Conducts women's professional tournaments

USA Bowling
5301 S. 76th St.
Greendale, WI 53129
(414) 421-9008
Develops amateur teams for international competitions

Women's International Bowling Congress (WIBC) (414) 421-9000
American Bowling Congress (414) 421-6400
Same address as USA Bowling; governing bodies for amateur women's and men's leagues.

Scoring

Scoring systems use both total points and won-lost records. Use the basic summary format in paragraph form, and use a comma for pinfalls more than 999.

Use the basic summary:

EXAMPLES:

Professional Bowlers Association
at St. Louis, June 8
(Second Round leaders and total pinfalls)
1. Bill Springer, Hamden, Conn., 2,820.
2. Garry Dickinson, Fort Worth, Texas, 2,759.
3. etc.

Alameda Open
at Alameda, Calif., June 8
(The 24 match play finalists with their match play records and
    total pinfall after four rounds — 26 games.)
1. Jay Robinson, Los Angeles, 5-3, 5,937.
2. Butch Soper, Huntington Beach, Calif., 3-5, 5,932
3. etc.

Boxing

Terms

bantamweight	KO'd
featherweight	middleweight
flyweight	outpointed
heavyweight	rabbit punch
kidney punch	welterweight
knockout	World Boxing Council (WBC)
KO	World Boxing Organization (WBO)

Governing Bodies

International Boxing Federation
134 Evergreen Place, 9th Floor
East Orange, NJ 07018
(201) 414-0300
International Governing Body

World Boxing Council (WBC)
Genova 33-DESP 503
Mexico D.F. 06600
Mexico
Conducts international matches, trains boxers and officials

World Boxing Organization (WBO)
412 Colorado Ave.
Aurora, IL 60506
(708) 897-4765
Regulates world boxing

USA Boxing
One Olympic Plaza
Colorado Springs, CO 80909
(719) 578-4506
Selects and trains amateurs for national team

Scoring

Use a match summary with the winning fighter's name, weight, hometown, result, losing fighter's name, weight, hometown, and number of rounds.

EXAMPLE:

> Robert Meyers, 155, Los Angeles outpointed John Smith, 154, New Orleans, 10.
> Muhammad Ali, 220, Chicago, knocked out Pierre Coopman, 202, Belgium, 5.
> George Foreman, 217-½, Hayward, Calif., stopped Joe Frazier, 214, Philadelphia, 2.

TALE OF THE TAPE:

EXAMPLE:

> SAN JUAN, Puerto Rico (AP)—The tale of the tape for the Jean Pierre Coopman-Muhammad Ali world heavyweight championship fight Friday night:

	Coopman	Ali
Age	29	34
Weight	202	220
Height	6-0	6-3
Reach	75	80
Chest normal	43	44
Chest expanded	45-½	46
Biceps	15	15
Forearm	13	13-½
Waist	34-½	34
Thigh	25-½	26
Calf	15	17
Neck	17	17-½
Wrist	7-½	8
Fist	12-½	13
Ankle	9	9-½

Scoring by Rounds:

EXAMPLE:

NEW YORK (UPI)—Scorecards for the Muhammad Ali-Joe Frazier heavyweight title fight Friday night:
Scoring by rounds:
Referee Tom Smith

| AAA | FFF | AAA | AFA | —FFF-A8-7 |

Judge Bill Swift

| AAA | FFF | FFF | AFA | —FFF-F10-5 |

Judge Ralph Cohen

| AAA | FFF | FFF | FFF | —AFF-F11-4 |

Scoring by points system:

Referee Tom Smith

| A | 10 | 10 | 10 | 10 | 10 | 10 | 10 | 10 | 10 | 10 | 9 | 9 | 9 | 9 | 10 |
| F | 10 | 9 | 9 | 9 | 9 | 9 | 9 | 10 | 10 | 9 | 10 | 10 | 10 | 10 | 10 |

Total—Ali 146, Frazier 143
Judge Bill Swift

| A | 10 | 10 | 10 | 9 | 9 | 9 | 9 | 10 | 9 | 9 | 9 | 10 | 9 | 10 | 9 |
| F | 9 | 9 | 9 | 10 | 10 | 10 | 10 | 10 | 10 | 10 | 10 | 9 | 10 | 9 | 10 |

Total—Frazier 145, Ali 141
Judge Ralph Cohen

| A | 10 | 9 | 10 | 10 | 10 | 10 | 10 | 10 | 10 | 10 | 10 | 9 | 9 | 9 | 9 |
| F | 9 | 10 | 10 | 9 | 9 | 9 | 9 | 9 | 10 | 10 | 9 | 10 | 10 | 10 | 10 |

Total—Ali 145, Frazier 143

Canoeing/Kayaking

Terms

beam	"J" stroke	shaft
blade	keel	stern
bow	petit-final	sweep
downstream gate	repêchage	thwart
draw	river left	upstream gate
Eskimo roll	river right	
gunwale	rudder	

Governing Bodies

United States Canoe and Kayak Team
Pan American Plaza
201 S. Capitol Ave Suite 610
Indianapolis, IN 46225
(317) 237-5690
Selects and trains national team

American Canoe Association
7422 Alban Station Blvd.
Suite B-226
Springfield, VA 22150
(703) 451-0141
National governing body

Scoring

Scoring is in points. List the top three finishers.
Follow this format:

> MEN
> Canoe Slalom Finals
> 1. Lukas Pollert, Czechoslovakia, 113.69; 2. Gareth Marriott,
>   Britain, 116.48; 3. etc.

> WOMEN
> Kayak Slalom Finals
> 1. Elisabeth Micheler, Germany, 126.41; 2. Danielle Ann Wood-
>   ward, Australia, 128.27; 3. Dana Chladek, Bloomfield Hills,
>   Mich., 131.75.

Chess

Terms

bishop	kingside
castle	pawn
check	queen
checkmate	queenside
king	rook

Usage

In stories, spell out the pieces and terms in lowercase: king, rook, queenside, black, white, etc.

Scoring

The news services notate the match in summaries. B is for bishop, K is for king, N is for knight, Q is for queen, R is rook, and P is pawn. Each row, or file, is given the name of the piece originally posted on it, and the ranks are numbered by squares from 1 to 8 away from the player. Each rank has a dual designation, depending on which player makes a move.

The moving piece is listed first, followed by a hyphen, followed by the destination square.

EXAMPLE:

> Moving a pawn to the fourth rank of the kingside rook file would be noted as P-KR4.

The indication of Q and K for queenside and kingside are used only if ambiguity would result.

The castle is noted by lowercase o's separated by a hyphen. A kingside castle is o-o, queenside is o-o-o.

To note a capture, use a lowercase x between the two initials instead of a hyphen, with the aggressor listed first. A queen capturing a pawn would be QxP.

The initials ch are used for a check; mate is used for checkmate.

EXAMPLE:

	White	Black
	Fischer	Kasparov
1.	P-K4	P-K4
2.	P-KB4	PxP
3.	B-B4	P-QN4
4.	BxNP	Q-R5ch
. . .		
21.	N-Pch	K-Q1
22.	Q-B6ch	NxQ
23.	B-K7, mate	

College Football and Basketball

See individual sports listings for scoring other collegiate-level sports.

Usage

ACC Spell out Atlantic Coast Conference on first reference, then ACC.

All- Capitalize All when it is part of a proper name.

> The All-Big Ten team will be named today.
> Four swimmers made the Academic All-Big Eight team.
> The National League won the All-Star Game 1-0.

All-America Use All-America in reference to a team or honor.

All-American Use All-American in reference to an individual.

Athletic Director Capitalize as a formal title before a name. A.D. is acceptable on second reference and in headlines.

Biletnikoff Receiver Award Sponsored by the Downtown Athletic Club of Orlando, Florida, this award was first presented in 1994 to the outstanding collegiate pass receiver. Use Fred Biletnikoff Award on first reference to this award named after the former Florida State All-American.

Bowl Alliance Participating teams come from the Atlantic Coast, Big East, Big Eight, Southeastern and Southwest conferences, and Notre Dame. The top six college football teams from these conferences and Notre Dame at the end of the season meet in three bowl games. The selection process rotates between the Fiesta, Sugar, and Orange bowls each year.
Sample Selection Order

> Sugar selects first and second
> Fiesta selects third and fifth
> Orange selects fourth and sixth

Bowl Coalition Poll The final Bowl Coalition Poll is determined by the combined point totals of the Associated Press and USA/CNN polls.

Broderick Award Award presented to the Division I or large school women's basketball Player of the Year.

Butkus Award Acceptable in all references to the award named for Dick Butkus. The Butkus Award is presented annually to the top collegiate linebacker. Use Butkus Award in all references.

Camp Award The Walter Camp award is given to the NCAA Division I Player of the Year and Coach of the Year.

College World Series Spell out College World Series on first reference to the Division I Men's Baseball Championship and the Division I Women's Softball Championship. Use the series, not CWS, on second reference.

Davis Award This award, named after Ernie Davis, 1961 Heisman winner, was first presented in 1992 to honor a Division I-AA college football player who overcame personal, athletic, or academic adversity to perform in an outstanding manner. Use Ernie Davis Award in first reference.

Division I, Division I-A Always use Roman numerals. Do not hyphenate as a modifier.

Is Pittsburgh a Division I or Division II team?

Eastman Trophy

Final Four This term is a registered trademark of the NCAA and must be capitalized in reference to the four remaining teams in the Division I Men's and Women's basketball championships.

Michigan advanced to the Final Four.

Do not capitalize final four in other uses.

North advanced to the high school tournament's final four.

games Capitalize games as part of a proper name.

> Two collegiate swimmers qualified for the Olympic Games.
> Hundreds will participate in the World University Games.

Groza Award Use Lou Groza Award on first reference to this annual award presented to the top collegiate placekicker.

Heisman Trophy This award, determined by sportswriters and presented at the Downtown Athletic Club in New York City, is given annually to the top collegiate football player.

Hill Trophy Award given to the Division II Football Player of the Year, named after former Chicago Bear and NFL MVP Harlon Hill. Use Harlon Hill Trophy on first reference.

majors Do not capitalize the name of a major unless the name is normally capitalized.

> Alberts is an engineering major.
> Kalin in an English major.

-man Do not change -man to -woman when it is used as a suffix or in the phrase man-to-man in sports references.

> Kara is the first baseman.
> The women's team plays man-to-man defense.

Lombardi Award Presented since 1970 by the Rotary Club of Houston, Texas, this award honors the outstanding college lineman of the year. Use Vince Lombardi Award on the first reference.

major, academic Do not capitalize an academic major unless it is normally capitalized.

> Johnson is a chemical engineering major.
> Van Etten is an English major.

Maxwell Award Award presented to the collegiate football player of the year, named after Robert "Tiny" Maxwell, who played lineman at the University of Chicago near the turn of the century. Use Maxwell Award in all references.

Naismith Trophy Named after James Naismith, inventor of basketball, this award is presented annually to the top male and female basketball players.

National Association of Intercollegiate Athletics Spell out on first reference. Use NAIA in headlines when space is limited and on second reference.

NCAA Acceptable in all references to the National Collegiate Athletic Association.

NIT Use National Invitation Tournament on first reference to this post-season collegiate tournament. Do not use the redundant NIT Tournament.

O'Brien Award This award, named after former TCU quarterback Davey O'Brien, is presented to the outstanding collegiate quarterback. Spell out Davey O'Brien award on the first reference.

Outland Trophy Award annually presented to the outstanding NCAA Division I interior lineman.

partial qualifier An incoming student who does not meet all the requirements established by Proposition 48 but who has graduated from high school and has met the requirements of the partial qualifier index scale. *See* Proposition 48.

Payton Award Voted on by Division I-AA sports information directors, this award is presented to the I-AA Player of the Year. Use Walter Payton Award on first reference.

preseason (n., adj.) Do not hyphenate.

---

professional vs. amateur An amateur becomes a professional when he or she:

> plays for a professional team
> puts his or her name on a draft list (except in baseball, where a student must declare intention to return to school within 30 days of the draft to maintain eligibility)
> receives pay or accepts the promise of pay for playing
> signs a contract or verbally commits with an agent of a professional sports organization
> uses skills to gain pay in commercials or other activity
> receives pay, awards, or educational expenses for playing on an amateur team (uniforms, equipment, and travel expenses are not considered pay)

Proposition 48 This NCAA rule establishes requirements that must be met by incoming students in order to participate in intercollegiate sports. To meet the requirements for a Division I school a student must:

> be a high school graduate
> have completed 13 core classes, one additional class in English, math, natural or physical science, and two additional academic courses
> have a grade-point average and combined SAT or ACT score that meets requirements based on a qualifier index scale

Proposition 48 requires students preparing to attend Division II schools to have:

> graduated from high school
> a grade-point average of 2.0 on a 4.0 scale in 13 core courses, and two additional courses in English, math, natural or physical science, and two additional academic courses
> a 700 combined score on the SAT or a 17 on the ACT

postseason (n., adj.) Do not hyphenate.

qualifier index This index establishes minimum requirements for incoming students hoping to participate in intercollegiate athletics. The index is a sliding scale that takes into account a student's GPA, and SAT or ACT score. For example, a student with a 2.5 GPA would need a 700 SAT score or 17 ACT score. A student with a 2.3 GPA would need an SAT score of 780 or a 19 on the ACT. *See* Proposition 48.

redshirt, redshirted, redshirting As a general rule, a collegiate athlete is allowed to redshirt for one year and still maintain four years of athletic eligibility.

regional Lowercase regional in phrases such as the East regional, Midwest regional semi-final.

Rupp Trophy Voted on by AP sportwriters, this award goes to the top male basketball player.

school Capitalize the proper names of schools within a university.

> Andrew was accepted to the Tridle School of Journalism.
> The school of journalism is located in Strong Hall.

student-athlete Hyphenate in all uses.

Thorpe Award This award, established in 1986 by the Jim Thorpe Athletic Club of Oklahoma City, honors the outstanding NCAA Division I defensive back. Use Jim Thorpe Award on first reference.

university Capitalize when part of a proper name.

> I attended the University of Iowa.
> Did you visit the university?

With the exception of UCLA, spell out the full name, and then use the acronym.

> Schwarz attends the University of Nevada-Las Vegas. UNLV has been 18-5 since he arrived last year.

Walker Award This award, given to the top Division I-A junior or senior running back for achievements on the field, in the classroom, and in the community, was first presented in 1990. Use Doak Walker Award on first reference.

Wooden Award Annual award to the nation's top male basketball player. Use John R. Wooden Award on first reference, then Wooden Award.

years Spell out freshman, sophomore, junior, senior, and fifth-year senior when referring to a player's year in school. Do not capitalize.

Governing Body

NCAA
6201 College Blvd.
Overland Park, KS 66211-2422
(913) 339-1906

Leagues and Teams

Following is a list of bowl games and their participants.

BOWL	CONFERENCE/TEAM	CONFERENCE/TEAM
Builder's Square Alamo	Big Ten No.4	Big Eight No.4
Carquest	Big East No.3	SEC No.5 or ACC No.4
CompUSA Florida Citrus	Big Ten No.2	SEC No.2
Federal Express Orange	Bowl Alliance	Alliance
Freedom	WAC No.3	Open
Gator	ACC No.2	Big East No.2
IBM/OS/2 Fiesta	Bowl Alliance	Alliance
Jeep Eagle Aloha	Pac-10 No.4	Big Eight No.5 or 6
Las Vegas	Mid-American No.1 team	Big West No.1

Mobil Cotton	WAC No.1 or Pac-10 No.2	Big Eight No.2
Nokia Sugar	Bowl Alliance	Alliance
Outback	Big Ten No.3	SEC No.3
Peach	ACC No.3	SEC No.4
Poulan/Weed Eater Independence	Open	Open
Rose	Pac-10 No.1	Big Ten No.1
St. Jude Liberty	Liberty Bowl Alliance	Open
Sun	Pac-10 No.3	Big Ten No.5
Thrifty Car Rental Holiday	WAC No.1 or Pac-10 No.2	Big Eight No.3
Weiser Lock Copper	WAC No.2	Big Eight No.5 or 6

Division I conferences

All of the basketball conferences listed are Division I. The football conferences are all Division I-A and Division I-AA.

American West Conference (basketball, football Division I-AA).

California Poly SLO Mustangs	Green & Gold
California State Northridge Matadors	Red, White & Black
California State-Sacramento Hornets	Green & Gold
Southern Utah Thunderbirds	Scarlet, Royal Blue & White

Atlantic Coast Conference (basketball, football Division I-A). Spell out on first reference, then ACC.

Clemson Tigers	Purple & Orange
Duke Blue Devils	Royal Blue & White
Florida State Seminoles	Garnet & Gold
Georgia Tech Yellow Jackets	Old Gold & White
University of Maryland Terrapins	Red, White, Black & Gold

North Carolina-Chapel Hill (UNC)
Tar Heels   Carolina Blue & White

North Carolina State (N.C. State)
Wolfpack   Red & White

University of Virginia Cavaliers   Orange & Black

Wake Forest Demon Deacons   Old Gold & Black

Atlantic Ten Conference (basketball). Atlantic 10 is acceptable in all references.

Dayton Blue Demons	Scarlet & Blue
Duquesne Dukes	Red & Blue
Fordham Rams	Maroon & White
George Washington Colonials	Buff & Blue
La Salle Explorers	Blue & Gold
Massachusetts (UMass) Minutemen	Maroon & White
Rhode Island Rams	Blue & White
St. Bonaventure Bonnies	Brown & White
St. Joseph's (Pa.) Hawks	Crimson & Gray
Temple Owls	Cherry & White
Virginia Tech Gobblers, Hokies	Orange & Maroon
Xavier (Ohio) Musketeers	Blue & White

Big East Conference (basketball).

Boston College Eagles	Maroon & Gold
University of Connecticut (UConn) Huskies	National Flag Blue & White
Georgetown Hoyas	Blue & Gray
Miami (Fla.) Hurricanes	Orange, Green & White
Notre Dame Fighting Irish	Gold & Blue
Pittsburgh Panthers	Blue & Gold
Providence Friars	Black & White
Rutgers Scarlet Knights	Scarlet
St. John's Red Storm	Red & White
Seton Hall Pirates	Blue & White
Syracuse Orangemen	Orange
Villanova Wildcats	Blue & White
West Virginia Mountaineers	Old Gold & Blue

Big East Conference (football Division I-A).

Boston College Eagles	Maroon & Gold
Miami (Fla.) Hurricanes	Orange, Green & White
Pittsburgh Panthers	Blue & Gold
Rutgers Scarlet Knights	Scarlet
Syracuse Orangemen	Orange
Temple Owls	Cherry & White
Virginia Tech Gobblers, Hokies	Orange & Maroon
West Virginia Mountaineers	Old Gold & Blue

Big Eight Conference* (all sports). Spell out Big Eight in stories. Big 8 is acceptable in headlines. The following teams make up this Division I-A conference.

Colorado Buffaloes	Silver, Gold & Black
Iowa State Cyclones	Cardinal & Gold
Kansas Jayhawks	Crimson & Blue
Kansas State Wildcats	Purple & White
Missouri Tigers	Old Gold & Black
Nebraska Cornhuskers	Scarlet & Cream
Oklahoma Sooners	Crimson & Cream
Oklahoma State Cowboys	Orange & Black

*As of June 30, 1996, the Big Eight Conference will be renamed the Big Twelve. Baylor, Texas, Texas A & M, and Texas Tech will all move from the dissolved Southwest Conference. *See* Southwest Conference.

Big Sky Conference (basketball, football Division I-AA).

Boise State Broncos	Orange & Blue
Eastern Washington Eagles	Red & White
Idaho Vandals	Silver & Gold
Idaho State Bengals	Orange & Black
Montana Grizzlies	Copper, Silver & Gold
Montana State Bobcats	Blue & Gold
Northern Arizona Lumberjacks	Blue & Gold
Weber State Wildcats	Royal Purple & White

Individual and Team Sports

Big South Conference (basketball).

Charleston Southern Buccaneers	Blue & Gold
Coastal Carolina Chanticleers	Coastal Green, Bronze & Black
Liberty Flames	Red, White & Blue
Maryland-Baltimore County Retrievers	
N.C.-Asheville Bulldogs	Royal Blue & White
Radford Highlanders	Blue, Red, Green & White
Winthrop Eagles	Garnet & Gold

Big Ten Conference (all sports). Big 10 is acceptable in all references. Although there are 11 teams in this Division I conference, do not refer to this conference as the Big 11.

Illinois Fighting Illini	Orange & Blue
Indiana Hoosiers	Cream & Crimson
Iowa Hawkeyes	Old Gold & Black
Michigan Wolverines	Maize & Blue
Michigan State Spartans	Green & White
Minnesota Golden Gophers	Maroon & Gold
Northwestern Wildcats	Purple & White
Ohio State Buckeyes	Scarlet & Gray
Penn State Nittany Lions	Blue & White
Purdue Boilermakers	Old Gold & Black
Wisconsin Badgers	Cardinal & White

Big West Conference (basketball).

California State-Fullerton Titans	Blue, Orange & White
UC Irvine Anteaters	Blue & Gold
UC Santa Barbara Gauchos	Blue & Gold
Long Beach State 49ers	Black & Gold
* Nevada-Las Vegas (UNLV) Rebels	Scarlet & Gray
Nevada-Reno Wolf Pack	Silver & Blue
New Mexico State Aggies	Crimson & White
Pacific Tigers	Orange & Black
* San Jose State Spartans	Gold, White & Blue
Utah State Aggies	Navy Blue & White

Big West Conference (football Division I-A).

Arkansas State Indians	Scarlet & Black
Louisiana Tech Bulldogs	Red & Blue
* Nevada-Las Vegas (UNLV) Rebels	Scarlet & Gray
Nevada-Reno Wolf Pack	Silver & Black
New Mexico State Aggies	Crimson & White
Northern Illinois Huskies	Cardinal & Black
Pacific Tigers	Orange & Black
* San Jose State Spartans	Gold, White & Blue
Southwestern Louisiana Ragin' Cajuns	Vermilion & White
Utah State Aggies	Navy Blue & White

* UNLV and San Jose State will join the Western Athletic Conference starting with the 1996-1997 season.

Colonial Athletic Association (basketball).

American University Eagles	Red, White & Blue
East Carolina Pirates	Purple & Gold
George Mason Patriots	Green & Gold
James Madison Dukes	Purple & Gold
Old Dominion Monarchs	Slate Blue & Silver
Richmond Spiders	Red & Blue
N.C.-Wilmington Seahawks	Green, Gold & Navy Blue
Virginia Commonwealth Rams	Black & Gold
William and Mary Tribe	Green, Gold & Silver

Conference USA (basketball).

Alabama-Birmingham Blazers	Green, Gold & White
Cincinnati Bearcats	Red & Black
DePaul Blue Demons	Scarlet & Blue
Louisville Cardinals	Red, Black & White
Marquette Golden Eagles	Blue & Gold
Memphis Tigers	Blue & Gray
N.C.-Charlotte 49ers	Green & White
St. Louis Billikens	Blue & White
South Florida Bulls	Green & Gold
Southern Mississippi Golden Eagles	Black & Gold
Tulane Green Wave	Olive Green & Sky Blue

Gateway Football Conference (football Division I-AA).

Eastern Ill. Panthers	Blue & Gray
Illinois State Redbirds	Red & White
Indiana State Sycamores	Blue & White
Northern Iowa Panthers	Purple & Old Gold
Southern Ill. Salukis	Maroon & White
Southwest Mo. State Bears	Maroon & White
Western Ill. Leathernecks	Purple & Gold

Ivy Group. Do not refer to as the Ivy League or Ivy Conference. The following teams make up this Division I basketball and Division I-AA football group.

Brown Bears	Seal Brown, Cardinal & White
Columbia Lions	Columbia Blue & White
Cornell Big Red	Carnelian & White
Dartmouth Big Green	Dartmouth Green & White
Harvard Crimson	Crimson, Black & White
Pennsylvania (Penn) Quakers	Red & Blue
Princeton Tigers	Orange & Black
Yale Bulldogs, Elis	Yale Blue & White

Metro Atlantic Athletic Conference (basketball).

Canisius Golden Griffins	Blue & Gold
Fairfield Stags	Cardinal Red
Iona Gaels	Maroon & Gold
Loyola (Md.) Greyhounds	Green & Grey
Manhattan Jaspers	Kelly Green & White
Niagara Purple Eagles	Purple, White & Gold
St. Peter's Peacocks	Blue & White
Siena Saints	Green & Gold

Individual and Team Sports   281

Metro Atlantic Athletic Conference (football Division I-AA).

Canisius Golden Griffins	Blue & Gold
Duquesne Dukes	Red & Blue
Iona Gaels	Maroon & Gold
Georgetown Hoyas	Blue & Gray
St. John's Red Storm	Red & White
St. Peters Peacocks	Blue & White
Siena Saints	Green & Gold

Mid-American Athletic Conference (basketball, football Division I-A).

Akron Zips	Blue & Gold
Ball State Cardinals	Cardinal & White
Bowling Green Falcons	Orange & Brown
Central Michigan Chippewas	Maroon & Gold
Eastern Michigan Eagles	Dark Green & White
Kent Golden Flashes	Navy Blue & Gold
Miami (Ohio) Redskins	Red & White
Ohio University Bobcats	Green & White
Toledo Rockets	Blue & Gold
Western Michigan Broncos	Brown & Gold

Mid-Continent Conference (basketball).

Buffalo Bengals	Orange & Black
Central Connecticut State Blue Devils	Blue & White
Chicago State Cougars	Green & White
Eastern Illinois Panthers	Blue & Gray
Missouri-Kansas City (UMKC) Kangaroos	Blue & Gold
Northeastern Illinois Golden Eagles	Royal Blue & Gold
Troy St. Trojans	Cardinal, Silver & Black
Valparaiso Crusaders	Brown & Gold
Western Illinois Leathernecks	Purple & Gold
Youngstown State Penguins	Red & White

Mid-Eastern Athletic Conference (football Division I-AA).

Bethune-Cookman Wildcats	Blue & Gold
Delaware State Hornets	Red & Black
Florida A & M Rattlers	Orange & Green
Howard Bison	Blue, White & Red
Morgan State Bears	Blue & Orange
North Carolina A & T Aggies	Blue & Gold
South Carolina State Bulldogs	Garnet & Blue

Mid-Eastern Athletic Conference (basketball).

Bethune-Cookman Wildcats	Blue & Gold
Coppin State Eagles	Royal Blue & Gold
Delaware State Hornets	Red & Black
Florida A & M Rattlers	Orange & Green
Hampton Pirates	Royal Blue & White
Howard Bison	Blue, White & Red
Maryland-Eastern Shore Hawks	Maroon & Gray
Morgan State Bears	Blue & Orange
North Carolina A & T Aggies	Blue & Gold
South Carolina State Bulldogs	Garnet & Blue

Midwestern Collegiate Conference (basketball).

Butler Bulldogs	Blue & White
Cleveland State Vikings	Green & White
Detroit Mercy Titans	White & Blue
Illinois of Chicago Flames	Indigo & Flame
Loyola (Ill.) Ramblers	Maroon & Gold
Northern Illinois Huskies	Cardinal & Black
Wisconsin-Green Bay Phoenix	Green, White & Phoenix Red
Wisconsin-Milwaukee Panthers	Black & Gold
Wright State Raiders	Green & Gold

Missouri Valley Conference (basketball).

Bradley Braves	Red & White
Creighton Bluejays	Blue & White
Drake Bulldogs	Blue & White
Evansville Purple Aces	Purple & White
Illinois State Redbirds	Red & White
Indiana State Sycamores	Blue & White
Northern Iowa Panthers	Purple & Old Gold
Southern Illinois Salukis	Maroon & White
Southwest Missouri State Bears	Maroon & White
Tulsa Golden Hurricane	Blue & Gold
Wichita State Shockers	Yellow & Black

North Atlantic Conference (basketball).

Boston University Terriers	Scarlet & White
Delaware Fightin' Blue Hens	Blue & Gold
Drexel Dragons	Navy Blue & Gold
Hartford Hawks	Scarlet & White
Hofstra Flying Dutchmen	Blue, White & Gold
Maine Black Bears	Blue & White
New Hampshire Wildcats	Blue & White
Northeastern Huskies	Red & Black
Towson State Tigers	Gold, White & Black
Vermont Catamounts	Green & Gold

Northeast Conference (basketball).

FDU-Teaneck Knights	Maroon, White & Blue
LIU-Brooklyn Blackbirds	Blue & White
Marist Red Foxes	Black, Red & White
Monmouth (N.J.) Hawks	Royal Blue & White
Mt. St. Mary's (Md.) Mountaineers	Blue & White
Rider Broncs	Cranberry & White
Robert Morris Colonials	Blue & White
St. Francis (N.Y.) Terriers	Red & Blue
St. Francis (Pa.) Red Flash	Red & White
Wagner Seahawks	Green & White

Individual and Team Sports

Ohio Valley Conference (basketball, football Division I-AA).

Austin Peay Governors	Red & White
Eastern Kentucky Colonels	Maroon & White
Middle Tennessee State Blue Raiders	Blue & White
Morehead State Eagles	Blue & Gold
Murray State Racers	Blue & Gold
Southeast Missouri State Indians	Red & Black
Tennessee-Martin Pacers	Orange, White & Royal Blue
Tennessee State Tigers	Royal Blue & White
Tennessee Tech Golden Eagles	Purple & Gold

Pacific-10 Conference (basketball, football Division I-A). Pac-10 is acceptable on second reference.

Arizona Wildcats	Cardinal & Navy
Arizona State Sun Devils	Maroon & Gold
California-Berkeley Golden Bears	Blue & Gold
Oregon Ducks	Green & Yellow
Oregon State Beavers	Orange & Black
Southern California Trojans	Cardinal & Gold
Stanford Cardinal	Cardinal & White
UCLA Bruins	Blue & Gold
Washington Huskies	Purple & Gold
Washington State Cougars	Crimson & Gray

Patriot League (football Division I-AA).

Bucknell Bison	Orange & Blue
Colgate Red Raiders	Maroon
Fordham Rams	Maroon & White
Holy Cross Crusaders	Royal Purple
Lafayette Leopards	Maroon & White
Lehigh Engineers	Brown & White

Patriot League (basketball).

Army Cadets, Black Knights	Black, Gold & Gray
Bucknell Bison	Orange & Blue
Colgate Red Raiders	Maroon
Fordham Rams	Maroon & White
Holy Cross Crusaders	Royal Purple
Lafayette Leopards	Maroon & White
Lehigh Engineers	Brown & White
Navy Midshipmen	Navy Blue & Gold

Pioneer Football League (Division I-AA).

Butler Bulldogs	Blue & White
Dayton Flyers	Red & Blue
Drake Bulldogs	Blue & White
Evansville Purple Aces	Purple & White
San Diego Toreros	Columbia Blue, Navy & White
Valparaiso Crusaders	Brown & Gold

Southeastern Conference (basketball, football Division I-A). SEC is acceptable on the second reference.

East Division

Florida Gators	Blue & Orange
Georgia Bulldogs	Red & Black
Kentucky Wildcats	Blue & White
South Carolina Fighting Gamecocks	Garnet & Black
Tennessee Volunteers	Orange & White
Vanderbilt Commodores	Black & Gold

West Division

Alabama Crimson Tides	Crimson & White
Arkansas Razorbacks	Cardinal & White
Auburn Tigers	Burnt Orange & Navy Blue
Louisiana State Tigers	Purple & Gold
Mississippi Rebels	Cardinal Red & Navy Blue
Mississippi State Bulldogs	Maroon & White

Individual and Team Sports

Southern Conference (football Division I-AA).

Appalachian State Mountaineers	Black & Gold
Citadel Bulldogs, Cadets	Blue & White
East Tennessee State Buccaneers	Blue & Gold
Furman Paladins	Purple & White
Georgia Southern Eagles	Blue & White
Marshall Thundering Herd	Green & White
Tennessee-Chattanooga Moccasins	Navy Blue & Gold
Virginia Military Keydats	Red, White & Yellow
Western Carolina Catamounts	Purple & Gold

Southern Conference (basketball).

Appalachian State Mountaineers	Black & Gold
Citadel Bulldogs, Cadets	Blue & White
Davidson Wildcats	Red & Black
East Tennessee State Buccaneers	Blue & Gold
Furman Paladins	Purple & White
Georgia Southern Eagles	Blue & White
Marshall Thundering Herd	Green & White
N.C.-Greensboro Spartans	Gold, White & Navy
Tennessee-Chattanooga Moccasins	Navy Blue & Gold
Virginia Military Keydats	Red, White & Yellow
Western Carolina Catamounts	Purple & Gold

Southland Conference (football Division I-AA).

McNeese State Cowboys	Blue & Gold
Nicholls State Colonels	Red & Gray
North Texas Mean Green Eagles	Green & White
Northeast Louisiana Indians	Maroon & Gold
Northwestern State Demons	Purple & White
Sam Houston State Bearkats	Orange & White
Southwest Texas State Bobcats	Maroon & Gold
Stephen F. Austin Lumberjacks	Purple & White

Southland Conference (basketball).

McNeese State Cowboys	Blue & Gold
Nicholls State Colonels	Red & Gray
North Texas Mean Green Eagles	Green & White
Northeast Louisiana Indians	Maroon & Gold
Northwestern State Demons	Purple & White
Sam Houston State Bearkats	Orange & White
Southwest Texas State Bobcats	Maroon & Gold
Stephen F. Austin Lumberjacks	Purple & White
Texas-Arlington Mavericks	Royal Blue & White
Texas-San Antonio Roadrunners	Orange, Navy Blue & White

Southwest Conference: As of June 30, 1996, this conference will dissolve. Baylor, Texas, Texas A & M, and Texas Tech will move to the Big Eight (which will be renamed the Big 12). Rice, SMU, and TCU will move to the Western Athletic Conference. Houston will be a Division I-A independent.

Baylor Bears	Green & Gold
Houston Cougars	Scarlet & White
Rice Owls	Blue & Gray
Southern Methodist Mustangs	Red & Blue
Texas Longhorns	Burnt Orange & White
Texas A & M Aggies	Maroon & White
Texas Christian Horned Frogs	Purple & White
Texas Tech Red Raiders	Scarlet & Black

Southwestern Athletic Conference (basketball, football Division I-AA).

Alabama State Hornets	Black & Old Gold
Alcorn State Braves	Purple & Gold
Grambling Tigers	Black & Gold
Jackson State Tigers	Blue & White
Mississippi Valley Delta Devils	Green & White
Prairie View A & M Panthers	Purple & White
Southern University and A & M Jaguars	Blue & Gold
Texas Southern Tigers	Maroon & Gray

Sun Belt Conference (basketball).

Arkansas Little Rock Trojans	Maroon & White
Arkansas State Indians	Scarlet & Black
Jacksonville (Fla.) Dolphins	Green & Gold
Lamar Cardinals	Red & White
Louisiana Tech Bulldogs	Red & Blue
New Orleans Privateers	Royal Blue & Silver
South Alabama Jaguars	Red, White & Blue
Southwestern Louisiana Ragin' Cajuns	Vermilion & White
Texas-Pan American Broncos	Green & White
Western Kentucky Hilltoppers	Red & White

Trans America Athletic Conference (basketball).

Campbell Fighting Camels	Orange & Black
Centenary College (La.) Gentleman	Maroon & White
Central Florida Golden Knights	Black & Gold
Charleston (S.C.) Cougars	Maroon & White
Florida Atlantic Owls	Blue & Gray
Florida International Golden Panthers	Blue & Yellow
Georgia State Panthers	Royal Blue, Crimson & White
Mercer Bears	Orange & Black
Samford Bulldogs	Crimson & Blue
Southeastern Louisiana Lions	Green & Gold
Stetson Hatters	Green & White

West Coast Conference (basketball).

Gonzaga Bulldogs, Zags	Blue, White & Red
Loyola Marymount Lions	Crimson & Blue
Pepperdine Waves	Blue & Orange
Portland Pilots	Purple & White
St. Mary's (Cal.) Gaels	Red & Blue
San Diego Toreros	Columbia Blue, Navy & White
San Francisco Dons	Green & Gold
Santa Clara Broncos	Bronco Red & White

Western Athletic Conference (basketball, football Division I-A).

Air Force Falcons	Blue & Silver
Brigham Young (Utah) Cougars	Royal Blue & White
Colorado State Rams	Green & Gold
Fresno State Bulldogs	Cardinal & Blue
Hawaii Rainbow Warriors	Green & White
New Mexico Lobos	Cherry & Silver
San Diego State Aztecs	Scarlet & Black
Texas El Paso (UTEP) Miners	Orange, White & Blue
Utah Utes	Crimson & White
Wyoming Cowboys	Brown & Yellow

Beginning June 30, 1996, the WAC will have a new configuration with the addition of six new teams: Rice, San Jose State, SMU, TCU, Tulsa, and UNLV.

QUAD 1:	QUAD 2:	QUAD 3:	QUAD 4:
Rice	Air Force	BYU	Fresno State
SMU	Colorado State	New Mexico	Hawaii
TCU	UNLV	Utah	San Diego State
Tulsa	Wyoming	UTEP	San Jose State

Yankee Conference (football Division I-AA).

MID-ATLANTIC DIVISION

Delaware Fightin' Blue Hens	Blue & Gold
James Madison Dukes	Purple & Gold
Northeastern (Mass.) Huskies	Red & Black
Richmond Spiders	Red & Blue
Villanova Wildcats	Blue & White
William & Mary Tribe	Green, Gold & Silver

NEW ENGLAND DIVISION

Boston University Terriers	Scarlet & White
Connecticut (UConn) Huskies	National Flag Blue & White
Maine Black Bears	Blue & White
Massachusetts (UMass) Minutemen	Maroon & White
New Hampshire Wildcats	Blue & White
Rhode Island Rams	Blue & White

Independents (basketball).

Oral Roberts Golden Eagles	Navy Blue, White & Vegas Gold
Wofford Terriers	Old Gold & Black
Houston Cougars (1996-1997 Season)	Scarlet & White

Independents (football Division I-A).

Army Cadets, Black Knights	Black, Gold & Gray
Cincinnati Bearcats	Red & Black
East Carolina Pirates	Purple & Gold
Louisville Cardinals	Red, Black & White
Memphis Tigers	Blue & Gray
Navy Midshipmen	Navy & Gold
Northeast Louisiana Indians	Maroon & Gold
Notre Dame Fighting Irish	Gold & Blue
Southern Mississippi Golden Eagles	Black & Gold
Tulane Green Wave	Olive Green & Sky Blue
Tulsa Golden Hurricane*	Blue & Gold

*Tulsa will join the Western Athletic Conference beginning with the 1996-1997 season.

Independents (football Division I-AA).

Alabama-Birmingham Blazers	Gold & White
Buffalo Bulls	Buffalo Blue, White & Red
Central Connecticut State Blue Devils	Blue & White
Central Florida Golden Knights	Blue & Gold
Charleston South Buccaneers	Blue & Gold
Davidson Wildcats	Red & Black
Hampton Pirates	Royal Blue & White
Hofstra Flying Dutchmen	Blue, Gold & White
Jacksonville State Gamecocks	Red & White
Liberty Flames	Red, White & Blue
Monmouth (N.J.) Hawks	Royal Blue & White
Robert Morris Colonials	Blue & White
St. Francis (Pa.) Red Flash	Red & White

St. Mary's (Calif.) Gaels	Red & Blue
Samford Bulldogs	Crimson & Blue
Towson State Tigers	Gold & White
Troy State Trojans	Cardinal, Gray & Black
Wagner Seahawks	Green & White
Western Kentucky Hilltoppers	Red & White
Wofford Terriers	Old Gold & Black
Youngstown State Penguins	Red & White

Scoring

Box Scores

Basketball: Follow the same format for professional basketball except for the standings, which should read:

	Conference			All Games		
	W	L	Pct	W	L	Pct
Wisconsin	12	2	.857	24	4	.857
etc.						

Football: Follow the same format for professional football except for the standings, which should read:

	Conference				All Games			
	W	L	T	Pts.	OP	W	L	T	Pts.	OP
N'western	7	3	0	240	150	10	5	0	405	288
etc.										

In standings, limit college team names to 9 letters or fewer.

Cross Country *See* running.

Cricket

Terms

batsman	wicket
fieldsman	side-bye
leg-bye	

Governing Body

World Cricket League
301 W. 57th St. Suite 5D
New York, NY 10019
(212) 582-8556

Scoring

Use the match summary:

EXAMPLE:

Surrey def. Hoscar, 12-6.

Curling

Terms

back line
foot line
hog line
skip
tee line

Governing Body

U.S. Curling Association
1100 Centerpoint Dr.
Stevens Point, WI 54481
(715) 344-1199

Cycling

Terms

break	gap	pull
breakaway	hammering	pursuit
bridge	jam	sitting in
contre la montre	jump	sprint
drafting	mass start	Tour de France
echelon	pace line (n.)	wind-out (n.)
field	pace-line (adj.)	wind-up (n.)
field sprint	pedal (n., v.)	
force the pace	pole line	

Governing Bodies

National Cycling League
532 La Guardia Place Suite 162
New York, NY 10012
(212) 777-3611
National league of professional outdoor teams

United States Professional Cycling Federation
7733 Brobst Hill Rd.
New Tripoli, PA 18066
(215) 298-3262
Governing body of national professional racing team

U.S. Cycling Federation
One Olympic Plaza
Colorado Springs, CO 80909
(719) 578-4628
Governing body of national amateur racing team

Leagues and Teams

National Cycling League teams are:

Amsterdam Flying Dutchman
Forza Milano

Houston Outlaws
London Lancers
Los Angeles Wings
Miami Wave
New York Ghost Riders
Pittsburgh Power
Portland Thunder
Tulsa Cyclones

Scoring

Scored in hours, minutes, seconds, and tenths and hundredths of a second when available. Use the basic summary format.

> Olympic finals at Montmerle
> Men's team road race final
> (100 kilometers)
> 1. Germany 2:01:39.00; 2. Italy 2:02:39.00l; 3. France 2:05:25.00; 4. etc.

> Women's individual road race
> 1. Kathryn Watt, Australia, 2:04:42; 2. Jeannie Longo-Ciprelli, France, 2:05:02; 3. Monique Knol, Netherlands, same time; 4. etc.

Decathlon *See* track and field.

Diving

Terms

armstand dive	platform
back dive	reverse dive
forward dive	straight
free	tuck
inward dive	twisting dive
layout (n., adj.)	springboard
pike	

Governing Body

United States Diving
201 S. Capitol Ave. Suite 510
Indianapolis, IN 46225
(317) 237-5252
Selects and trains diving team for international competition

Scoring

Scoring is in points, based on a combination of scores from a panel
of judges. Use the basic summary.

EXAMPLE:

> WOMEN
> Springboard preliminary rounds
> (top 12 advance to tomorrow's finals)
> > 1. Irina Lachko, Unified Team, 334.890 points; 2. Brit Pia Bal-
> > dus, Germany, 312.900; 3. etc.

Dog Racing

Usage

When writing about dogs, do not use a personal pronoun unless
gender has been established or the dog has a name.

> The dog won its race.
> Kansas Sue won her third race.

Governing Body

American Greyhound Council
1065 N.E. 125th St. Suite 219
N. Miami, FL 33161-5832
(305) 893-2101
Promotes greyhound racing in the U.S.

Scoring

See horse racing for examples.

Equestrian

Terms

American Horse Shows Association (AHSA)
aids
canter
course
dressage
distance fault
Fédération Equestre Internationale
fence
grand prix dressage
grand prix jumping
hazard
on the flat
stride
test
trot
United States Equestrian Team (USET)
walk
walking the course

Governing Bodies

American Horse Shows Association
220 East 42nd St.
New York, NY 10017-5876
(212) 972-2472

Fédération Equestre Internationale
Bollingenstrasse 54
Boite Postale
Berne 32, CH-3000
Switzerland
+41 +31/429 342

United States Equestrian Team (USET)
Potterville Rd.
Gladstone, NJ 07934
(908) 234-1251
Sponsors and trains national team

Scoring

Scoring is in points. Use the basic summary, noting type of competition. In individual events, list rider, country or city, horse, and points or time. In team events, include team members.

EXAMPLE:

Equestrian
Individual Show Jumping
1. Pierre Durand, France, Jappeloup, 1.25; 2. Greg Best, United States, Gem Twist, 4.00 (won jump off); 3. Karsten Huck, Germany, Nepomuk, 4.00.

Team Dressage
1. Switzerland, 4,164, Otto Hofer, Christine Stuekelberger, Daniel Ramseier, Samuel Schatzmann; 2. Canada, 3,969, Cynthia Ishoy, Eva Maria Pracht, Gina Smith, Ashley Nicoll; 3. etc.

Fencing

Terms

advance	engagement	piste
attack	en guard	pommel
beat	enveloppement	president
closing in	épée	recover
composite attack	feint	remise
counterattack	flèche	riposte
counter-party	foil	sabre
counter-riposte	glide	simple
coupé	guard	stop thrust
director	jump	strip
disengage	lunge	taking
double touch	parry	thrust

Governing Bodies

United States Fencing Association
One Olympic Plaza
Colorado Springs, CO 80909
(719) 578-4511
Selects and trains national team

Federation Internationale D'Escrime
32, rue de la Boetie
Paris, 75008
France
+33 +1/4561-1484
International governing body

Scoring

Use match summary for early rounds of major events, for lesser dual meets, and for tournaments.

Use basic summary for final results of major championships.

EXAMPLE:

> MEN
> Individual épée
> Championship match
> Eric Srecki, France, def. Pavel Kolokov, Unified Team, 6-5, 5-2.
>
> Final standings
> 1. Eric Srecki, France; 2. Pavel Kolokov, Unified Team; 3. Jean-Michel Henry, France.

For major events, where competitors are divided into pools and meet in a round-robin tournament, follow this form:

> Épée, first round (four qualify for semi-finals) Pool 1—Joe Smith, Springfield, Mass., 4-1; Enrique Lopez, Chile, 3-2; etc.

Field Hockey

Terms

corner hit
free hit
obstruction
offside

penalty corner
penalty stroke
push back (n.)

Governing Bodies

United States Field Hockey Association
One Olympic Plaza
Colorado Springs, CO 80909
(719) 578-4567
Selects and trains national team

Federation Internationale de Hockey
1, Ave des Arts (Boite 5)
Bruxelles, B-1040
Belgium
+32 +2/319 4537
International governing body

Scoring

Show standings and final results.

EXAMPLE:

Field Hockey
MEN
Pool A

	W	L	T	GF	GA	Pts.
Australia	3	0	1	14	2	7
Germany	3	0	1	14	3	7
Britain	3	1	0	7	4	6
etc.						

Championship game:
Australia def. Pakistan, 3-2.

Final standings:
1. Australia; 2. Pakistan; 3. etc.

Figure Skating

Terms

axel	Salchow
compulsory routine	short program
death spiral	spin
flip	split jump
ice dancing	three turn
long program	throw jumps
loop	toe loop
Lutz	double-toe loop
pairs skating	triple-toe loop
Russian split	U.S. Figure Skating Association (USFSA)

Governing Bodies

U.S. Figure Skating Association
20 First St.
Colorado Springs, CO 80906
(719) 635-5200
Selects and trains national skating team

Scoring

Use the basic summary format with the skater's name, hometown or country, points and ordinals. In pairs, list the woman's name, her partner's name, their country or hometown, and their score.

Figure skating—Women's final
1. Dorothy Hamill, Riverside, Conn. 9.0 ordinals, 215 points; 2. Dianne de Leeuw, Netherlands, 20.0, 236; 3. etc.

Pairs final
1. Ekaterina Gordeeva, Sergei Grinkov, Soviet Union, 1.4 ordinals, 220 points; 2. Elena Valova, Oleg Vassiliev, Soviet Union, 2.8, 246; 3. etc.

Fishing

Terms

BASS Masters Classic
fly-fishing
gamefish
IGFA
jig
jigging
waders

Governing Bodies

International Game Fish Association
1301 East Atlantic Blvd.
Pompano Beach, FL 33060
(305) 941-3474
Governing body for freshwater, saltwater, and fly fishing

Bassing America
4398 Sunbelt Dr.
Dallas, TX 75248
(214) 380-2656
Sponsors bass fishing events

Scoring

Use match summary.

BASS Masters Classic at Birmingham, Ala.
Leaders after the first day of the BASS Masters Classic on Lake
Logan Martin, with angler's hometown, number of fish, and
weight in pounds and ounces.

1. Denny Brauer, Camdenton, Mo. 7, 22-13; 2. Rick Clunn, Mont-
gomery, Texas, 7, 21-0; 3. etc.

Football

Terms

All-Pro (n., adj.)
all-purpose yards
audible
audibilize
backfield
backup
ball carrier
ballclub
blitz (n., v.)
bootleg
bump-and-run
clip (n.)
clipping (v.)
cornerback
crackback block
crossbar
delay of game
delay-of-game (adj.)
down-and-in
down-and-out
downfield
drop back (v.)
drop-back (adj.)
drop kick (n.)
drop-kick (v.)
encroachment
end line
end zone
fair catch
fair catch signal
field goal
field-goal attempt
first-and-10
first quarter (n.)
first-quarter (adj.)
flea flicker
fourth-and-one
4-3 defense
free-blocking zone
free kick (n.)

free-kick (v.)
fullback
game clock
goal line
goal-line stand
goal post
halfback
hand off (v.)
handoff (n.)
hash mark
kicker
kick off (v.)
kickoff (n., adj.)
I-formation
inadvertent whistle
injured-reserve list
intentional ground-
 ing
left guard
linebacker
line judge
lineman (player)
line of scrimmage
linesman (official)
locker room
loss of down
man in motion
muff
nickel package
nose guard
nose tackle
off-setting penalties
offside
onside kick
out of bounds (n.)
out-of-bounds (adj.)
pass interference
pick-and-roll
pitch out (v.)
pitchout (n.)

placekicker
play-action pass
play off (v.)
playoff (n., adj.)
point after (n.)
point-after attempt
quarterback
runback
running back
safety
scoreboard
shovel pass
sideline
spearing
special teams
special teams coach
split end
square-out
straight-arm (n., v.)
tailback
T-formation
3-4 defense
tight end
timeout
touchback
touchdown
triple-option of-
 fense
turnover
TV timeout
two-minute warn-
 ing
unsportsmanlike
 conduct
walk-on
weak side (n.)
weak-side (adj.)
wide receiver
wishbone

Usage

AFC Acronym is acceptable on first reference for American Football Conference.

Arena Football League Spell out Arena Football League on first reference, then AFL.

Canadian Football League CFL is acceptable on first reference.

Eastern Division Acceptable if it is an obvious reference to the NFC or the AFC individually.

franchise player Under the NFL's Collective Bargaining Agreement, a franchise player is one whose team must offer a one-year contract at the average of the five highest-paid players at the franchise player's position or a 20 percent increase, whichever is greater. A transition player is one whose team must tender a one-year contract at the average of the 10 highest-paid players at the transition player's position or a 20 percent raise, whichever is greater.

free agent The NFL Collective Bargaining Agreement defines an unrestricted free agent as a player with four or more seasons of free agency experience. A restricted free agent is defined as a player with three seasons of free agency experience who is subject to compensation and/or right of first refusal.

Do not hyphenate free agent before a player's name or as a noun.

> The Reds picked up free agent Bob Lowden.
> Coldwell is an unrestricted free agent.

Hyphenate free-agent when it is used before a word other than a player's name.

> Dax wants to test the free-agent market.

Grey Cup The Grey Cup has been awarded to the CFL champion since 1954.

Lombardi Trophy Spell out Vince Lombardi Trophy on first reference. The trophy is awarded to the winner of the Super Bowl.

NFC Acronym is acceptable on first reference for National Football Conference.

National Football League NFL is acceptable on all references. The NFL is made up of six divisions in two conferences.

numbers Use figures for yardage. The 5-yard line, the 10-yard line, an 8-yard pass. Exception: a third-and-seven play.

> The Texas eleven won the game.
> The score was 17-15.
> The team record is 4-5-1.

Spell out numbers one through nine as in the following examples:

> Bradshaw completed four of five passes.
> The kicker was three for six.
> The Raiders faced a fourth-and-four situation.
> We took the lead in the third quarter.
> The Panthers passed on second down.

Use figures for numbers greater than nine and as in the following examples:

> Did the Bears retire Walter Payton's No. 34?
> Who will be the No. 1 draft pick?
> Bradeck ran to the 9-yard line.
> Meiners had a 5-yard return.
> The team gained 3 yards.
> Schwartz tied the game with a field goal with .5 seconds on the clock.

Pro Bowl The NFL All-Star game.

Pro Bowler

Rozelle Award Spell out Pete Rozelle Award on first reference. The award is given to the Most Valuable Player in the Super Bowl.

Super Bowl Note spelling, the championship game played between the NFC and AFC is not the superbowl.

The first championship game was played on Jan. 15, 1967, between the Green Bay Packers and Kansas City Chiefs in Los Angeles, but it was not called the Super Bowl. It was referred to as the World Championship Game.

uniforms Uniforms have the following numbers:

1-19	quarterback, placekicker, punter
10-19	wide receiver (if 80-89 are otherwise assigned)
20-49	running back, defensive back, safety, cornerback, full back
50-59	center, linebacker
60-69	center (if 50-59 are unavailable)
70-79	offensive guard, tackle, defensive lineman
80-89	wide receiver, tight end
90-99	defensive lineman (if 60-79 are unavailable)
90-99	linebacker (if 50-59 are unavailable)

Western Division Acceptable if it is an obvious reference to either the AFC or the NFC singly.

Governing Bodies

NFL
410 Park Ave.
New York, NY 10022
(212) 758-1500

CFL
Fifth Floor
110 Eglinton Ave. West
Toronto, ON M4R 1A3
Canada
(416) 322-9650

Arena Football League
220 W. Commercial Blvd. Suite 101
Ft. Lauderdale, FL 33309
(305) 777-2700

Leagues and Teams

National Football League

National Football Conference

EAST	CENTRAL	WEST
Dallas Cowboys	Chicago Bears	Atlanta Falcons
N.Y. Giants	Detroit Lions	L.A. Rams
Philadelphia Eagles	Green Bay Packers	New Orleans Saints
Arizona Cardinals	Minnesota Vikings	San Francisco 49ers
Washington Redskins	Tampa Bay Buccaneers	Carolina Panthers

American Football Conference

EAST	CENTRAL	WEST
Buffalo Bills	Cincinnati Bengals	Denver Broncos
Indianapolis Colts	Cleveland Browns	Kansas City Chiefs
Miami Dolphins	Houston Oilers	L.A. Raiders
New England Patriots	Pittsburgh Steelers	San Diego Chargers
N.Y. Jets	Seattle Seahawks	Jacksonville Jaguars

Canadian Football League

NORTH DIVISION	SOUTH DIVISION
British Columbia Lions	Baltimore Stallions
Calgary Stampeders	Birmingham Barracudas
Edmonton Eskimos	Memphis Mad Dogs
Hamilton Tiger-Cats	San Antonio Texans
Ottawa Rough Riders	Shreveport Pirates
Saskatchewan Roughriders	
Toronto Argonauts	
Winnipeg Blue Bombers	

Arena Football League

CENTRAL DIVISION	EASTERN DIVISION
Iowa Barnstormers	Albany Firebirds
Memphis Pharaohs	Charlotte Rage
St. Louis Stampede	Connecticut Coyotes

WESTERN DIVISION	SOUTHERN DIVISION
Anaheim Piranhas	Houston
Arizona Rattlers	Florida Bobcats
San Jose SaberCats	Tampa Bay Storm

Scoring

Always list the visiting team first.

Field goals are measured from where the ball was kicked (not the line of scrimmage) to the goal posts (not the end zone).

Abbreviate team names to four or fewer letters on scoring and statistical lines.

The passing line shows, in this order: completions-attempts-had intercepted.

EXAMPLE:

(Timing is elapsed time, not time remaining.)

Northwestern	7	3	7	0-17
Notre Dame	0	9	0	6-15

How They Scored
First Quarter
NU—Beazley 7 pass from Schnur (Valenzisi)

Second Quarter
ND—FG Kopka 35
NU—FG Valenzisi 37
ND—Farmer 5 run (kick failed)

Third Quarter
NU—Bates 26 pass from Schnur (Valenzisi)

Fourth Quarter
ND—Kinder 2 run (pass failed)
A—53,134

	NU	ND
First downs	17	17
Rushes—yards	15-95	48-238
Passing yards	215	67
Sacks by—yards	4-28	2-16
3rd down eff.	4-10-40.0	10-19-53.0
4th down eff.	0-0-0.0	1-1-1.0
Passes	20-38-5	11-20-0
Punts	4-39.8	11-20.0
Punt return—yards	1-11	1-11

KO returns—yards	4-48	3-72
Fumbles—lost	1-1	2-2
Penalties—yards	7-54	2-19
Time of Possession	24:16	35:44

Individual Statistics:

RUSHING—Northwestern—D. Autry 33-160, A. Autry 1-5, Hartl 1-4, Schnur 4-(minus 4), Notre Dame—Farmer 16-85, Kinder 12-68, Edwards 10-49, Stokes 2-15, Mosley 1-3, Powlus 6-(minus 24).

PASSING—Northwestern—Schnur 14-28-0-166, Washington—Powlus 17-26-0-175.

RECEIVING—Northwestern—Bates 4-58, Musso 2-42, Beazley 2-28, Hartl 2-25, D. Autry 2-8, Graham 1-3, Drexler 1-2.

Notre Dame—Mayes 8-94, Edwards 4-37, Mosley 1-26, Chryplewicz 1-13, Farmer 1-6, Wallace 1-5, Kinder 1-(minus 6).

SACKS—Northwestern—Baker 1-10, Grooms 1-6. Notre Dame—Mann 3-18.

INTERCEPTIONS—Northwestern—None. Notre Dame—Kaufman 1-10, Cherry 1-22, Green 1-0.

MISSED FIELD GOALS—Northwestern—None. Notre Dame—Kopka 42.

Stadiums

The following is a list of NFL teams, their phone numbers, home field, its address, phone number, and seating capacity.

TEAM	STADIUM	PERMANENT SEATING CAPACITY
Arizona Cardinals (602) 379-0101	Sun Devil Stadium Arizona State University I.C.A. Building Stadium Drive & College Ave. Tempe, AZ 85287 (602) 965-2666	73,521
Atlanta Falcons (404) 945-1111	Georgia Dome One Georgia Dome Drive N.W. Atlanta, GA 30313-1591 (404) 223-9200	71,280

Buffalo Bills (716) 648-1800	Rich Stadium 1 Bills Drive Orchard Park, NY 14127 (716) 649-0015	80,024
Carolina Panthers (704) 358-1644	Carolina Stadium 800-1 South Mint St. Charlotte, NC 28202 (704) 358-1644	n/a
Chicago Bears (708) 295-6600	Soldier Field 425 E. McFetridge Drive Chicago, IL 60605 (312) 294-4557	66,950
Cincinnati Bengals (513) 621-3550	Riverfront Stadium 201 E. Pete Rose Way Cincinnati, OH 45202 (513) 352-5400	60,389
Cleveland Browns (216) 891-5000	Cleveland Stadium W. 3rd St. Tower B Cleveland, OH 44114 (216) 891-5000	78,512
Dallas Cowboys (214) 556-9900	Texas Stadium 2401 E. Airport Freeway Irving, TX 75062 (214) 438-7676	65,024
Denver Broncos (303) 649-9000	Mile High Stadium 2755 W. 17th Ave. Denver, CO 80204 (303) 458-4850	76,273
Detroit Lions (313) 335-4131	Pontiac Silverdome 11200 Featherstone Road Pontiac, MI 48342 (810) 858-7358	80,365

Green Bay Packers (414) 496-5700	Lambeau Field 1265 Lombardi Ave. Green Bay, WI 54307 (414) 496-5738	59,543
Houston Oilers (713) 797-9111	The Astrodome 8400 Kirby Drive Houston, TX 77054 (713) 799-9500	59,905
Indianapolis Colts (317) 297-2658	RCA Dome 100 S. Capitol Ave. Indianapolis, IN 46225 (317) 262-3685	60,127
Kansas City Chiefs (816) 924-9300	Arrowhead Stadium One Arrowhead Drive Kansas City, MO 64129 (816) 924-9300	77,872
Jacksonville Jaguars (904) 663-6000	Jacksonville Municipal Stadium One Stadium Place Jacksonville, FL 32202 (904) 633-6000	73,000
Miami Dolphins (305) 620-5000	Joe Robbie Stadium 2269 N.W. 199th St. Miami, FL 33056 (305) 626-7400	74,916
Minnesota Vikings (612) 828-6500	Hubert H. Humphrey Metrodome 900 S. Fifth St. Minneapolis, MN 55415 (612) 332-0386	63,000

New England Patriots (508) 543-8200	Foxboro Stadium Route 1 Foxboro, MA 02035 (508) 543-0350	60,290
New Orleans Saints (504) 733-0255	Louisiana Superdome Sugar Bowl Drive New Orleans, LA 70112 (504) 587-3663	69,065
New York Jets (516) 538-6600	Giant Stadium 50 Route 120 E. Rutherford, NJ 07073 (201) 460-4204	77,121
New York Giants (201) 935-8111	Giant Stadium 50 Route 120 E. Rutherford, NJ 07073 (201) 460-4204	77,541
Oakland Raiders n/a	Oakland-Alameda County Coliseum 7000 Coliseum Way Oakland, CA 94621 (510) 639-7700	n/a
Philadelphia Eagles (215) 463-2500	Veterans Stadium Broad St. & Pattison Ave. Philadelphia. PA 19148 (215) 685-1500	62,382
Pittsburgh Steelers (412) 323-1200	Three Rivers Stadium 400 Stadium Circle Pittsburgh, PA 15212 (412) 321-0650	59,600

St. Louis Rams (314) 982-7267	Trans World Dome 701 Convention Plaza St. Louis, MO 63101 (314) 342-5036	65,000
San Diego Chargers (619) 280-2111	San Diego Jack Murphy Stadium 9449 Friars Road San Diego, CA 92108 (619) 525-8266	60,789
San Francisco 49ers (408) 562-4949	3 Com Park Giants Dr. and Gilman Ave. San Francisco, CA 94124 (415) 467-1994	70,207
Seattle Seahawks (206) 827-9777	The Kingdome 201 S. Kings St. Seattle, WA 98104 (206) 296-3663	66,400
Tampa Bay Buccaneers (813) 870-2700	Tampa Stadium 4201 N. Dale Mabry Hwy. Tampa, FL 33607 (813) 872-7977	74,296
Washington Redskins (703) 478-8900	Robert F. Kennedy Stadium* 2400 E. Capitol St. Washington, DC 20003 (202) 547-9077	56,454

*Scheduled for September, 1996, the Redskins will play in Redskins Stadium, with 78,600 seats.

Golf

Terms

apron
best-ball tourna-
    ment
birdie (n., v.)
bogey (s.)
bogeys (pl.)
British Open
bunker
caddie
caddies, caddied,
    caddying
casual water
dogleg
double bogey (n.)
double-bogey (v.)
double eagle (n.)
double-eagle (v.)
draw
du Marier Classic
eagle (n., v.)
fade
fairway

fore
handicap
hole in one
hook
Ladies Professional
    Golf Association
    (LPGA)
ladies' tee
lay up (v.)
The Masters
match play
medal play
mulligan
par, parred,
    parring
Professional
    Golfers' Associa-
    tion (PGA)
PGA Tour
President's Cup
pull shot
push shot

putt (n., v.), putted,
    putting
putter (n.)
Ryder Cup
scramble
Skins Game
slice
Solheim Cup
stroke play
summer rules
Tradition
triple bogey (n.)
triple-bogey (v.)
U.S. Golf Associa-
    tion (USGA)
U.S. Open
U.S. Women's
    Open
Vardon Trophy
Vare Trophy
Walker Cup
winter rules

Usage

Use figures when referring to number of shots, scores, clubs, and final totals.

Nelson shot a 6-under-par 66.
He has a 2-stroke lead.
Watson shot an eagle 3 on the first hole.
He sank a 6-foot putt.
Sheehan used a 9 iron on the third hole.
He has a 7-handicap.
The hole is a 265-yard par-4.

Hyphenate final scores: 65-68-62-195

A birdie is one shot under par.
An eagle is two shots under par.
A bogey is one shot over par.

Governing Bodies

PGA
100 Ave. of the Champions
Palm Beach Gardens, FL 33410
(407) 624-8400
Sponsors and governs men's professional tournaments

LPGA
2570 W. International Speedway Blvd. Suite B
Daytona Beach, FL 32114
(904) 254-8800
Sponsors and governs women's professional tournaments

USGA
P.O. Box 708
Far Hills, NJ 07931-0708
(908) 234-2300
Governing body for amateur golf

Scoring

Stroke (Medal) play

List in ascending order. Use a dash before the final figure and hyphens between others. On the first day of a tournament, list a player's score on each of nine holes; on subsequent days, list the player's daily scores. In the final round of professional tournaments, include prize money.

First round:
Nick Price   35-36 — 71
Ernie Els   36-36 — 72
etc.

Second round:
Nick Price   71-70 — 141
Ernie Els   72-70 — 142
etc.

Nick Price, $50,000   71-70-68-70 — 279
Ernie Els, $25,000   72-70-68-71 — 280

Use hometowns, if ordered, only on national championship amateur tournaments. Use home countries for major international events. The hometown or country should be on a second line, indented.

Nick Price   71-70-68-70 — 279
    England
Ernie Els   72-70-68-71 — 280
    United States

Use the following form for cards:

Par out	443	443	545-36
Daly out	453	333	555-36
Watson out	443	543	435-35
Par in	454	344	454-37
Daly in	344	344	444-34
Watson in	444	454	344-36

Match play
    List winner, loser, and number of holes margin. Add "and number of holes skipped" if a player skips holes with a large lead. Add "-up" if the match goes to 18 holes. Add "(last hole #)" if extra holes are needed to break a tie.

Sam Snead def. Chi Chi Rodriguez, 2 and 1.
Calvin Peete def. Raymond Floyd, 2-up.
Jack Nicklaus def. Lee Trevino, 1-up (19).

Greyhound racing *See* dog racing.

Gymnastics

Terms

aerial
all-around
balance beam
flip-flop
floor exercise
full-twisting (adj.)
giant
half-in
half-out
hecht
horizontal bar
horse vault
kip
Kovac
Moore
parallel bars
pike position
pirouette

planche
pommel horse
rings
rhythmic gymnastics
Russian
salto
somersault
Stockli
Stutz
Tkatchev
Tsukahara
tuck
uneven bars
U.S. Gymnastic Federation (USGF)
Valdez
vault
walkover
Yurchenko

Governing Body

USA Gymnastics
Pan American Plaza
201 S. Capitol Ave. Suite 300
Indianapolis, IN 46225
(317) 237-5050
Selects national team

Scoring

Identify separate events. Scoring is in points, down to the thousandth of a point. A score of 10.000 is also called a perfect score; a perfect 10 is redundant.

EXAMPLE:

WOMEN
Vault
1. Henrietta Onodi, Hungary, and Lavinia Corina Milosovci, Romania, 9.925 points; 3. Tatiana Lisenko, Unified Team, 9.912; 4. etc.

Uneven bars
1. Lu Li, China, 10.000; 2. Tatiana Gutsu, Unified Team, 9.975; 3. etc.

Handball *See* team handball.

Hockey

Terms

backcheck	empty-net goal	play off (v.)
blue line	game-winning goal	playoff (n., adj.)
board-check	give-and-go	power play
boarding	goalie	power-play goal
body check (n.)	goal line	red line
body-check (v.)	goal post	right wing
breakaway	goals against aver-	shootout
butt-ending	age	short-handed
center circle	goaltender	short-hand goal
center line	hat trick	sideboard
crease	high-sticking (v.)	slap shot
cross-checking	icing	Stanley Cup
deke	left wing	sweep check
face off (v.)	one-timer	tip-in
faceoff (n., adj.)	offside (n., adj.)	two-on-one break
forecheck	penalty box	

Usage

Adams Award Presented to the NHL Coach of the Year, the award is named after Jack Adams, a former coach and general manager of the Detroit Red Wings.
Spell out Jack Adams Award on first reference.

Byng Memorial Trophy Awarded to the NHL player who best exemplifies sportsmanship, the trophy is named after Lady Evelyn Byng.
Spell out Lady Byng Memorial Trophy on first reference.

Calder Memorial Trophy Awarded to the NHL Rookie of the Year, the trophy is named after former NHL president Frank Calder.
Calder Memorial Trophy is acceptable in all references.

Hart Memorial Trophy Awarded to the player voted most valuable to his team, the trophy is named after Cecil Hart, a former coach of the Montreal Canadiens.
Hart Memorial Trophy is acceptable in all references.

Jennings Trophy Awarded to the NHL goalie with best goals against average in regular season.

King Clancy Trophy Award presented to the NHL player who displays outstanding leadership on the ice and through humanitarian contributions to the community.

Masterton Memorial Trophy Awarded to the NHL player exhibiting most sportsmanship, the trophy is named after Bill Masterton, a rookie who died of a head injury in 1968.
Spell out Bill Masterton Trophy on first reference.

Norris Memorial Trophy Award given to NHL's top defenseman is named after James Norris, a former owner of the Detroit Red Wings.
Spell out James Norris Memorial Trophy on first reference.

numbers Spell out numbers one through nine as in the following examples:

> The Red Wings had a three-on-one break.
> Bure scored two goals.
> The game was tied late in the third period.

Use figures for numbers greater than nine and as in the following examples:

> Newman's goals against average is 2.94.
> Ford may be Sharks' No.1 draft pick.
> Gretzky wears No. 99.
> The Lightning defeated the Jets 3-2.
> Washington finished the season 39-37-8.
> New York won Game 5 of the Stanley Cup Final.

Pearson Award Presented to the NHL's most outstanding player, the award is named after former Canadian Prime Minister Lester Pearson.

Spell out Lester Pearson Award on first reference.

power play (n., adj.)

> Sykes scored on the power play.
> His team has scored 10 power play goals this season.

Ross Trophy Award given to the NHL leader in points scored during the regular season is named after Art Ross, a former general manager of the Boston Bruins.

Spell out Art Ross Trophy on first reference, then Ross Trophy.

Selke Trophy Award given to the NHL's top defensive forward is named after Frank Selke, a former general manager of the Montreal Canadiens.

Spell out Frank Selke Trophy on first reference.

short-handed (adj.) The Flyers scored a short-handed goal.

Smythe Trophy Award given to the Most Valuable Player in the Stanley Cup playoffs is named after Conn Smythe, a former Toronto Maple Leafs coach, owner, and general manager.

Spell out Conn Smythe Trophy on first reference, then Smythe Trophy.

Stanley Cup Awarded to the winner of NHL playoffs. Cup is named after Sir Frederick Arthur Stanley, who donated the cup.

Vezina Trophy Award given to the NHL's top goaltender is named after Georges Vezina, who played for the Montreal Canadiens and died of tuberculosis in 1926.

Vezina Trophy is acceptable in all references.

Governing Bodies

NHL
1800 McGill College Rd.
Suite 2600
Montreal Quebec Canada H3A 3J6
(514) 288-9220
Governing body of the national professional league

International Hockey League (IHL)
1577 N. Woodward Ave. Suite 212
Bloomfield Hills, MI 48304
(810) 258-0580
Governing body with professional league affiliated with the NHL

Sunshine Hockey League
700 W. Lemon St.
Box 1808
Lakeland, FL 33802-1808
(813) 499-8112
Governing body of Florida league

East Coast Hockey League
AA520 Mart Office Bldg.
800 Briar Creek Rd.
Charlotte, NC 28205
(704) 358-3658
Governing body of eastern U.S. league

Leagues and Teams
National Hockey League
The NHL is made up of four divisions in two conferences:

EASTERN CONFERENCE

Atlantic Division
Florida Panthers
New Jersey Devils
N.Y. Islanders
N.Y. Rangers
Philadelphia Flyers
Tampa Bay Lightning
Washington Capitals

Northeast Division
Boston Bruins
Buffalo Sabres
Hartford Whalers
Montreal Canadiens
Ottawa Senators
Pittsburgh Penguins

WESTERN CONFERENCE

Central Division
Chicago Blackhawks
Dallas Stars
Detroit Red Wings
St. Louis Blues
Toronto Maple Leafs
Winnipeg Jets

Pacific Division
Anaheim Mighty Ducks
Calgary Flames
Edmonton Oilers
Los Angeles Kings
San Jose Sharks
Vancouver Canucks
Colorado Avalanche

Following are the International Hockey League teams, the NHL teams they are affiliated with, and the conferences and divisions in which they play.

EASTERN CONFERENCE

Northern Division
Chicago Wolves (Independent)
Cleveland Lumberjacks (Pittsburgh Penguins)
Detroit Vipers (Independent)
Kalamazoo Wings (Dallas Stars)

Midwest Division
Cincinnati Cyclones (Florida Panthers)
Fort Wayne Komets (Independent)
Indianapolis Ice (Chicago Blackhawks)
Peoria Rivermen (St. Louis Blues)

WESTERN CONFERENCE
Central Division
Atlanta Knights (Tampa Bay Lightning)
Houston Aeros (Independent)
Kansas City Blades (San Jose Sharks)
Milwaukee Admirals (Independent)
Minnesota Moose (Independent)

Southwest Division
Denver Grizzlies (New York Islanders)
Las Vegas Thunder (Independent)
Phoenix Roadrunners (Los Angeles Kings)
San Diego Gulls (Mighty Ducks of Anaheim)

SUNSHINE HOCKEY LEAGUE
Daytona Beach Sun Devils
Fresno Falcons
Jacksonville Bullets
Lakeland Ice Warriors
West Palm Beach Blaze

East Coast Hockey League Teams and Divisions

NORTH DIVISION	SOUTH DIVISION	EAST DIVISION
Columbus Chill	Birmingham Bulls	Charlotte Checkers
Dayton Bombers	Jacksonville Lizard	Hampton Roads
Erie Panthers	Kings	Admirals
Huntington Blizzard	Knoxville Cherokees	Raleigh IceCaps
Johnstown Chiefs	Louisiana IceGators	Richmond Renegades
Louisville River Frogs	Mobile Mysticks	Roanoke Express
Toledo Storm	Nashville Knights	S.Carolina Stingrays
Wheeling Thunderbirds	Tallahassee Tiger	
	Sharks	

Scoring

Box Score:

```
                  Whalers 2,  Panthers 1
Hartford   1    1    0   -    2
Florida    0    0    1   -    1
```

First period—1, Hartford, Harkins 1 (Potvin, Propp), :56.
Second period—2, Hartford, Sanderson 33 (Verbeek, Nylander), 13:36.
Third period—3, Florida, Niedermayer 9 (Fitzgerald, Severyn), 10:09.
Shots on goal— Hartford 11-10-10—31. Florida 9-10-19—38.
Power-play opportunities—Hartford 0 of 4; Florida 0 of 6.
Goalies—Hartford, Burke, 13-17-4 (38 shots-37 saves). Florida, Vanblesbrouck, 17-19-8 (31-29). Announced attendance—14,697.

Arenas

The following is a list of NHL teams, their phone numbers, arenas, arena phone numbers, and addresses.

TEAM	ARENA	PERMANENT SEATING CAPACITY
Mighty Ducks of Anaheim	Arrowhead Pond 2695 E. Katella Ave. Anaheim, CA 92806 (714) 704-2400	19,400
Boston Bruins (617) 557-1310	FleetCenter One FleetCenter Boston, MA 02114 (617) 624-1050	17,565
Buffalo Sabres (716) 856-7300	Buffalo Memorial Stadium 140 Main St. Buffalo, NY 14202 (716) 851-5663	16,248

Calgary Flames (403) 261-0475	Olympic Saddledome 555 Saddledome Rise S.E. P.O. Box 1540-Station M Calgary, AB T2P 3B9 Canada (403) 261-0475	20,240
Chicago Blackhawks (312) 455-7000	United Center 1901 W. Madison St. Chicago, IL 60612 (312) 455-4500	20,500
Colorado Avalanche (303) 893-0614	McNichols Sports Arena 1635 Clay Street Denver, CO 80204 (303) 893-0614	16,061
Dallas Stars (214) 712-2890	Reunion Arena 777 Sports St. Dallas, TX 75207 (214) 939-2770	16,853
Detroit Red Wings (313) 396-7544	Joe Louis Arena 600 Civic Center Drive Detroit, MI 48226 (313) 396-7444	19,275
Edmonton Oilers (403) 474-8561	Northlands Coliseum 7300 116th Ave. Edmonton, AB T5J 2N5 Canada (403) 471-7159	17,503
Florida Panthers (305) 768-1900	Miami Arena 100 Northeast Third Avenue Tenth Floor Fort Lauderdale, FL 33301 (305) 768-1900	14,703
Hartford Whalers (860) 728-3366	Hartford Civic Center 1 Civic Center Blvd. Hartford, CT 06103 (860) 249-6633	15,635

Los Angeles Kings (310) 419-3160	Great Western Forum 3900 W. Manchester Blvd. Inglewood, CA 90306 (310) 419-3100	17,505
Montreal Canadiens	Montreal Forum 2313 St. Catherine St. W. Montreal, PQ H3H 1N2 Canada (514) 932-2582	17,909
New Jersey Devils (201) 935-6050	Brendan Byrne Arena 50 Route 120 E. Rutherford, NJ 07073 (201) 460-4296	19,020
New York Islanders (516) 794-4100	Nassau Veterans Memorial Coliseum 1255 Hempstead Turnpike Uniondale, NY 11553 (516) 794-9303	16,285
New York Rangers (212) 465-6486	Madison Square Garden 4 Penn Plaza New York, NY 10001 (212) 465-6000	19,941
Ottawa Senators (613) 721-0115	Ottawa Civic Center 301 Modine Drive Nepean, ON K2H 9C4 Canada (613) 721-0115	10,585
Philadelphia Flyers (215) 465-4500	CoreStates Spectrum Broad & Pattison Ave. Philadelphia, PA 19148 (215) 336-3600	17,337
Pittsburgh Penguins (412) 642-1800	Pittsburgh Civic Arena 300 Auditorium Place Pittsburgh, PA 15219 (412) 642-1800	17,500

St. Louis Blues (314) 781-5300	Kiel Center 1401 Clark Ave. St. Louis, MO 63103 (314) 622-5410	18,500
San Jose Sharks (408) 287-7070	San Jose Arena 525 W. Santa Clara St. San Jose, CA 95113 (408) 287-7070	17,310
Tampa Bay Lightning (813) 229-2658	Thunderdome One Stadium Drive St. Petersburg, FL 33705 (813) 825-3111	24,000
Toronto Maple Leafs (416) 977-1641	Maple Leaf Gardens 60 Carlton St. Toronto, ON M5B 1L1 Canada (416) 977-1641	15,642
Vancouver Canucks (604) 254-5141	General Motors Place 780 Beatty St., 3rd Floor Vancouver, BC V6B 2M1 Canada (604) 681-2280	19,000
Winnipeg Jets (204) 982-5387	Winnipeg Arena 1430 Maroons Road Winnipeg, MB R3G 0L5 Canada (204) 982-5400	15,393
Washington Capitals (301) 386-7000	USAir Arena 1 Harry S. Truman Dr. Landover, MD 20785 (301) 386-7000	18,130

Horse Racing

Terms

Belmont Stakes	Kentucky Derby
Breeders' Cup	mare
broodmare	matinee
bug boy	mutuel field
colt	Preakness Stakes
entry	Run for the Roses
filly	stallion
furlong	stirrup
gelding	thoroughbred
half-mile pole	Triple Crown
harness racing	United States Trotting Association (USTA)

Usage

When writing about horses, do not use a personal pronoun unless gender has been established or the animal has a name.

> The horse won its race.
> Holy Bull won his third race.

Governing Body

United States Trotting Association
750 Michigan Ave.
Columbus, OH 43215-1191
(614) 224-2291
Governing body for harness racing

Scoring

EXAMPLE:

> Belmont Park thoroughbred results

Weather clear, track fast
FIRST-T-1:16 2/5, clmg. 6-1/2 f
9 Rag Top	12.20	6.90	5.00
4 Firm Decree		4.10	3.20
6 Can't Believeit		4.10	
Scratched—Medal Winner
Exacta $81.50

Jai Alai

Terms

cesta
pelota

Governing Body

Federacion Internacional De Pelota Vasca
Sede Central, Aldamar, 5-1 Dcha.
San Sebastian, 20003
Spain
+34 +43/428 415
International governing body

See racquetball for a scoring summary.

Judo *See* martial arts.

Jujitsu *See* martial arts.

Karate *See* martial arts.

Kayaking *See* canoeing.

Kendo *See* martial arts.

Kung fu *See* martial arts.

Lacrosse

Terms

> attackman
> defenseman
> flipoff (n.)
> midfielder

Governing Bodies

Major Indoor Lacrosse League
2310 W. 75th St.
Prairie Village, KS 66208
(913) 384-8960
Sponsors national professional lacrosse league

Lacrosse Foundation
113 W. University Parkway
Baltimore, MD 21210
(410) 235-6882
Promotes lacrosse in the United States

Leagues and Teams

MILL teams include

> Baltimore Thunder
> Boston Blazers
> Buffalo Bandits
> New York Saints
> Philadelphia Wings
> Rochester (N.Y.) Knighthawks

Scoring

Use match summary.

EXAMPLE:

> Baggataway League
> at Boston College
>
> Bull Dogs def. Lexington, 10-2.
> Lawrence Academy def. Rebels, 9-7.

Luge *See* bobsledding.

Marathon

Term

marathoner

Scoring

A marathon is 26.2 miles long. Use a basic summary.

EXAMPLE:

> Boston Marathon
> Women's Results
> 1. Wanda Panfil, Poland, 2:24:18 (39th overall); 2. Kim Jones, Spokane, Wash., 2:26:40; 3. etc.

Martial Arts

Terms

aikido	karate	masutemi waza
ashiwaza	kendo	tae kwon do
jujitsu	koshiwaza	tewaza
judo	kung fu	yokosutemi waza

Governing Bodies

United States Judo
P.O. Box 10013
El Paso, TX 79991
(915) 565-8754
Selects and trains national team

International Judo Federation
PSF 380
Berlin, 106
Germany
+37 +2/229 1633
International governing body

International Aikido Federation
c/o Dr. Peter Goldsbury
Ushita Honmanchi 3-29
4-Chome Higashi-ku
Hiroshima, 732
Japan
+81 +82/211 1271
International governing body of aikido

USA Karate Federation
1300 Kenmore Blvd.
Akron, OH 44314
(216) 753-3114
National governing body for karate

U.S. Tae kwon do Union
One Olympic Plaza
Colorado Springs, CO 80909
(719) 578-4632
Selects and trains national tae kwon do team

World Tae kwon do Federation
635 Yuksamdong, Kangnamku
Seoul, 135
Korea
+82 +2/566 2505
International governing body for tae kwon do

Scoring

Use the basic summary by weight divisions for major tournaments; match summary can be used for lesser tournaments. In judo, include the name of the winning throw.

EXAMPLE:

> MEN
> 143-pound final
> Rogerio Sampaio Cardoso, Brazil, def. Jozsef Csak, Hungary, ashi-waza.
>
> Final standings:
> 41. Rogerio Sampaio Cardoso, Brazil; 2. Jozsef Csak, Hungary; 3. Uno Gunter Quetimeiz, Germany, and Israel Hemandez Planas, Cuba.

Modern Pentathlon *See* pentathlon.

Motorboat Racing *See* boating.

Motorcycle Racing *See* auto racing.

Olympics

Terms

WINTER GAMES EVENTS INCLUDE

Alpine Skiing	Ice Hockey
Biathlon	Luge
Bobsled	Nordic Skiing
Cross Country Skiing	Ski Jumping
Figure Skating	Speed Skating

SUMMER GAMES EVENTS INCLUDE

Archery	Rowing
Badminton	Shooting
Baseball	Soccer
Basketball	Swimming
Boxing	Synchronized Swimming
Canoe/Kayak	Table Tennis
Cycling	Team Handball
Diving	Tennis
Equestrian	Track and Field
Fencing	Volleyball
Field Hockey	Water Polo
Gymnastics	Weightlifting
Judo	Wrestling
Modern Pentathlon	Yachting

Usage

Capitalization Always capitalize Olympic and Games in reference to the Olympics.

> Carl Lewis won four gold medals during the '84 Summer Olympics.
> Mark Spitz dominated the '72 Games.
> Janet Evans swam in an Olympic-sized pool.

Capitalize Opening Ceremony in reference to the Winter and Summer Olympic Opening Ceremonies. Also capitalize Closing Ceremonies.

Cities in which games have been held:

Year	Summer Games	Winter Games
1896	Athens	
1900	Paris	
1904	St. Louis	
1906	Athens	
1910	London	
1912	Stockholm	
1916	canceled due to World War I	
1920	Antwerp	
1924	Paris	Chamonix
1928	Amsterdam	St. Moritz
1932	Los Angeles	Lake Placid
1936	Berlin	Garmisch-Partenkirchen
1940	canceled due to World War II	
1944	canceled due to World War II	
1948	London	St. Moritz
1952	Helsinki	Oslo
1956	Melbourne	Cortina d'Ampezzo
1960	Rome	Squaw Valley
1964	Tokyo	Innsbruck
1968	Mexico City	Grenoble
1972	Munich	Sapporo
1976	Montreal	Innsbruck
1980	Moscow	Lake Placid
1984	Los Angeles	Sarajevo
1988	Seoul	Calgary
1992	Barcelona	Albertville
1994		Lillehammer
1996	Atlanta	
1998		Nagano
2000	Sydney	
2002		Salt Lake City

numbers Follow the same general rules under numbers in Part I.

medal Do not capitalize gold, silver, or bronze medal. Do not use medal as a verb.

Use "the" instead of "a" when referring to the gold, silver, or bronze medal in events. Each event only awards one of each medal.

It is acceptable to simply say the gold, the silver, or the bronze when referring to Olympic medals.

> WRONG: Bonnie Blair medalled in the 500.
> WRONG: Bonnie Blair won a Gold Medal in the 500.
> RIGHT: Bonnie Blair won the gold in the 500.

professional vs. amateur An amateur becomes a professional when he or she:

> plays for a professional team
> puts his or her name on a draft list (except in baseball, where a student must declare intention to return to school within 30 days of the draft to maintain eligibility)
> receives pay or accepts the promise of pay for playing
> signs a contract or verbally commits with an agent of a professional sports organization
> uses skills to gain pay in commercials or other activity
> receives pay, awards, or educational expenses for playing on an amateur team (uniforms, equipment, and travel expenses are not considered pay)

record Only note one record; if a swimmer creates a world record, he or she has also created an Olympic record, a pool record, a personal record, etc. It is sufficient to note that the swimmer has set a new world record.

Governing Bodies

United States Olympic Committee (USOC)
One Olympic Plaza
Colorado Springs, CO 80909
(719) 632-5551
National governing body of the U.S. Olympic Team

International Olympic Committee (IOC)
Chauteau de Vidy
Case Postale 356
CH-1001 Lausanne, Switzerland
21 253271
International governing body of the Summer and Winter Games

Scoring

See individual sports for how to summarize each event.

For overall medals, chart the numbers of gold, silver, bronze, and overall medals, from the most medals to the least.

When several countries have the same number of medals, order the countries with the most golds to the fewest; if countries have the same number of gold medals, list the country with more silver medals first.

If two or more countries win the same number and kind of medal, order them alphabetically.

EXAMPLE:

Day 3, Barcelona Olympics

	Gold	Silver	Bronze	Total
China	1	3	0	4
United States	1	1	1	3
Unified Team	2	0	0	2
Bulgaria	1	1	0	2
Hungary	1	1	0	2
Australia	1	0	1	2
Germany	1	0	1	2
France	0	1	1	2
Sweden	0	1	1	2

Pelota *See* jai alai.

Pentathlon

Term

pentathlete

Governing Body

U.S. Modern Pentathlon Association
530 McCullough Ave, Suite 619
San Antonio, TX 78215
(210) 246-3000
Selects and trains national team

Scoring

Box scores should follow the formats for each individual event. Final results should use a basic summary. See decathlon in track and field for an example.

Ping-Pong *See* table tennis.

Racquetball

Terms

lob
z-serve

Governing Bodies

American Amateur Racquetball Association
1685 Unitah St.
Colorado Springs, CO 80904-2921
(719) 635-6085
National governing body of amateur racquetball

International Racquetball Federation (IRF)
same address
(719) 635-5391
International governing body for racquetball

Scoring

Games go to 21; winner can win by one point. Matches are usually a best-of-three games format. Use the match summary:

EXAMPLE:

> Joseph Kleinschmidt, Winona, Minn., def. Jacob Mayfield, Bloomington, Ind., 21-9, 15-21, 21-20.

Polo

Terms

> chukker
> mallet

Governing Body

U.S. Polo Association
4059 Iron Works Pike
Lexington, KY 40511
(606) 255-0593

Scoring

Use the match summary:

EXAMPLE:

> Chairman's Cup
> at Myopia Polo Club, Hamilton, Mass.
> Mill Pond def. North Cliff, 10-7.

Riflery *See* shooting.

Rodeo

Terms

All-Around Cowboy
Bareback Riding
Bull Riding
Calf Roping
Professional Rodeo Cowboys Association (PRCA)
Saddle Bronc Riding
Steer Roping
Steer Wrestling
Team Roping

Governing Body

Professional Rodeo Cowboys Association (PRCA)
101 Pro Rodeo Dr.
Colorado Springs, CO 80919
(719) 593-8840
Sponsors national events and tournaments

Scoring

Use the basic summary format by event.

EXAMPLE:

Saddle Bronc Riding (10 rides)
1. Dan Mortensen, Manhattan, Mont., 791; 2. Billy Etbauer, Edmond, Okla., 715; 3. etc.

Roller Hockey/In-line Hockey

Governing Bodies

Roller Hockey International (RHI)
1388 Sutter, Suite 710
San Francisco, CA 94109
(415) 673-5396

National In-Line Hockey Association
1221 Brickell Ave. 9th Floor
Miami, FL 33131
(305) 358-8988
National governing body for amateur in-line hockey

Leagues and Teams

RHI League

WESTERN CONFERENCE

Pacific Division:
Anaheim Bullfrogs
Los Angeles Blades
Phoenix Cobras
San Diego Barracudas
Oklahoma Coyotes

Northwest Division:
Oakland Skates
Sacramento River Rats
San Jose Rhinos
Vancouver VooDoo

EASTERN CONFERENCE

Central Division:
Buffalo Stampede
Chicago Cheetahs
Detroit Mustangs
Minnesota Blue Ox
St. Louis Vipers

Atlantic Division:
Montreal Roadrunners
Orlando RollerGators
Ottawa Loggers
New Jersey Rockin' Rollers
Philadelphia Bulldogs

Scoring

See hockey.

Rowing

Terms

coxless
coxswain
oarsman
oarsmen
shell
scull

Governing Body

U.S. Rowing Association
Pan American Plaza
201 S. Capitol Ave. Suite 400
Indianapolis, IN 46225
(317) 237-5656
Select and train national team

Scoring

Scoring is in minutes, seconds, and tenths of a second. Use hundredths of a second when available. Follow the basic summary format.

EXAMPLE:

Men's single sculls
1. Thomas Lange, Germany, 6:51.40; 2. Vaclav Chalupa, Czechoslovakia, 6:52.93; 3. etc.

Women's coxless pairs
1. Canada (Marnie McBean, Kathleen Haddle) 7:06.22; 2. Germany (Stefani Werremeier, Ingeburg Schwertzmann) 7:07.96; 3. etc.

Rugby

Term

drop goal

Governing Bodies

U.S.A. Rugby
3595 E. Fountainhead Blvd.
Colorado Springs, CO 80910
(719) 637-1022
Promotes rugby in the U.S.

Federation Internationale de Rugby Amateur
7, cite d'Antin
Paris, 75009
France
+33 +1/48 74 84 75
International governing body

Scoring

Use the match summary.

Springfield def. Jamestown, 5-3.

Running

Governing Body

AAU National Headquarters
3400 W. 86th St.
Indianapolis, IN 46268
(317) 872-2900

Scoring

Scoring for running events is in minutes, seconds, tenths of a second, and hundredths, if available.

EXAMPLE:

> National AAU Championship
> Cross Country
> 1. Frank Shorter, Miami, 5:25.67; 2. Tom Coster, Los Angeles,
>   5:30.72; 3. etc.

Adapt the basic summary to paragraph form under a dateline if the field has more than 10 competitors. *See* auto racing for an example.

Sailing *See* boating.

Shooting

Terms

airgun	free rifle
bore	metallic sight
bull	National Rifle Association (NRA)
bunker	offhand
caliber	pits
cartridge	sighters
challenge	string
chamber	stock
crossfire	ten-ring
firing line	.22
free pistol	

Usage

Ten Olympic classifications:

Air Pistol	Three-position
Free Pistol	Air Rifle
Rapid Fire Pistol	Running Target
Sport Pistol	Trap
Men's Smallbore Free Rifle Prone	Skeet

Governing Body

International Shooting Sports
One Olympic Plaza
Colorado Springs, CO 80909
(719) 578-4670
Selects and trains national team

Scoring

Use the basic summary format, and note the classification.

EXAMPLE:

> Men's Running Game Target Final
> 1. Michael Jakosits, Germany, 673.0 points; 2. Anatoll Asrabaev, Unified Team, 672.0; 3. etc.

Skating *See* figure skating, speed skating.

Skiing

Terms

Alpine	Nordic
combined	ski jump
downhill	super-G
freestyle	super giant slalom

Governing Body

U.S. Skiing
1500 Kerns Blvd.
Bldg. F, Suite F200
Park City, UT 84060
(801) 649-9090
Selects and trains national team

Scoring

Alpine and Nordic cross country skiing are scored in minutes, seconds, tenths of seconds, and hundredths when available. Use basic summary format.

> Women's Slalom
> 1. Vreni Schneider, Switzerland, 1:36.69; 2. Mateja Svet, Yugoslavia, 1:38.37; 3. etc.

Ski jumping is scored in points; use the match summary.

Soccer

Terms

advantage rule	goalie
APSL	goalkeeper
banana shot	goaltender
bend	head
bicycle kick	indirect-free kick (n.)
boot	linesman
box	mark
cannonball shot	Major Indoor Soccer League (MISL)
center circle	National Professional Soccer League (NPSL)
challenge	offside
charge	overhead kick
clogger	penalty area
corner kick	shinguard
FIFA	stopper
forward	striker
free kick	touchline
goal area	World Cup
goal kick	yellow card

Governing Bodies

American Professional Soccer League (American Soccer League and World Soccer League merger)
2 Village Rd. Suite 5
Horsham, PA 19044
(215) 657-7440
Professional soccer league

Continental Indoor Soccer League (CISL)
16027 Ventura Blvd. Suite 605
Encino, CA 91436
(818) 906-7627
Professional indoor soccer league

FIFA
Hitzigweg 11
Postfach 85
CH-8030 Zurich, Switzerland
International governing body

National Professional Soccer League (NPSL)
229 3rd St. N.W.
Canton OH 44702
(216) 455-4625
Professional soccer league

U.S. Soccer Federation
1801-1811 S. Prairie Ave.
Chicago, IL 60616
(312) 808 1300
Creates all national teams

Major League Soccer
2029 Century Park East
Suite 400
Los Angeles, CA 90067
(310) 772-2600

Leagues and Teams

APSL Teams:

Atlanta Ruckus	New York Centaurs
Colorado Foxes	Seattle Sounders
Montreal Impact	Vancouver 86ers

CISL Teams:

EASTERN DIVISION	SOUTHERN DIVISION	WESTERN DIVISION
Dallas Sidekicks	Anaheim Splash	Las Vegas Dust Devils
Detroit Neon	Arizona Sandsharks	Portland Pride
Monterey La Raza	Houston Hotshots	Sacramento Knights
Pittsburgh Stingers	Mexico Toros	San Jose Grizzlies
Washington Warthogs	San Diego Sockers	Seattle SeaDogs

NPSL Teams:

Baltimore Spirit	Harrisburg Heat
Buffalo Blizzard	Kansas City Attack
Canton Invaders	Milwaukee Wave
Chicago Power	St. Louis Ambush
Cincinnati Silverbacks	Tampa Bay Terror
Detroit Rockers	Wichita Wings

MLS Teams:

Colorado Rapids	New England Revolution
Columbus Crew	NY/ NJ MetroStars
Dallas Burn	San Jose Clash
Kansas City Wiz	Tampa Bay Mutiny
Los Angeles Galaxy	Washington D.C. United

Scoring

Use a match summary and follow with a box score, with each team's score in each half, followed by a dash and the final score. Note the last names of the scoring players and the time elapsed when they scored. Also note players who received yellow or red cards, and the elapsed time of the penalty.

Friendship Cup
at Los Angeles

Columbia def. United States, 1-0.
Columbia   1   0 — 1
United States   0   0 — 0

Scoring: Columbia, Valencia 33.00
Yellow Card: Acosta, US, 65.00 Red Cards: None.

Softball

Terms

base on balls	ground-rule double
batter's box	on-deck circle
catcher's box	sacrifice fly
dead ball	windup

Governing Bodies

USA Softball
2801 N.E. 50th St.
Oklahoma City, OK 73111
(405) 424-5266
National governing body

International Softball Federation
(405) 427-5700
International governing body

Scoring

For box scores and scoring summaries, *see* baseball.

Speed Skating

Terms

long-track speed skating
short-track speed skating

Governing Body

U.S. International Speedskating Association
P.O. Box 16157
Rocky River, OH 44116
(216) 899-0128
Selects and trains national team

Scoring

Use basic summary, with name, hometown or country, and points.

Women's 500 meters
1. Bonnie Blair, Champaign, Ill., 39.10; 2. Christa Rothenburger, Germany, 39.12; 3. etc.

Squash

Governing Body

U.S. Squash Racquets Association
P.O. Box 1216
Bala-Cynwyd, PA 19004-1216
(610) 667-4006
National governing body

Scoring

Matches are usually played in a best-of-three format; top score in a game is 21. For a match summary example, *see* racquetball.

Swimming

Terms

backstroke
banana heat
breaststroke
butterfly
flip turn
freestyle
gravity wave
lane
lanelines
long course

medley relay
negative split
Olympic-style pool
relay exchange
roll
short-course pool
sidestroke
split
swimmer's ear
touchpad

Governing Body

U.S. Swimming
One Olympic Plaza
Colorado Springs, CO 80909
(719) 578-4669
Select and train national team

Scoring

Scoring is in minutes, seconds, tenths and hundredths of a second.
Use the match summary format.

Women's 400-meter freestyle
1. Janet Evans, USA, 4:03.85; 2. Heike Friedrich, Germany,
4:06.62; 3. etc.

Synchronized Swimming

Terms

back pike
ballet leg
ballet leg double
bent knee/vertical

castle, vertical
crane
flamingo
front pike

knight
split
tuck
vertical

Governing Body

U.S. Synchronized Swimming
Pan American Plaza
201 S. Capitol Ave. Suite 510
Indianapolis, IN 46225
(317) 237-5700

Scoring

Scoring is in points. *See* figure skating for an example.

Table Tennis

Terms

block	loop	push
chop	penhold	Seemiller
hit	Ping-Pong	shakehands
kill		

Governing Body

USA Table Tennis
One Olympic Plaza
Colorado Springs, CO 80909
(719) 578-4583

Scoring

Games go to 21 points with a two-point spread. Use the match summary. *See* racquetball for a match summary example.

Team Handball

Governing Bodies

U.S. Handball Association
2333 N. Tucson Blvd.
Tucson, AZ 85716-2726
(602) 795-0434

U.S. Team Handball Federation
One Olympic Plaza
Colorado Springs, CO 80909
(719) 578-4582

Scoring

Games are won by the first player to score 21 points with a two-point spread. In a tie-breaker, the winner must score 11 points. Most matches are best-of-three games.

Use match summary. *See* racquetball for an example.

Tennis

Terms

ace
ad-in
ad-out
all
Association of Tennis
    Professionals (ATP)
back court
backhand
baseline
Big Four
center mark
Centre Court
deuce
dink
double fault (n.)
double-fault (v.)
drop shot
earned point
error
fault (n., v.)
foot fault (n.)
foot-fault (adj., v.)
forecourt
Grand Slam
ground stroke
hard court (n.)

hard-court (adj.)
hold serve
International Tennis
    Federation (ITF)
kill
let
linesman
lob
love
match point
midcourt (n., adj.)
poach
seed
service line
set
set point
smash
straight sets
TEAMTENNIS or TeamTennis
United States Tennis
    Association (USTA)
U.S. Open
volley
Wimbledon
Women's Tennis Association
    (WTA)

Governing Bodies

World TeamTennis
445 N. Wells, Suite 404
Chicago, IL 60610
(312) 245-5300

United States Tennis Association
70 W. Red Oak Lane
White Plains, NY 10604
(914) 696-7000
Establishes rules for professional and amateur tennis

Association of Tennis Professionals (ATP) Tour
200 ATP Tour Blvd.
Ponte Verde Beach, FL 32802
(904) 285-8000
Sponsors men's professional tournaments

Women's Tennis Association (WTA) Tour
133 First St. N.E.
St. Petersburg, FL 33701
(813) 895-5000
Sponsors women's professional tournaments

Leagues and Teams

World TeamTennis is a national professional tennis league. Each team consists of two men and two women. The teams are

EAST DIVISION:	WEST DIVISION:
Atlanta Thunder	Idaho Shakers
Charlotte Express	Kansas City Explorers
Florida Twist	Sacramento Capitals
New Jersey Stars	St. Louis Aces
New York OTBzz	Wichita Advantage

Scoring

In major tournaments, men play a best-of-5 match; women play a best-of-3.

Use match summary with game scores; tie breaker should be in parentheses following the game.

> Women's singles
> Monica Seles, Germany, def. Martina Navratilova, Colorado
>   Springs, Colo., 6-1, 3-6, 7-6 (7-5).

Thoroughbred racing *See* horse racing.

Track and Field

Terms

anchor leg	long jump (n.)
decathlon	long-jump (v., adj.)
discus	marathon
false start	middle distance
Fosbury flop	pole vault
hammer throw	pole vaulter
heptathalon	shot put
high jump (n.)	starting block
high-jump (v.)	steeplechase
hurdle (n., v.)	triple jump (n.)
javelin	triple-jump (v.)

Governing Body

USA Track & Field
One Hoosier Dome Suite 140
Indianapolis, IN 46225
(317) 261-0500
National governing body: choose athletes for national team

Scoring

Score running events in minutes, seconds, tenths and hundredths of a second.

Throwing events, long jump, and triple jump are measured in distances; pole vault and high jump are measured in heights. When writing distances, note on first reference whether the distance is measured in meters, feet, or yards.

In decathlon and heptathlon, note event points and cumulative points.

Use the basic summary format.

> Decathlon
> (Group A)
>
> 100-meter dash—1. Fred Dixon, Los Angeles, 10.8 seconds, 854 points; 2. Bruce Jenner, San Jose State, 11:09, 783.3; 3. etc.
> Long jump—1. Dixon, 24-7 (7.34m), 889, 1,743; 2. Jenner, 23-6 (7.17m), 855, 1,638; 3. etc.
> Decathlon final—1. Bruce Jenner, San Jose State, 8,524 points; 2. Fred Dixon, Los Angeles, 8,277; 3. etc.

Triathlon

Term

Ironman

Governing Body

Triathlon Federation USA
3595 E. Fountain Blvd. F-1
Colorado Springs, CO 80910
(719) 597-9090
800 TRI-1USA

Scoring

See decathlon in track and field

Volleyball

Terms

advantage	center line	red card
attack line	collective screen	serve
backcourt	dink	service zone
backline	fault	set
back row (n.)	front row (n.)	spike
back-row (adj.)	front-row (adj.)	USA Volleyball
block	rally-point (adj.)	yellow card

Governing Bodies

Indoor:
U.S. Volleyball Association
3595 E. Fountain Blvd. I-2
Colorado Springs, CO 80910-1740
(719) 637-8300
Selects and trains national team

Professional Beach Volleyball:
Association of Volleyball Professionals
15260 Ventura Blvd. Suite 2250
Sherman Oaks, CA 91403
(818) 386-2486

Women's Professional Volleyball Association
1730 Oak St.
Santa Monica, CA 90405
(310) 392-4210

Scoring

Use the match summary.

Women's World Grand Prix
at Tapei

United States def. Japan, 3-1 (15-10, 13-15, 15-10, 15-10).

For professional beach volleyball events, follow match summary:

> Men's Pro Beach Tour
> at Hermosa Beach, Calif.

> Adam Johnson and Jose Loiola ($100,00) def. Karch Kiraly and
> Scott Ayakatubby, 15-5.

Water Polo

Governing Body

U.S. Water Polo
Pan American Plaza
201 S. Capitol Ave.
Indianapolis, IN 46225
(317) 237-5599
Selects and trains national team

Scoring

Use the match summary.

EXAMPLE:

> First round
> Pool A results
> Unified Team def. Czechoslovakia, 10-6; United States def. Aus-
> tralia, 8-4; etc.

> Final round
> Yugoslavia def. United States, 5-4.

> Final standings
> 1. Yugoslavia (Dragan Andric, Perika Bukic . . .); 2. United States
> (James Bergeson, Greg Boyer, etc.).

Weightlifting

Terms

bench press
clean-and-jerk
snatch

Governing Body

U.S. Weightlifting Federation
One Olympic Plaza
Colorado Springs, CO 80909
(719) 578-4508
Selects and trains national team

Scoring

Use the basic summary. Note whether weights are in pounds or kilograms.

52 kilograms final
Barcelona
1. Lin Qisheng, China, 253 pounds; 2. Zhang Zairong, China, 253; 3. etc.

Wrestling

Terms

fall	nelson
Greco-Roman wrestling	pin
half nelson	takedown

Governing Body

USA Wrestling
6155 Lehman Dr.
Colorado Springs, CO 80918
(719) 598-8181
Selects and trains national team

Scoring

For early rounds, list results in a match summary. For final round, follow the summary with final standings.

> Greco-Roman wrestling
> 100 kilograms
> Group A First Round
> Dennis Koslowski, St. Louis Park, Minn. def. Andrzej Wronski, Poland, 2-0; Ion Ieremciuc, Romania, def. Stipe Damjanovic, Croatia, 7-0; etc.

Yachting *See* boating.

SUMMARIES

Most of the sports listed here use the basic summary or the match summary.

Basic Summary

The basic summary lists the winners of events or meets from first to last place. The paragraph should be headed by the event name (if necessary), followed by a dash. List the place, the athlete's full name, hometown or club affiliation, and his or her winning score (in time, distance, points, or any other applicable unit).

If the winners are listed by team, list the team name, the members' last names in parentheses, and the winning score.

If a competitor is from outside the United States, list his or her country.

EXAMPLE:

> 100 hurdles
> Heat 1—1. Jackie Joyner-Kersee, Canoga Park, Calif., 12.85 seconds, 1,147 points; 2. Liliana Nastase, Romania, 12.86, 1,146; 3. etc.

Match Summary

The match summary lists the winner, followed by the abbreviation def., the loser, and the score. This type of summary is used most often in competitions where only two teams or individuals compete.

EXAMPLE:

U.S. Open
Second round
Monica Seles def. Mary Pierce, 6-3, 4-6, 6-1.

Frequently Misspelled Names

The following is a list of sports figures whose names are often misspelled.

Aaron, Hank	baseball
Abdul-Jabbar, Kareem (Lew Alcindor)	basketball
Abdul-Rauf, Mahmoud	basketball
Adelman, Rick	basketball
Agassi, Andre	tennis
Aguilera, Rick	baseball
Aikman, Troy	football
Albright, Tenley	figure skating
Alexeyev, Vasily	weightlifting
Alou, Felipe	baseball
Alou, Moises	baseball
Ali, Muhammad	boxing
Alicea, Luis	baseball
Andretti, Mario	auto racing
Andreychuk, Dave	hockey
Aouita, Said	running
Ashe, Arthur	tennis
Assenmacher, Paul	baseball
Auerbach, Red	football
Azinger, Paul	golf
Baerga, Carlos	baseball
Baggio, Roberto	soccer
Bagwell, Jeff	baseball
Baiul, Oksana	figure skating
Ballesteros, Seve	golf
Baumgartner, Bruce	wrestling
Baylor, Elgin	basketball
Beamon, Bob	track and field
Bedrosian, Steve	baseball

Beebe, Don	football
Belle, Albert	baseball
Beliveau, Jean	hockey
Benes, Andy	baseball
Bere, Jason	baseball
Berroa, Geronimo	baseball
Bettis, Jerome	football
Bettman, Gary	hockey
Beuerlein, Steve	football
Bieniemy, Eric	football
Biletnikoff, Fred	football
Biondi, Matt	swimming
Biggio, Craig	baseball
Bledsoe, Drew	football
Bodine, Geoff	auto racing
Bogues, Muggsy	basketball
Bol, Manute	basketball
Bonaly, Surya	figure skating
Borg, Bjorn	tennis
Bosio, Chris	baseball
Bourque, Ray	hockey
Bowe, Riddick	boxing
Bruguera, Sergi	tennis
Bryant, Paul "Bear"	football
Bubka, Sergey	track and field
Budig, Gene	baseball
Buechele, Steve	baseball
Bure, Pavel	hockey
Burrell, Leroy	track and field
Butkus, Dick	football
Campanella, Roy	baseball
Capriati, Jennifer	tennis
Caray, Harry	baseball
Carbajal, Michael	boxing
Carter, Cris	football
Caulkins, Tracy	swimming
Cawley, Evonne Goolagong	tennis
Ceballos, Cedric	basketball
Cedeno, Andujar	baseball
Chamberlain, Wilt	basketball
Chavez, Julio Cesar	boxing
Cianfrocco, Archi	baseball

Clemente, Roberto	baseball
Cochrane, Mickey	baseball
Comaneci, Nadia	gymnastics
Connolly, Maureen	tennis
Courier, Jim	tennis
Cousey, Bob	basketball
Crum, Denny	basketball
Csonka, Larry	football
Daly, Chuck	basketball
Daugherty, Brad	basketball
Dawes, Dominique	gymnastics
de Coubertin, Pierre	Olympics
Del Greco, Al	football
Demir, Mahmut	wrestling
Dempsey, Jack	boxing
de Varona, Donna	swimming
Devereaux, Mike	baseball
Devers, Gail	track and field
Durocher, Leo	baseball
DiMaggio, Joe	baseball
DiSarcina, Gary	baseball
Divac, Vlade	basketball
Dorsett, Tony	football
Drechsler, Heike	track and field
Earnhardt, Dale	auto racing
Eckersley, Dennis	baseball
Edberg, Stefan	tennis
Ederle, Gertrude	swimming
Ehlo, Craig	basketball
Eisenreich, Jim	baseball
Ellis, LaPhonso	basketball
Els, Ernie	golf
Esiason, Boomer	football
Esposito, Phil	hockey
Evans, Chick	golf
Evert, Chris	tennis
Favre, Brett	football
Federov, Sergei	hockey
Fermin, Felix	baseball
Fernandez, Mary Joe	tennis
Fischer, Bobby	chess
Fittipaldi, Emerson	auto racing

Fleming, Peggy	ice skating
Fosbury, Dick	track and field
Foxx, Jimmie	baseball
Foyt, A. J.	auto racing
Frazier, Joe	boxing
Frazier, Walt	basketball
Friesz, John	football
Gaetti, Gary	baseball
Gagne, Greg	baseball
Galarraga, Andres	baseball
Gammons, Peter	baseball
Gastineau, Mark	football
Gehrig, Lou	baseball
Gipp, George	football
Glanville, Jerry	football
Go for Gin	horse racing
Graf, Steffi	tennis
Grange, Harold "Red"	football
Graziano, Rocky	boxing
Gretzky, Wayne	hockey
Griese, Bob	football
Griffey, Ken Jr.	baseball
Grissom, Marquis	baseball
Gubicza, Mark	baseball
Guillen, Ozzie	baseball
Gugliotta, Tom	basketball
Guthrie, Janet	auto racing
Halas, George	football
Hamill, Dorothy	figure skating
Harbaugh, Jim	football
Hardaway, Anfernee	basketball
Hasek, Dominik	hockey
Havlicek, John	basketball
Hayes, Woody	football
Hebert, Bobby	football
Heiden, Eric and Beth	speed skating
Henderson, Rickey	baseball
Henie, Sonja	figure skating
Henke, Tom	baseball
Hentgen, Pat	baseball
Hill, Glenallen	baseball
Hogan, Ben	golf

Hoge, Merril	football
Holyfield, Evander	boxing
Hornacek, Jeff	basketball
Hornsby, Rogers	baseball
Hornung, Paul	football
Hostetler, Jeff	football
Howe, Gordie	hockey
Hrbek, Kent	baseball
Huizenga, Wayne	businessman
Incaviglia, Pete	baseball
Indurain, Miguel	cycling
Ismail, Rahib "Rocket"	football
Ito, Midori	figure skating
Ivanisevic, Goran	tennis
Jackson, Reggie	baseball
Joyner, Florence Griffith	track and field
Joyner-Kersee, Jackie	track and field
Jurgensen, Sonny	football
Kaline, Al	baseball
Kamieniecki, Scott	baseball
Karros, Eric	baseball
Kasparov, Garry	chess
Kidd, Jason	basketball
King, Billie Jean	tennis
Killy, Jean-Claude	skiing
Kiraly, Karch	volleyball
Knoblauch, Chuck	baseball
Koncak, Jon	basketball
Korbut, Olga	gymnastics
Koss, Johann Olav	speed skating
Kotashaan	horse racing
Koufax, Sandy	baseball
Krone, Julie	horse racing
Krystkowiak, Larry	basketball
Krzyzewski, Mike	basketball
Kukoc, Toni	basketball
Laettner, Christian	basketball
Landis, Kenesaw Mountain	baseball
Lapchick, Joe	basketball
Lemieux, Mario	hockey
LeMond, Greg	cycling
Lendl, Ivan	tennis

Lindros, Eric	hockey
Lombardi, Vince	football
Louganis, Greg	diving
Maddux, Greg	baseball
Mahomes, Pat	baseball
Mahre, Phil and Steve	skiing
Majerle, Dan	basketball
Majkowski, Don	football
Mantle, Mickey	baseball
Manwaring, Kirt	baseball
Maradona, Diego	soccer
Maravich, Pete	basketball
Maris, Roger	baseball
Martinez, Conchita	tennis
Marciano, Rocky	boxing
Massimino, Rollie	basketball
Mazeroski, Bill	baseball
Mathewson, Christy	baseball
McCall, Oliver	boxing
McCallum, Napoleon	football
McDuffie, O. J.	football
McNall, Bruce	hockey
Means, Natrone	football
Messier, Mark	hockey
Metzelaars, Pete	football
Mikita, Stan	hockey
Milburn, Rodney Jr.	track and field
Mirer, Rick	football
Moe, Tommy	skiing
Moorer, Michael	boxing
Mulholland, Terry	baseball
Murdoch, Rupert	businessman
Muresan, Gheorghe	basketball
Murray, Ty	rodeo
Musial, Stan	baseball
Mutombo, Dikembe	basketball
Nagy, Charles	baseball
Nagurski, Bronko	football
Naismith, James	basketball
Namath, Joe	football
Nastase, Ilie	tennis
Navratilova, Martina	tennis

Nettles, Graig	baseball
Nicklaus, Jack	golf
Nilsson, Dave	baseball
Nomo, Hideo	baseball
Novacek, Jay	football
Novotna, Jana	tennis
Odomes, Nate	football
Oerter, Al	track and field
O'Neal, Shaquille	basketball
Olajuwon, Hakeem	basketball
Olazabol, Jose Maria	golf
Ontiveros, Steve	baseball
Orosco, Jesse	baseball
Orr, Bobby	hockey
Orsulak, Joe	baseball
Ott, Mel	baseball
Owens, Jesse	track and field
Paige, Satchel	baseball
Pagnozzi, Tom	baseball
Palmeiro, Rafael	baseball
Pelé	soccer
Pettit, Bob	basketball
Petty, Richard	auto racing
Pfund, Randy	basketball
Penske, Roger	auto racing
Pippen, Scottie	basketball
Pippig, Uta	marathon
Plante, Jacques	hockey
Podoloff, Maurice	basketball
Polonia, Luis	baseball
Proehl, Ricky	football
Radja, Dino	basketball
Reveiz, Fuad	football
Ripken, Cal	baseball
Richardson, Nolan	basketball
Rizzuto, Phil	baseball
Robertson, Oscar	basketball
Robinson, Brooks	baseball
Robinson, Frank	baseball
Robinson, Jackie	baseball
Rockne, Knute	football
Roenick, Jeremy	hockey

Roffe-Steinrotter, Diann	skiing
Romario	soccer
Rudolph, Wilma	track and field
Rupp, Adolph	basketball
Rypien, Mark	football
Sabatini, Gabriela	tennis
Saberhagen, Bret	baseball
Salisbury, Sean	football
Sampras, Pete	tennis
Samuelson, Joan Benoit	marathon
Sanchez, Rey	baseball
Sanders, Deion	baseball, football
Sayers, Gale	football
Schembechler, Bo	football
Schott, Marge	baseball
Schottenheimer, Marty	football
Schrempf, Detlef	basketball
Schroeder, Jay	football
Sealy, Malik	basketball
Secretariat	horse racing
Seitzer, Kevin	baseball
Seles, Monica	tennis
Selig, Bud	baseball
Senna, Ayrton	auto racing
Sharpe, Sterling	football
Sheehan, Patty	golf
Shoemaker, Willie	horse racing
Shuler, Heath	football
Smith, Emmitt	football
Spahn, Warren	baseball
Spitz, Mark	swimming
Sprague, Ed	baseball
Sprewell, Latrell	basketball
Stagg, Amos Alonzo	football
Starr, Bart	football
Stenerud, Jan	football
Stengel, Casey	baseball
Stenmark, Ingemar	skiing
Stottlemyre, Todd	baseball
Stoyanovich, Pete	football
Stojko, Elvis	figure skating
Strawberry, Darryl	baseball

Street, Picabo	skiing
Swoopes, Sheryl	basketball
Tagliabue, Paul	football
Testaverde, Vinny	football
Theismann, Joe	football
Thomas, Isiah	basketball
Thompson, Daley	decathlon
Thorpe, Jim	football
Tobasco Cat	horse racing
Tomczak, Mike	football
Trachsel, Steve	baseball
Trammell, Alan	baseball
Trudeau, Jack	football
Turner, Norv	football
Ueberroth, Peter	Olympic organizer
Uecker, Bob	baseball
Unitas, Johnny	football
Valentin, John	baseball
Vanbiesbrouck, John	hockey
VanLandingham, Bill	baseball
Van Slyke, Andy	baseball
Vaughn, Mo	baseball
Van Exel, Nick	basketball
Vicario, Arantxa Sanchez	tennis
Vizquel, Omar	baseball
Walker, Herschel	football
Webb, Spud	basketball
Weber, Dick	bowling
Wenzel, Hanni	skiing
Wetteland, John	baseball
Whitaker, Pernell	boxing
Wilander, Mats	tennis
Wilkens, Lenny	basketball
Wilkins, Dominique	basketball
Williamson, Corliss	basketball
Wilmsmeyer, Klaus	football
Wisniewski, Steve	football
Witt, Katarina	ice skating
Wohlers, Mark	baseball
Wooden, John	basketball
Yamaguchi, Kristi	ice skating
Yastrzemski, Carl	football

Zaharias, Mildred "Babe" Didrikson	track, golf
Zeile, Todd	baseball
Zmeskal, Kim	gymnastics
Zurbriggen, Pirmin	skiing

REFERENCES

The following sources were used to gather ideas, names, information, and definitions for the *Sports Style Guide and Reference Manual*.

American Heritage Dictionary. Dell Publishing Group, Inc., New York, 1983.

American League Red Book. The Sporting News Publishing Co., St. Louis, 1994.

Associated Press Stylebook and Libel Manual, edited by Norm Goldstein. Associated Press Publishing, New York, 1994.

Atlanta Journal-Constitution

The Baseball Encyclopedia, 9th edition, edited by Rick Wolf. Macmillan Publishing Co., New York, 1993.

Boston Globe

Carroll, Bob. *The Hidden Game of Football*. Warner Books, New York, 1988.

Chicago Manual of Style, 14th edition. University of Chicago Press, Chicago, 1993.

Chicago Sun-Times

Chicago Tribune

Connors, Martin, Diane L. Dupris, and Brad Morgan. *The Olympics Factbook*. Visible Ink Press, Detroit, 1992.

Dallas Morning News

Information Please Sports Almanac, edited by Mike Meserole. Houghton Mifflin Co., Burlington, Mass., 1995.

Kansas City Star

Make the Right Call: National Football League. Triumph Books, Chicago, 1995.

May, John Allan. *Complete Book of Golf*. Gallery Books, New York, 1991.

National Hockey League Official Records 1994-1995. Triumph Books, Chicago, 1994.

National League Green Book. The Sporting News Publishing Co., St. Louis, 1994.

1995 PGA Tour Book, edited by PGA Tour Creative Services. Triumph Books, Chicago, 1995.

1995 Senior PGA Tour Book, edited by PGA Tour Creative Services. Triumph Books, Chicago, 1995.

Official NCAA Basketball Records Book, edited by Laura E. Bollig. NCAA, Overland Park, Kan., 1995.

Official NCAA Football Records Book, edited by J. Gregory Summers. NCAA, Overland Park, Kan., 1995.

Official Rules of Major League Baseball. Triumph Books, Chicago. 1995.

Official Rules of the NHL. Triumph Books, Chicago, 1994.

Official Rules of Soccer. Triumph Books, Chicago, 1995.

Professional Rodeo USA. Triumph Books, Chicago, 1995.

The Rule Book, edited by The Diagram Group. St. Martin's Press, New York, 1983.

Sports Market Place. Sportsguide, Princeton, N.J., 1984.

Strunk Jr., William, and E. B. White. *Elements of Style*, 3rd edition. Macmillan, New York, 1979.

United Press International Stylebook, 3rd edition. National Textbook Company, Lincolnwood, Ill., 1993.

USA Today

Webster's Sports Dictionary. G.C. Merriam Co., Springfield, Mass., 1976.

WTA Tour Media Guide, compiled by the WTA Tour Communications Staff. WTA Tour, New York, 1995